# स ।।

## Upāsanā

# Cosmic Pūjā



By

स्वामी सत्यानन्द सरस्वती

Swami Satyananda Saraswati

and

स्वामी विट्ठलानन्द सरस्वती

Swami Vittalananda Saraswati

Published By

Devi Mandir Publications

समष्टि उपासना **Cosmic Pūjā**


by Devi Mandir Publications
5950 Highway 128
Napa, CA 94558 USA
Communications: Phone and Fax 1-707-966-2802
E-Mail swamiji@shreemaa.org
Please visit us on the World Wide Web at
http://www.shreemaa.org


ISBN 1-887472-83-5
Library of Congress Catalog Card Number
CIP 2001 126147

समष्टि उपासना **Cosmic Pūjā**
Swami Satyananda Saraswati
1. Hindu Religion. 2. Worship. 3. Spirituality.
4. Philosophy. I. Saraswati, Swami Satyananda;
Saraswati, Swami Vittalananda

# Table of Contents

## Introduction

*Samaṣṭi* means universal, infinite, beyond the realm of sensory knowledge, Cosmic. It is often contrasted with *Vyāṣṭi*, which indicates a particular, individual form, something definable by the minds of humans. *Upāsanā* means worship or meditation. It is derived from the same word roots as *Upāṇisād*, *upa* meaning near, and *āsana*, to sit. This was used in reference to the practice of the Vedic ṛṣis giving discourses to their disciples, who were literally sitting near, perhaps under a tree or some other conducive environment. These dissertations have become known as *Vedānta*, the teachings that come at the end or the apex of the Vedas, the teachings of the highest union with God.

Therefore this Samaṣṭi Upāsanā, or *Cosmic Pūjā*, as we have called it, is the meditation or worship on the universal divinity, the Infinite, beyond the realms of sensory knowledge, or all the forms of the divinity of existence. *Pū* means *Puṇya*, merits; *Jā* means *Jāta*, to give birth. *Pūjā* describes the actions that give birth to merits. The action of the greatest merit is to guide one's awareness into the presence of God, and to maintain that presence as long as possible. To that objective this work is intended to lead us.

Included within the Chaṇḍī Paṭh are three secrets called The Most Preeminent Secret, The Modified Secret and The Secret of the Manifestations. The first two of these secrets describe the origin of existence as we know it and the Cosmic Pūjā, worship of all the deities of the universe. The third secret deals with manifestations that are yet to appear, and hence, is not dealt with in the present text. It is from this Chaṇḍī Paṭh, and especially from the secrets of the Upasaṃhāra Pūjā, that this Cosmic Pūjā is derived.

Specifically we are directed to worship on three levels. The first level of worship reveals on the left Mahā Kālī with ten heads, ten arms and ten feet. Her ten faces see in the ten directions: the eight cardinal points of the compass, plus above and below. They indicate the ten Mahā Vidyās, the ten great forms of knowledge, personified as Goddesses: Kālī, Bagalā, Chinnamastā, Bhuvaneśvarī, Mātaṅginī, Ṣorosī, Dhumāvatī, Tripurasundarī, Tārā and Bhairavī.

Her ten arms perform all the karma of the universe and indicate the five karmendriyas, or organs of action (upper appendages, lower appendages, tongue, reproductive organ and anus), and the five jñāna indriyas, or organs of knowledge (eyes, ears, nose, tongue and skin) with which all interaction with the universe takes place. Her ten feet perform the cosmic dance of Nature: Mother Nature dancing on the stage of Consciousness, Kālī upon the chest of Śiva.

She originally manifested to take the life from two demons named Too Much and Too Little. Mahā Kālī is the Goddess of the Divine Balance, perfection in harmony, with neither Too Much nor Too Little.

In the center is the eighteen-armed form of Durgā and Mahā Lakṣmī. Comprised of the unity of light emitted from all the Gods, She is Mahiṣaśura-Mardinī, the slayer of the Great Ego. In Her eighteen hands She wields the weapons with which to combat the excesses of Egotism. She demands surrender of the Ego, and no one is able to resist Her. She cuts down the generals of the immense armies of egotistical thought: Devoid of Clear Understanding, Fickleness, Disbelief, Arrogance, Memories, Anxiety, Blindness, Violent Temper, Passion, The Great Deceiver, Hypocrisy, Irresistible Temptation, Foul Mouth, Wandering To and Fro, Haughtiness, the Great Frustration, Want of Resolution, the Great Ego and other generals as well. All meet their death at the hands of the Divine Mother.

To her right sits the eight-armed Mahā Sarasvatī, the Slayer of the armies of Self-Conceit and Self-Deprecation: Anger, Passion, the Seeds of Desire. Because of Her incomparable Knowledge, even Self-Conceit and Self-Deprecation meet their demise when they encounter the Divine Goddess.

Let us meditate to surrender Too Much and Too Little, to cut down Self-Conceit and Self-Deprecation, along with their armies, even to surrender the Great Ego itself to the feet of the Divine Mother Goddess. When we are able to do this, then we can raise our perception from the first row, the gross level of existence, to the second row, the subtle body of existence.

There we will be able to see that all that is perceivable, all of existence, is merely the dance of the three guṇas, Mahā Kālī, Mahā Lakṣmi and Mahā Sarasvatī, the sattva, raja and tama qualites of existence: being, becoming, and rest; desire, activity and wisdom.

*Kal* means Darkness, and Kālī takes away the darkness of all beings. She Herself is dark because She takes away the darkness to Herself. She is dark to the outside, but radiates light within. *Kāl* means time, and *ī* means the cause: Kālī, the Cause of Time, or She Who is Beyond Time. By virtue of the darkness of Her time, She is the night of wisdom. She gives rest and respite to all beings. Of the nature of Tama Guṇa, She is the quality of darkness, the quality of rest.

In the center is Mahā Lakṣmī, the Great Goddess Who Defines All. She is the Being of this existence, Mūla Prakṛti, the natural state of all existence, even prior to manifestation. Of the nature of Sattva Guṇa, She is Being, existence as it is, the energy of activity, Kriya Śakti, Energy in motion, Pure Light.

And on the right is Mahā Sarasvatī, of the nature of Raja Guṇa, the energy of desire. While Mahā Lakṣmī is Being, Mahā Sarasvatī is Becoming. Mahā Kālī is the state of rest. The three guṇas of nature, nature's three qualities, are light, wisdom, peace; activity, passion, motion; desire, knowledge, action. This is the second row of deities worshipped in the Cosmic Pūjā.

When we can put these three attitudes into balance, so that no one is predominant over the other two, then we can rise to the perception of the third level. Here we can perceive that this entire līlā, the entire dance of existence, is orchestrated by Brahmā, Viṣṇu and Śiva, the three aspects of the One God; Generator-Organizer-Dissolver, the GOD of Divinity.

In the upper left-hand corner is the five-faced Śiva, the Consciousness of Infinite Goodness. His five faces are, from left to right:

Sadhyo Jāta, who continually gives birth to truth
Vāma Deva, the Beloved Deity
In the center, Aghora, who is free from fear
Tat Puruṣa, that Universal Consciousness
Īsāna, the Ruler of All

These are five attributes of the One Consciousness of Infinite Goodness, Lord Śiva who presides over the transformation of all that is.

Next to Śiva is Durgā. *Durgaṃ* means confusion, and Durgā takes away the *durgaṃ*: the Reliever of Confusion, she is the wife of Lord Śiva. Her other name is Gaurī, She who is Rays of Light. She rides on the great Lion who is Dharma. She is the Energy of Continuous Transformation. Durgā energizes Śiva in creating change.

In the center is Brahmā, the Creator of All. He has four faces by means of which he sees in the four directions, and from which he expounds the four Vedas. He rides on the swan of vital breath, the *haṃ saḥ* that makes our breath regular in the processes of Prāṇāyām.

Beside Brahmā is his wife Sarasvatī, the Goddess of Knowledge, Art, Philosophy and Music. She is the Creative Energy. Together they create the perceivable universe.

To Her right is Lord Viṣṇu, who is all blue, the color of the sky, the color of infinity. *Viṣ* means the universe, *ṇu*, to pervade: *Viṣṇu*, He who Pervades All of the Universe; the Infinite Consciousness that, while pervading the entire universe, is the universe. He protects the entire universe, and is the circumstance of all the beings of the universe.

Next to Viṣṇu is his wife Lakṣmī, the Goddess of True Wealth. *Lakṣya* mean the goal, and therefore Lakṣmī is the Ultimate Goal. *Lakṣya* also means the definition, and therefore Lakṣmī defines the creation and all that is in it, and at the same time She energizes it with the circumstances of each and every being.

Brahmā and Sarasvatī create, Viṣṇu and Lakṣmī are protecting the circumstances of all beings and Śiva and Durgā transform all that is, even as it is becoming.

Samaṣṭi Upāsanā
North

| | | |
|---|---|---|
| Śiva and Durgā | Brahmā and Sarasvatī | Viṣṇu and Lakṣmī |
| Mahā Kālī 4 arms | Mahā Lakṣmī 4 arms | Mahā Sarasvatī 4 arms |
| Mahā Kālī 10 arms | Mahā Lakṣmī 18 arms | Mahā Sarasvatī 8 arms |

In addition to worshipping Brahmā, Viṣṇu and Śiva; Durgā, Sarasvatī and Lakṣmi; Mahā Kālī, Mahā Lakṣmī and Mahā Sarasvatī in their four-armed appearance and with eight, ten and eighteen arms as well, it is customary in every pūjā to worship Gaṇeśa, the Lord of Wisdom, the Guru and the Nava Grahaṇ, the Sun and Nine Planets. This completes what is known as the *Pañca Devatā Pūjā*, the worship of the five divisions of Hindu Dharma: Śiva, Śakti, Viṣṇu, Gaṇeśa and the Nine Planets.

Accompanying the Goddess are a number of Her entourage, including the sarvato bhadramaṅḍala devatās, the sixty-four yogiṇīs, as well as Her weapons of war, the nine forms of Durgā, the eight forms of energy, the sixteen mothers, and all of the dhyānas and nyāsas pertinent to such worship.

There is no end to the amount of systems of worship one might perform. If you perform this *paddhoti* (system of worship) straight through, it should take at least two and a half to three hours at the fastest and well-practiced pace. If you cannot sit that long, choose the mantras and viddhis that are most applicable to your worship, and use them as a basis to create your own pūjās, according to your capacity. The objective is to dedicate as much time as you can to the exclusive concentration on the Divine Mother and Her divine family. Through pūjā we cultivate the habit to offer the best we possibly can to God, and to give as *prasād* (a sanctified offering) all that is appropriate to anyone who may ask.

Pūjā is a way of life more than a practice. Just as with any desired trait, we begin by practice until the behavior becomes instinctual. We practice worship until our lives become instinctually an offering of respect in which the most important criteria for success is the quality of peace that we are aware of at any moment. This Cosmic Pūjā, the worship of all the divine beings of the universe, is designed to guide our meditations into that quality of true reverence in which we actually pay attention, even go beyond into absorption, where union between the perceiver and the object of perception is the proof of the transcendence of duality.

I would like to thank Viṭṭalānanda and Janārdānanda for their invaluable assistance, and the entire staff of the Devi Mandir, especially our Divine Mother, Shree Maa. You cannot know what the completion of this saṃkalpa means to me. For the last three years I have sat within the Devi Mandir without going outside, every day performing this pūjā, along with chanting the entire Chaṇḍī Pāṭh and the Devi Gītā before the sacred homa fire. Now I am trying to share even a portion of that light. Divine Mother, I bow to you. Please accept this offering.

Swami Satyananda Saraswati
Devi Mandir, 1991

Here it is ten years later, and we are called upon to bring out a new edition of the Cosmic Pūjā. You can imagine my joy to be able to share the love of my life! Now spiritual people around the world are increasing the presence of God in their lives, and it is such a privilege to explain the mantras and techniques by which the ṛṣis became established in God.

Shree Maa joins me in our prayer that all the powers of divinity join to bless us all with the greatest goodness.

Swami Satyananda Saraswati
Devi Mandir, 2001

## देवता प्रणाम्
## devatā praṇām

श्रीमन्महागणाधिपतये नमः

**śrīmanmahāgaṇādhipataye namaḥ**

We bow to the Respected Great Lord of Wisdom.

लक्ष्मीनारायणाभ्यां नमः

**lakṣmīnārāyaṇābhyāṃ namaḥ**

We bow to Lakṣmī and Nārāyaṇa, The Goal of all Existence and the Perceiver of All.

उमामहेश्वराभ्यां नमः

**umāmaheśvarābhyāṃ namaḥ**

We bow to Umā and Maheśvara, She who protects existence, and the Great Consciousness or Seer of All.

वाणीहिरण्यगर्भाभ्यां नमः

**vāṇīhiraṇyagarbhābhyāṃ namaḥ**

We bow to Vāṇī and Hiraṇyagarbha, Sarasvatī and Brahmā, who create the cosmic existence.

शचीपुरन्दराभ्यां नमः

**śacīpurandarābhyāṃ namaḥ**

We bow to Śacī and Purandara, Indra and his wife, who preside over all that is divine.

मातापितृभ्यां नमः

**mātāpitṛbhyāṃ namaḥ**

We bow to the Mothers and Fathers.

इष्टदेवताभ्यो नमः

**iṣṭadevatābhyo namaḥ**

We bow to the chosen deity of worship.

कुलदेवताभ्यो नमः

**kuladevatābhyo namaḥ**

We bow to the family deity of worship.

ग्रामदेवताभ्यो नमः

**grāmadevatābhyo namaḥ**

We bow to the village deity of worship.

वास्तुदेवताभ्यो नमः

**vāstudevatābhyo namaḥ**

We bow to the particular household deity of worship.

स्थानदेवताभ्यो नमः

**sthānadevatābhyo namaḥ**

We bow to the established deity of worship.

सर्वेभ्यो देवेभ्यो नमः

**sarvebhyo devebhyo namaḥ**

We bow to all the Gods.

सर्वेभ्यो ब्राह्मणेभ्यो नमः

**sarvebhyo brāhmaṇebhyo namaḥ**
We bow to all the Knowers of Divinity.

**dhyānam**
meditations

खड्गं चक्रगदेषुचापपरिघाञ्छूलं भुशुण्डीं शिरः
शङ्खं संदधतीं करैस्त्रिनयनां सर्वाङ्गभूषावृताम् ।
नीलाश्मद्युतिमास्यपाददशकां सेवे महाकालिकां
यामस्तौत्स्वपिते हरौ कमलजो हन्तुं मधुं कैटभम् ॥

**khaḍgaṃ cakra gadeṣu cāpa**
**parighāñ chūlaṃ bhuśuṇḍīṃ śiraḥ**
**śaṅkhaṃ saṃdadhatīṃ karai**
**strinayanāṃ sarvāṅga bhūṣāvṛtām |**
**nīlāś madyutimāsya pāda**
**daśakāṃ seve mahākālikāṃ**
**yāmastaut svapite harau**
**kamalajo hantuṃ madhuṃ kaiṭabham ||**

Bearing in Her ten hands the sword of worship, the discus of revolving time, the club of articulation, the bow of determination, the iron bar of restraint, the pike of attention, the sling, the head of egotism and the conch of vibrations, She has three eyes and displays ornaments on all Her limbs. Shining like a blue gem, She has ten faces. I worship that Great Remover of Darkness whom the lotus-born Creative Capacity praised in order to slay Too Much and Too Little when the Supreme Consciousness was asleep.

अक्षस्रक्परशुं गदेषुकुलिशं पद्मं धनुः कुण्डिकां
दण्डं शक्तिमसिं च चर्म जलजं घण्टां सुराभाजनम् ।
शूलं पाशसुदर्शने च दधतीं हस्तैः प्रसन्नाननां
सेवे सैरिभमर्दिनीमिह महालक्ष्मीं सरोजस्थिताम् ॥

**akṣasrak paraśuṃ gadeṣu**
**kuliśaṃ padmaṃ dhanuḥ kuṇḍikāṃ**
**daṇḍaṃ śaktīm asiṃ ca carma**
**jalajaṃ ghaṇṭāṃ surābhājanam |**
**śūlaṃ pāśa sudarśane ca**
**dadhatīṃ hastaiḥ prasannānanāṃ**
**seve sairibha mardinī**
**miha mahālakṣmīṃ sarojasthitām ||**

She with the beautiful face, the Destroyer of the Great Ego, is seated upon the lotus of Peace. In Her hands She holds the rosary of alphabets, the battle axe of good actions, the club of articulation, the arrow of speech, the thunderbolt of illumination, the lotus of peace, the bow of determination, the water-pot of purification, the staff of discipline, energy, the sword of worship, the shield of faith, the conch of vibrations, the bell of continuous tone, the wine cup of joy, the pike of concentration, the net of unity and the discus of revolving time named Excellent Intuitive Vision. I worship that Great Goddess of True Wealth.

घण्टाशूलहलानि शङ्खमुसले चक्रं धनुः सायकं
हस्ताब्जैर्दधतीं घनान्तविलसच्छीतांशुतुल्यप्रभाम् ।
गौरीदेहसमुद्भवां त्रिजगतामाधारभूतां महा-
पूर्वामत्र सरस्वतीमनुभजे शुम्भादिदैत्यार्दिनीम् ॥

**ghaṇṭā śūla halāni śaṅkha**
**musale cakraṃ dhanuḥ sāyakaṃ**
**hastābjair dadhatīṃ ghanānta**
**vilasacchītāṃ śutulya prabhām |**
**gaurīdeha samudbhavāṃ**
**trijagatām ādhārabhūtāṃ mahā-**
**pūrvāmatra sarasvatīm**
**anubhaje śumbhādi daityārdinīm**

Bearing in Her lotus hands the bell of continuous tone, the pike of concentration, the plow sowing the seeds of the Way of Truth to Wisdom, the conch of vibrations, the pestle of refinement, the discus of revolving time, the bow of determination and the arrow of speech, whose radiance is like the moon in autumn, whose appearance is most beautiful, who is manifested from the body of She Who is Rays of Light, and is the support of the three worlds, I worship that Great Goddess of All-Pervading Knowledge, who destroyed Self-Conceit and other thoughts.

या चण्डी मधुकैटभादिदैत्यदलनी या माहिषोन्मूलिनी
या धूम्रेक्षणचण्डमुण्डमथनी या रक्तबीजाशनी ।
शक्तिः शुम्भनिशुम्भदैत्यदलनी या सिद्धिदात्री परा
सा देवी नवकोटीमूर्तिसहिता मां पातु विश्वेश्वरी ॥

**yā caṇḍī madhukaiṭabhādidaityadalanī**
**yā māhiṣonmūlinī**
**yā dhūmrekṣaṇacaṇḍamuṇḍamathanī**
**yā raktabījāśanī**
**śaktiḥ śumbhaniśumbhadaityadalanī**
**yā siddhidātrī parā**
**sā devī navakoṭīmūrtisahitā māṃ pātu viśveśvarī**

That Caṇḍī, who slays the negativities of Too Much and Too Little and other Thoughts; Who is the origin of the Great Ego, and the Destroyer of Sinful Eyes, Passion and Anger, and the Seed of Desire; the Energy that tears asunder Self-Conceit and Self-Deprecation, the Grantor of the highest attainment of perfection: may that Goddess who is represented by ninety million divine images, the Supreme Lord of the Universe, remain close and protect me.

ॐ अग्निर्ज्योतिर्ज्योतिरग्निः स्वाहा ।
सूर्यो ज्योतिर्ज्योतिः सूर्यः स्वाहा ।
अग्निर्वर्चो ज्योतिर्वर्चः स्वाहा ।
सूर्यो वर्चो ज्योतिर्वर्चः स्वाहा ।
ज्योतिः सूर्यः सूर्यो ज्योतिः स्वाहा ॥

**oṃ agnir jyotir jyotir agniḥ svāhā**
**sūryo jyotir jyotiḥ sūryaḥ svāhā**
**agnir varco jyotir varcaḥ svāhā**
**sūryo varco jyotir varcaḥ svāhā**
**jyotiḥ sūryaḥ sūryo jyotiḥ svāhā**

Oṃ The Divine Fire is the Light, and the Light is the Divine Fire; I am One with God! The Light of Wisdom is the Light, and the Light is the Light of Wisdom; I am One with God! The Divine Fire is the offering, and the Light is the Offering; I am

One with God! The Light of Wisdom is the Offering, and the Light is the Light of Wisdom; I am One with God!

(wave light)

ॐ अग्निर्ज्योती रविर्ज्योतिश्चन्द्रो ज्योतिस्तथैव च ।

ज्योतिषामुत्तमो देवी दीपोऽयं प्रतिगृह्यताम् ॥

एष दीपः ॐ ऐं ह्रीं क्लीं चामुण्डायै विच्चे

**oṃ agnirjyotī ravirjyotiścandro jyotistathaiva ca**
**jyotiṣāmuttamo devī dīpo-yaṃ pratigṛhyatām**
**eṣa dīpaḥ oṃ aiṃ hrīṃ klīṃ cāmuṇḍāyai vicce**

Oṃ The Divine Fire is the Light, the Light of Wisdom is the Light, the Light of Devotion is the Light as well. The Light of the Highest Bliss, Oh Goddess, is in the Light that we offer, the Light that we request you to accept. With the offering of Light oṃ aiṃ hrīṃ klīṃ cāmuṇḍāyai vicce.

(wave incense)

ॐ वनस्पतिरसोत्पन्नो गन्धात्ययी गन्ध उत्तमः ।

आघ्रेयः सर्वदेवानां धूपोऽयं प्रतिगृह्यताम् ॥

एष धूपः ॐ ऐं ह्रीं क्लीं चामुण्डायै विच्चे

**oṃ vanaspatirasotpanno**
**gandhātyayī gandha uttamaḥ**
**āghreyaḥ sarvadevānāṃ dhūpo-yaṃ pratigṛhyatām**
**eṣa dhūpaḥ oṃ aiṃ hrīṃ klīṃ cāmuṇḍāyai vicce**

Oṃ Spirit of the Forest, from you is produced the most excellent of scents. The scent most pleasing to all the Gods, that scent we request you to accept. With the offering of fragrant scent oṃ aiṃ hrīṃ klīṃ cāmuṇḍāyai vicce.

ārātrikam

ॐ चन्द्रादित्यौ च धरणी विद्युदग्निस्तथैव च ।

त्वमेव सर्वज्योतीषिं आरात्रिकं प्रतिगृह्यताम् ॥

ॐ ऐं ह्रीं क्लीं चामुण्डायै विच्चे आरात्रिकं समर्पयामि

**oṃ candrādityau ca dharaṇī vidyudagnistathaiva ca**
**tvameva sarvajyotīṣiṃ ārātrikaṃ pratigṛhyatām**
**oṃ aiṃ hrīṃ klīṃ cāmuṇḍāyai vicce ārātrikaṃ samarpayāmi**

Oṃ All knowing as the Moon, the Sun and the Divine Fire, you alone are all light, and this light we request you to accept. With the offering of light oṃ aiṃ hrīṃ klīṃ cāmuṇḍāyai vicce.

ॐ पयः पृथिव्यां पय ओषधीषु

पयो दिव्यन्तरिक्षे पयो धाः ।

पयःस्वतीः प्रदिशः सन्तु मह्यम् ॥

**oṃ payaḥ pṛthivyāṃ paya oṣadhīṣu**
**payo divyantarikṣe payo dhāḥ**
**payaḥsvatīḥ pradiśaḥ santu mahyam**

Oṃ Earth is a reservoir of nectar, all vegetation is a reservoir of nectar, the divine atmosphere is a reservoir of nectar, and also above. May all perceptions shine forth with the sweet taste of nectar for us.

ॐ अग्निर्देवता वातो देवता सूर्यो देवता चन्द्रमा देवता

वसवो देवता रुद्रो देवता ऽदित्या देवता मरुतो देवता विश्वे

देवा देवता बृहस्पतिर्देवतेन्द्रो देवता वरुणो देवता ॥

**oṃ agnirdevatā vāto devatā sūryo devatā candramā devatā vasavo devatā rudro devatā-dityā devatā maruto devatā viśve devā devatā bṛhaspatirdevatendro devatā varuṇo devatā**

Oṃ The Divine Fire (Light of Purity) is the shining God, the Wind is the shining God, the Sun (Light of Wisdom) is the shining God, the Moon (Lord of Devotion) is the shining God, the Protectors of the Wealth are the shining Gods, the Relievers of Sufferings are the shining Gods, the Sons of the Light are the shining Gods; the Emancipated seers (Maruts) are the shining Gods, the Universal Shining Gods are the shining Gods, the Guru of the Gods is the shining God, the Ruler of the Gods is the shining God, the Lord of Waters is the shining God.

ॐ भूर्भुवः स्वः ।

तत् सवितुर्वरेण्यम् भर्गो देवस्य धीमहि ।

धियो यो नः प्रचोदयात् ॥

**oṃ bhūr bhuvaḥ svaḥ**
**tat savitur vareṇyam bhargo devasya dhīmahi**
**dhiyo yo naḥ pracodayāt**

Oṃ the Infinite Beyond Conception, the gross body, the subtle body and the causal body; we meditate on that Light of Wisdom that is the Supreme Wealth of the Gods. May it grant to us increase in our meditations.

ॐ भूः

**oṃ bhūḥ**

Oṃ the gross body

ॐ भुवः

**oṃ bhuvaḥ**
Oṃ the subtle body

ॐ स्वः

**oṃ svaḥ**
Oṃ the causal body

ॐ महः

**oṃ mahaḥ**
Oṃ the great body of existence

ॐ जनः

**oṃ janaḥ**
Oṃ the body of knowledge

ॐ तपः

**oṃ tapaḥ**
Oṃ the body of light

ॐ सत्यं

**oṃ satyaṃ**
Oṃ the body of truth

ॐ तत् सवितुर्वरेण्यम् भर्गो देवस्य धीमहि ।
धियो यो नः प्रचोदयात् ॥

**oṃ tat savitur vareṇyam bhargo devasya dhīmahi dhiyo yo naḥ pracodayāt**

Oṃ we meditate on that Light of Wisdom that is the Supreme Wealth of the Gods. May it grant to us increase in our meditations.

ॐ आपो ज्योतीरसोमृतं ब्रह्म भूर्भुवस्स्वरोम् ॥

**oṃ āpo jyotīrasomṛtaṃ brahma bhūrbhuvassvarom**

Oṃ May the divine waters luminous with the nectar of immortality of Supreme Divinity fill the earth, the atmosphere and the heavens.

ॐ मां माले महामाये सर्वशक्तिस्वरूपिणि ।

चतुर्वर्गस्त्वयि न्यस्तस्तस्मान्मे सिद्धिदा भव ॥

**oṃ māṃ māle mahāmāye sarvaśaktisvarūpiṇi**
**catur vargas tvayi nyastas**
**tasmān me siddhidā bhava**

Oṃ My Rosary, The Great Measurement of Consciousness, containing all energy within as your intrinsic nature, give to me the attainment of your Perfection, fulfilling the four objectives of life.

ॐ अविघ्नं कुरु माले त्वं गृह्णामि दक्षिणे करे ।

जपकाले च सिद्ध्यर्थं प्रसीद मम सिद्धये ॥

**oṃ avighnaṃ kuru māle tvaṃ gṛhṇāmi dakṣiṇe kare**
**japakāle ca siddhyarthaṃ prasīda mama siddhaye**

Oṃ Rosary, You please remove all obstacles. I hold you in my right hand. At the time of recitation be pleased with me. Allow me to attain the Highest Perfection.

ॐ अक्षमालाधिपतये सुसिद्धिं देहि देहि सर्वमन्त्रार्थसाधिनि साधय साधय सर्वसिद्धिं परिकल्पय परिकल्पय मे स्वाहा ॥

**oṃ akṣa mālā dhipataye susiddhiṃ dehi dehi sarva mantrārtha sādhini sādhaya sādhaya sarva siddhiṃ parikalpaya parikalpaya me svāhā**

Oṃ Rosary of rudrākṣa seeds, my Lord, give to me excellent attainment. Give to me, give to me. Illuminate the meanings of all mantras, illuminate, illuminate! Fashion me with all excellent attainments, fashion me! I am One with God!

एते गन्धपुष्पे ॐ गं गणपतये नमः

**ete gandhapuṣpe oṃ gaṃ gaṇapataye namaḥ**

With these scented flowers oṃ we bow to the Lord of Wisdom, the Lord of the Multitudes.

एते गन्धपुष्पे ॐ आदित्यादिनवग्रहेभ्यो नमः

**ete gandhapuṣpe oṃ ādityādi navagrahebhyo namaḥ**

With these scented flowers oṃ we bow to the Sun, the Light of Wisdom, along with the nine planets.

एते गन्धपुष्पे ॐ शिवादिपञ्चदेवताभ्यो नमः

**ete gandhapuṣpe oṃ śivādipañcadevatābhyo namaḥ**

With these scented flowers oṃ we bow to Śiva, the Consciousness of Infinite Goodness, along with the five primary deities (Śiva, Śakti, Viṣṇu, Gaṇeśa, Sūrya).

एते गन्धपुष्पे ॐ इन्द्रादिदशदिक्पालेभ्यो नमः

**ete gandhapuṣpe oṃ indrādi daśadikpālebhyo namaḥ**

With these scented flowers oṃ we bow to Indra, the Ruler of the Pure, along with the Ten Protectors of the ten directions.

एते गन्धपुष्पे ॐ मत्स्यादिदशावतारेभ्यो नमः

**ete gandhapuṣpe oṃ matsyādi daśāvatārebhyo namaḥ**

With these scented flowers oṃ we bow to Viṣṇu, the Fish, along with the Ten Incarnations that He assumed.

एते गन्धपुष्पे ॐ प्रजापतये नमः

**ete gandhapuṣpe oṃ prajāpataye namaḥ**

With these scented flowers oṃ we bow to the Lord of All Created Beings.

एते गन्धपुष्पे ॐ नमो नारायणाय नमः

**ete gandhapuṣpe oṃ namo nārāyaṇāya namaḥ**

With these scented flowers oṃ we bow to the Perfect Perception of Consciousness.

एते गन्धपुष्पे ॐ सर्वेभ्यो देवेभ्यो नमः

**ete gandhapuṣpe oṃ sarvebhyo devebhyo namaḥ**

With these scented flowers oṃ we bow to All the Gods.

एते गन्धपुष्पे ॐ सर्वाभ्यो देवीभ्यो नमः

**ete gandhapuṣpe oṃ sarvābhyo devībhyo namaḥ**

With these scented flowers oṃ we bow to All the Goddesses.

एते गन्धपुष्पे ॐ श्री गुरवे नमः

**ete gandhapuṣpe oṃ śrī gurave namaḥ**

With these scented flowers oṃ we bow to the Guru.

एते गन्धपुष्पे ॐ ब्राह्मणेभ्यो नमः

**ete gandhapuṣpe oṃ brāhmaṇebhyo namaḥ**

With these scented flowers oṃ we bow to All Knowers of Wisdom.

Recite while tying a piece of string around wrist.

ॐ कुशासने स्थितो ब्रह्मा कुशे चैव जनार्दनः ।

कुशे ह्याकाशवद् विष्णुः कुशासन नमोऽस्तु ते ॥

**oṃ kuśāsane sthito brahmā kuśe caiva janārdanaḥ**
**kuśe hyākāśavad viṣṇuḥ kuśāsana namo-stu te**

Oṃ Brahmā is in the shining light (or kuśa grass), in the shining light resides Janārdana, the Lord of Beings. The Supreme all-pervading Consciousness, Viṣṇu, resides in the shining light. Oh Repository of the shining light, we bow down to you, the seat of kuśa grass.

## आचमन

## **ācamana**

ॐ केशवाय नमः स्वाहा

**oṃ keśavāya namaḥ svāhā**

Oṃ We bow to the one of beautiful hair.

ॐ माधवाय नमः स्वाहा

**oṃ mādhavāya namaḥ svāhā**

Oṃ We bow to the one who is always sweet.

ॐ गोविन्दाय नमः स्वाहा

**oṃ govindāya namaḥ svāhā**

Oṃ We bow to He who is one-pointed light.

ॐ विष्णुः ॐ विष्णुः ॐ विष्णुः

**oṃ viṣṇuḥ oṃ viṣṇuḥ oṃ viṣṇuḥ**

Oṃ Consciousness, oṃ Consciousness, oṃ Consciousness.

ॐ तत् विष्णोः परमं पदम् सदा पश्यन्ति सूरयः ।

दिवीव चक्षुराततम् ॥

**oṃ tat viṣṇoḥ paramaṃ padam**
**sadā paśyanti sūrayaḥ divīva cakṣurā tatam**

Oṃ That Consciousness of the highest station, who always sees the Light of Wisdom, give us Divine Eyes.

ॐ तद् विप्र स पिपानोव जुविग्रन्सो सोमिन्द्रते ।

विष्णुः तत् परमं पदम् ॥

**oṃ tad vipra sa pipānova juvigranso somindrate**
**viṣṇuḥ tat paramaṃ padam**

Oṃ That twice-born teacher who is always thirsty for accepting the nectar of devotion, Oh Consciousness, you are in that highest station.

ॐ अपवित्रः पवित्रो वा सर्वावस्थां गतोऽपि वा ।

यः स्मरेत् पुण्डरीकाक्षं स बाह्याभ्यन्तरः शुचिः ॥

**oṃ apavitraḥ pavitro vā sarvāvasthāṃ gato-pi vā**
**yaḥ smaret puṇḍarīkākṣaṃ**
**sa bāhyābhyantaraḥ śuciḥ**

Oṃ The Impure and the Pure reside within all objects. Who remembers the lotus-eyed Consciousness is conveyed to radiant beauty.

ॐ सर्वमङ्गलमाङ्गल्यम् वरेण्यम् वरदं शुभं ।
नारायणं नमस्कृत्य सर्वकर्माणि कारयेत् ॥

**oṃ sarva maṅgala māṅgalyam**
**vareṇyam varadaṃ śubhaṃ**
**nārāyaṇaṃ namaskṛtya sarvakarmāṇi kārayet**

Oṃ All the Welfare of all Welfare, the highest blessing of Purity and Illumination, with the offering of respect we bow down to the Supreme Consciousness who is the actual performer of all action.

ॐ सूर्य्यश्चमेति मन्त्रस्य ब्रह्मा ऋषिः प्रकृतिश्छन्दः आपो
देवता आचमने विनियोगः ॥

**oṃ sūryyaścameti mantrasya brahmā ṛṣiḥ**
**prakṛtiśchandaḥ āpo devatā ācamane viniyogaḥ**

Oṃ these are the mantras of the Light of Wisdom, the Creative Capacity is the Seer, Nature is the meter, the divine flow of waters is the deity, being applied in washing the hands and rinsing the mouth.

Draw the following yantra with some drops of water
and/or sandal paste at the front of your seat.
Place a flower on the bindu in the middle, while reciting:

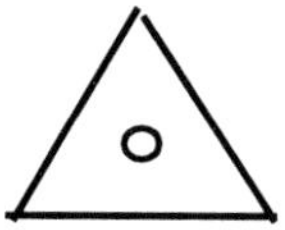

ॐ आसनस्य मन्त्रस्य मेरुपृष्ठ ऋषिः सुतलं छन्दः कूर्म्मो
देवता आसनोपवेशने विनियोगः ॥

**oṃ āsanasya mantrasya merupṛṣṭha ṛṣiḥ sutalaṃ**
**chandaḥ kūrmmo devatā āsanopaveśane viniyogaḥ**

Oṃ Introducing the mantras for the purification of the seat. The Seer is He whose back is Straight, the meter is of very beautiful form, the tortoise who supports the Earth is the deity. These mantras are applied to make the seat free from obstructions.

एते गन्धपुष्पे ॐ ह्रीं आधारशक्तये कमलासनाय नमः ॥

**ete gandhapuṣpe oṃ hrīṃ ādhāraśaktaye kamalāsanāya namaḥ**

With these scented flowers oṃ hrīṃ we bow to the Primal Energy situated in this lotus seat.

ॐ पृथ्वि त्वया धृता लोका देवि त्वं विष्णुना धृता ।
त्वञ्च धारय मां नित्यं पवित्रं कुरु चासनम् ॥

**oṃ pṛthvi tvayā dhṛtā lokā devi tvaṃ viṣṇunā dhṛtā tvañca dhāraya māṃ nityaṃ pavitraṃ kuru cāsanam**

Oṃ Earth! You support the realms of the Goddess. You are supported by the Supreme Consciousness. Also bear me eternally and make pure this seat.

ॐ गुरुभ्यो नमः

**oṃ gurubhyo namaḥ**

Oṃ I bow to the Guru.

ॐ परमगुरुभ्यो नमः

**oṃ paramagurubhyo namaḥ**

Oṃ I bow to the Guru's Guru.

ॐ परापरगुरुभ्यो नमः

**oṃ parāparagurubhyo namaḥ**

Oṃ I bow to the Gurus of the lineage.

ॐ परमेष्ठिगुरुभ्यो नमः

**oṃ parameṣṭhigurubhyo namaḥ**

Oṃ I bow to the Supreme Gurus.

ॐ गं गणेशाय नमः

**oṃ gaṃ gaṇeśāya namaḥ**

Oṃ I bow to the Lord of Wisdom.

ॐ अनन्ताय नमः

**oṃ anantāya namaḥ**

Oṃ I bow to the Infinite One.

ॐ ऐं ह्रीं क्लीं चामुण्डायै विच्चे

**oṃ aiṃ hrīṃ klīṃ cāmuṇḍāyai vicce**

Oṃ Creation, Circumstance, Transformation are known by Consciousness.

ॐ नमः शिवाय

**oṃ namaḥ śivāya**

Oṃ I bow to the Consciousness of Infinite Goodness.

Clap hands three times and snap fingers in the ten directions (N S E W NE SW NW SE UP DOWN) repeating

ॐ ऐं ह्रीं क्लीं चामुण्डायै विच्चे

**oṃ aiṃ hrīṃ klīṃ cāmuṇḍāyai vicce**

Oṃ Creation, Circumstance, Transformation are known by Consciousness.

### सङ्कल्प

### sankalpa

विष्णुः ॐ तत् सत्। ॐ अद्य जम्बूद्वीपे ( ) देशे ( )

प्रदेशे ( ) नगरे ( ) मन्दिरे ( ) मासे ( ) पक्षे ( )

तिथौ ( ) गोत्र श्री ( ) कृतैतत् श्रीचण्डिका कामः

पूजाकर्माहं करिष्ये ॥

**viṣṇuḥ oṃ tat sat oṃ adya jambūdvīpe (Country) deśe (State) pradeśe (City) nagare (Name of house or temple) mandire (month) māse (śukla or kṛṣṇa) pakṣe (name of day) tithau (name of) gotra śrī (your name) kṛtaitat śrī caṇḍikā kāmaḥ pūjā karmāhaṃ kariṣye**

The Consciousness Which Pervades All, oṃ That is Truth. Presently, on the Planet Earth, Country of (Name), State of (Name), City of (Name), in the Temple of (Name), (Name of Month) Month, (Bright or Dark) fortnight, (Name of Day) Day, (Name of Sādhu Family), Śrī (Your Name) is performing the worship for the satisfaction of the Respected Caṇḍī by reciting the Universal Worship.

ॐ यज्जाग्रतो दूरमुदेति दैवं तदु सुप्तस्य तथैवैति ।

दूरङ्गमं ज्योतिषां ज्योतिरेकं तन्मे मनः शिवसङ्कल्पमस्तु ॥

**oṃ yajjāgrato dūramudeti**
**daivaṃ tadu suptasya tathaivaiti**
**dūraṅgamaṃ jyotiṣāṃ jyotirekaṃ**
**tanme manaḥ śiva saṅkalpamastu**

Oṃ May our waking consciousness replace pain and suffering with divinity as also our awareness when asleep. Far extending be our radiant aura of light, filling our minds with light. May that be the firm determination of the Consciousness of Infinite Goodness.

या गुङ्गूर्या सिनीवाली या राका या सरस्वती ।
ईन्द्राणीमह्व ऊतये वरुणानीं स्वस्तये ॥

**yā guṅgūryā sinīvālī yā rākā yā sarasvatī**
**īndrāṇīmahva ūtaye varuṇānīṃ svastaye**

May that Goddess who wears the Moon of Devotion protect the children of Devotion. May that Goddess of All-Pervading Knowledge protect us. May the Energy of the Rule of the Pure rise up. Oh Energy of Equilibrium grant us the highest prosperity.

ॐ स्वस्ति न इन्द्रो वृद्धश्रवाः स्वस्ति नः पूषा विश्ववेदाः ।
स्वस्ति नस्तार्क्ष्यो अरिष्टनेमिः स्वस्ति नो बृहस्पतिर्दधातु ॥

**oṃ svasti na indro vṛddhaśravāḥ**
**svasti naḥ pūṣā viśvavedāḥ**
**svasti nastārkṣyo ariṣṭanemiḥ**
**svasti no bṛhaspatirdadhātu**

Oṃ The Ultimate Prosperity to us, Oh Rule of the Pure, who perceives all that changes; the Ultimate Prosperity to us, Searchers for Truth, Knowers of the Universe; the Ultimate

Prosperity to us, Oh Divine Being of Light, keep us safe; the Ultimate Prosperity to us, Oh Spirit of All-Pervading Delight, grant that to us.

ॐ गणानां त्वा गणपति꣡ हवामहे
प्रियाणां त्वा प्रियपति꣡ हवामहे
निधीनां त्वा निधिपति꣡ हवामहे वसो मम ।
आहमजानि गर्ब्भधमा त्वमजासि गर्ब्भधम् ॥

**oṃ gaṇānāṃ tvā gaṇapati guṃ havāmahe**
**priyāṇāṃ tvā priyapati guṃ havāmahe**
**nidhīnāṃ tvā nidhipati guṃ havāmahe vaso mama**
**āhamajāni garbbhadhamā tvamajāsi garbbhadham**

Oṃ We invoke you with offerings, Oh Lord of the Multitudes; we invoke you with offerings, Oh Lord of Love; we invoke you with offerings, Oh Guardian of the Treasure. Sit within me, giving birth to the realm of the Gods within me; yes, giving birth to the realm of the Gods within me.

ॐ गणानां त्वा गणपति꣡ हवामहे
कविं कवीनामुपमश्रवस्तमम् ।
ज्येष्ठराजं ब्रह्मणां ब्रह्मणस्पत
आ नः शृण्वन्नूतिभिः सीद सादनम् ॥

**oṃ gaṇānāṃ tvā gaṇapati guṃ havāmahe**
**kaviṃ kavīnāmupamaśravastamam**
**jyeṣṭharājaṃ brahmaṇāṃ brahmaṇaspata**
**ā naḥ śṛṇvannūtibhiḥ sīda sādanam**

Oṃ We invoke you with offerings, Oh Lord of the Multitudes, Seer among Seers, of unspeakable grandeur. Oh Glorious

King, Lord of the Knowers of Wisdom, come speedily hearing our supplications and graciously take your seat amidst our assembly.

ॐ अदितिर्द्यौरदितिरन्तरिक्षमदितिर्माता स पिता

स पुत्रः । विश्वे देवा अदितिः पञ्च जना

अदितिर्जातमदितिर्जनित्वम् ॥

**oṃ aditir dyauraditirantarikṣamaditirmātā**
**sa pitā sa putraḥ**
**viśve devā aditiḥ pañca janā**
**aditirjātamaditirjanitvam**

Oṃ The Mother of Enlightenment pervades the heavens; the Mother of Enlightenment pervades the atmosphere; the Mother of Enlightenment pervades Mother and Father and child. All Gods of the Universe are pervaded by the Mother, the five forms of living beings, all Life. The Mother of Enlightenment, She is to be known.

ॐ त्वं स्त्रीस्त्वं पुमानसि त्वं कुमार अत वा कुमारी ।

त्वं जिर्नो दण्डेन वञ्चसि त्वं जातो भवसि विश्वतोमुखः ॥

**oṃ tvaṃ strīstvaṃ pumānasi**
**tvaṃ kumāra ata vā kumārī**
**tvaṃ jirno daṇḍena vañcasi**
**tvaṃ jāto bhavasi viśvatomukhaḥ**

Oṃ You are Female, you are Male; you are a young boy, you are a young girl. You are the word of praise by which we are singing; you are all creation existing as the mouth of the universe.

ॐ श्रीश्च ते लक्ष्मीश्च पत्न्यावहोरात्रे पार्श्वे नक्षत्राणि रूपमश्विनौ व्यात्तम् । इष्णं निषाणामुं म ऽइषाण सर्वलोकं म ऽइषाण ॥

**oṃ śrīśca te lakṣmīśca patnyāvahorātre pārśve nakṣatrāṇi rūpamaśvinau vyāttam**
**iṣṇaṃ niṣāṇāmuṃ ma -iṣāṇa sarvalokaṃ ma-iṣāṇa**

Oṃ the Highest Respect to you, Goal of all Existence, wife of the full and complete night (the Unknowable One), at whose sides are the stars, and who has the form of the relentless search for Truth. Oh Supreme Divinity, Supreme Divinity, my Supreme Divinity, all existence is my Supreme Divinity.

ॐ अम्बेऽम्बिकेऽम्बालिके न मा नयति कश्चन ।
ससस्त्यश्वकः सुभद्रिकां काम्पीलवासिनीम् ॥

**oṃ ambe-mbike-mbālike na mā nayati kaścana**
**sasastyaśvakaḥ subhadrikāṃ kāmpīlavāsinīm**

Oṃ Mother of the Perceivable Universe, Mother of the Conceivable Universe, Mother of the Universe of Intuitive Vision, lead me to that True Existence. As excellent crops (or grains) are harvested, so may I be taken to reside with the Infinite Consciousness.

ॐ शान्ता द्यौः शान्तापृथिवी शान्तमिदमुर्वन्तरिक्षम् ।
शान्ता उदन्वतिरापः शान्ताः नः शान्त्वोषधीः ॥

**oṃ śāntā dyauḥ śāntā pṛthivī śāntam idamurvantarikṣam**
**śāntā udanvatirāpaḥ śāntāḥ naḥ śāntvoṣadhīḥ**

Oṃ Peace in the heavens, Peace on the earth, Peace upwards and permeating the atmosphere; Peace upwards, over, on all sides and further; Peace to us, Peace to all vegetation;

ॐ शान्तानि पूर्वरूपाणि शान्तं नोऽस्तु कृताकृतम् ।
शान्तं भूतं च भव्यं च सर्वमेव शमस्तु नः ॥

**oṃ śāntāni pūrva rūpāṇi śāntaṃ no-stu kṛtākṛtam**
**śāntaṃ bhūtaṃ ca bhavyaṃ ca**
**sarvameva śamastu naḥ**

Oṃ Peace to all that has form, Peace to all causes and effects; Peace to all existence, and to all intensities of reality, including all and everything; Peace be to us.

ॐ पृथिवी शान्तिरन्तरिक्षं शान्तिर्द्यौः
शान्तिरापः शान्तिरोषधयः शान्तिः वनस्पतयः शान्तिर्विश्वे
मे देवाः शान्तिः सर्वे मे देवाः शान्तिर्ब्रह्म शान्तिरापः शान्तिः
सर्वं शान्तिरेधि शान्तिः शान्तिः सर्व शान्तिः सा मा शान्तिः
शान्तिभिः ॥

**oṃ pṛthivī śāntir antarikṣaṃ śāntir dyauḥ**
**śāntir āpaḥ śāntir oṣadhayaḥ śāntiḥ vanaspatayaḥ**
**śāntir viśve me devāḥ śāntiḥ sarve me devāḥ śāntir**
**brahma śāntirāpaḥ śāntiḥ sarvaṃ śāntiredhi śāntiḥ**
**śāntiḥ sarva śāntiḥ sā mā śāntiḥ śāntibhiḥ**

Oṃ Let the earth be at Peace, the atmosphere be at Peace, the heavens be filled with Peace. Even further may Peace extend, Peace be to waters, Peace to all vegetation, Peace to All Gods of the Universe, Peace to All Gods within us, Peace to Creative Consciousness, Peace to Brilliant Light, Peace to All, Peace to

Everything, Peace, Peace, altogether Peace, equally Peace, by means of Peace.

ताभिः शान्तिभिः सर्वशान्तिभिः समया मोहं यदिह घोरं यदिह क्रूरं यदिह पापं तच्छान्तं तच्छिवं सर्वमेव समस्तु नः ॥

**tābhiḥ śāntibhiḥ sarva śāntibhiḥ samayā moham yadiha ghoram yadiha krūram yadiha pāpam tacchāntam tacchivam sarvameva samastu naḥ**

Thus by means of Peace, altogether one with the means of Peace, Ignorance is eliminated, Violence is eradicated, Improper Conduct is eradicated, Confusion (sin) is eradicated, all that is, is at Peace, all that is perceived, each and everything, altogether for us,

ॐ शान्तिः शान्तिः शान्तिः ॥

**oṃ śāntiḥ śāntiḥ śāntiḥ**

Oṃ Peace, Peace, Peace

## गणेश पूजा

## gaṇeśa pūjā

worship of gaṇeśa

ॐ विश्वेशं माधवं ढुण्ढिं दण्डपाणिं च भैरवम् ।
वन्दे काशीं गुहां गङ्गां भवानीं मणिकर्णिकाम् ॥

**oṃ viśveśaṃ mādhavaṃ ḍhuṇḍhiṃ**
**daṇḍapāṇiṃ ca bhairavam**
**vande kāśīṃ guhāṃ gaṅgāṃ**
**bhavānīṃ maṇikarṇikām**

Oṃ the Lord of the Universe, Lord Viṣṇu Mādhava, who holds the club in his hand and is fearless, worships He Who dwells in the cave at Benaris, who holds aloft the Gaṅgā, who is the Lord of the Universe, He who wears jeweled earrings.

### gaṇeśa gāyatrī

ॐ तत् पुरुषाय विद्महे वक्रतुण्डाय धीमहि ।
तन्नो दन्ती प्रचोदयात् ॥

**oṃ tat puruṣāya vidmahe vakratuṇḍāya dhīmahi**
**tanno dantī pracodayāt**

Oṃ we meditate on that Perfect Consciousness, we contemplate the One with a broken tooth. May that One with the Great Tusk grant us increase.

एते गन्धपुष्पे ॐ गं गणपतये नमः

**ete gandhapuṣpe oṃ gaṃ gaṇapataye namaḥ**

With these scented flowers oṃ we bow to the Lord of Wisdom, Lord of the Multitudes.

## gaṇeśa dhyānam

meditation

ॐ सुमुखश्चैकदन्तश्च कपिलो गजकर्णकः ।
लम्बोदरश्च विकटो विघ्ननाशो विनायकः ॥

**oṃ sumukhaścaika dantaśca kapilo gaja karṇakaḥ**
**lambodaraśca vikaṭo vighnanāśo vināyakaḥ**

Oṃ He has a beautiful face with only one tooth (or tusk), of red color with elephant ears; with a big belly and a great tooth he destroys all obstacles. He is the Remover of Obstacles.

धूम्रकेतुर्गणाध्यक्षो भालचन्द्रो गजाननः ।
द्वादशैतानि नामानि यः पठेच्छृणुयादपि ॥

**dhūmraketurgaṇādhyakṣo bhāla candro gajānanaḥ**
**dvādaśaitāni nāmāni yaḥ paṭhecchṛṇu yādapi**

With a grey banner, the living spirit of the multitudes, having the moon on his forehead, with an elephant's face. Whoever will recite or listen to these twelve names

विद्यारम्भे विवाहे च प्रवेशे निर्गमे तथा ।
संग्रामे संकटे चैव विघ्नस्तस्य न जायते ॥

**vidyārambhe vivāhe ca praveśe nirgame tathā**
**saṃgrāme saṃkate caiva vighnastasya na jāyate**

at the time of commencing studies, getting married, or on entering or leaving any place; on a battlefield of war, or in any difficulty, will overcome all obstacles.

शुक्लाम्बरधरं देवं शशिवर्णं चतुर्भुजम् ।
प्रसन्नवदनं ध्यायेत् सर्वविघ्नोपशान्तये ॥

**śuklāmbaradharaṃ devaṃ śaśivarṇaṃ caturbhujam**
**prasannavadanaṃ dhyāyet sarvavighnopaśāntaye**

Wearing a white cloth, the God has the color of the moon and four arms. That most pleasing countenance is meditated on who gives peace to all difficulties.

अभीप्सितार्थसिद्ध्यर्थं पूजितो यः सुरासुरैः ।
सर्वविघ्नहरस् तस्मै गणाधिपतये नमः ॥

**abhīpsitārtha siddhyarthaṃ pūjito yaḥ surā suraiḥ**
**sarvavighna haras tasmai gaṇādhipataye namaḥ**

For gaining the desired objective, or for the attainment of perfection, he is worshipped by the Forces of Union and the Forces of Division alike. He takes away all difficulties, and therefore, we bow down in reverance to the Lord of the Multitudes.

मल्लिकादि सुगन्धीनि मालित्यादीनि वै प्रभो ।
मयाऽहृतानि पूजार्थं पुष्पाणि प्रतिगृह्यताम् ॥

**mallikādi sugandhīni mālityādīni vai prabho**
**mayā-hṛtāni pūjārthaṃ puṣpāṇi pratigṛhyatām**

Various flowers, such as mallikā and others of excellent scent, are being offered to you, Our Lord. All these flowers have come from the devotion of our hearts for your worship. Please accept them.

एते गन्धपुष्पे ॐ गं गणपतये नमः

**ete gandhapuṣpe oṃ gaṃ gaṇapataye namaḥ**

With these scented flowers oṃ we bow to the Lord of Wisdom, the Lord of the Multitudes.

वक्रतुण्ड महाकाय सूर्यकोटिसमप्रभ ।
अविघ्नं कुरु मे देव सर्वकार्येषु सर्वदा ॥

**vakratuṇḍa mahākāya sūrya koṭi samaprabha**
**avighnaṃ kuru me deva sarva kāryeṣu sarvadā**

With a broken (or bent) tusk, a great body shining like a million suns, make us free from all obstacles, Oh God. Always remain (with us) in all actions.

एकदन्तं महाकायं लम्बोदरं गजाननम् ।
विघ्ननाशकरं देवं हेरम्बं प्रणामाम्यहम् ॥

**ekadantaṃ mahākāyaṃ lambodaraṃ gajānanam**
**vighnanāśakaraṃ devaṃ**
**herambaṃ praṇāmāmyaham**

With one tooth, a great body, a big belly and an elephant's face, he is the God who destroys all obstacles to whom we are bowing down with devotion.

## puṇyā havācana, svasti vācana

proclamation of merits and eternal blessings

ॐ शान्तिरस्तु

**oṃ śāntirastu**

Oṃ Peace be unto you.

ॐ पुष्टिरस्तु

**oṃ puṣṭirastu**

Oṃ Increase (Nourishment) be unto you.

ॐ तुष्टिरस्तु

**oṃ tuṣṭirastu**

Oṃ Satisfaction be unto you.

ॐ वृद्धिरस्तु

**oṃ vṛddhirastu**

Oṃ Positive Change be unto you.

ॐ अविघ्नमस्तु

**oṃ avighnamastu**

Oṃ Freedom from Obstacles be unto you.

ॐ आयुष्यमस्तु

**oṃ āyuṣyamastu**

Oṃ Life be unto you.

ॐ आरोग्यमस्तु

**oṃ ārogyamastu**

Oṃ Freedom from Disease be unto you.

ॐ शिवमस्तु

**oṃ śivamastu**

Oṃ Consciousness of Infinite Goodness be unto you.

ॐ शिवकर्माऽस्तु

**oṃ śivakarmā-stu**

Oṃ Consciousness of Infinite Goodness in all action be unto you.

ॐ कर्मसमृद्धिरस्तु

**oṃ karmasamṛddhirastu**

Oṃ Progress (Increase) in all action be unto you.

ॐ धर्मसमृद्धिरस्तु

**oṃ dharmasamṛddhirastu**

Oṃ Progress (Increase)in all Ways of Truth be unto you.

ॐ वेदसमृद्धिरस्तु

**oṃ vedasamṛddhirastu**

Oṃ Progress (Increase) in all Knowledge be unto you.

ॐ शास्त्रसमृद्धिरस्तु

**oṃ śāstrasamṛddhirastu**

Oṃ Progress (Increase) in Scriptures be unto you.

ॐ धन-धान्यसमृद्धिरस्तु

**oṃ dhana-dhānyasamṛddhirastu**

Oṃ Progress (Increase) in Wealth and Grains be unto you.

ॐ इष्टसम्पदस्तु

**oṃ iṣṭasampadastu**

Oṃ May your beloved deity be your wealth.

ॐ अरिष्टनिरसनमस्तु

**oṃ ariṣṭanirasanamastu**

Oṃ May you remain safe and secure, without any fear.

ॐ यत्पापं रोगमशुभमकल्याणं तद्दूरे प्रतिहतमस्तु

**oṃ yatpāpaṃ rogamaśubhamakalyāṇaṃ taddūre pratihatamastu**

Oṃ May sin, sickness, impurity and that which is not conducive unto welfare leave from you.

ॐ ब्रह्म पुण्यमहर्यच्च सृष्ट्युत्पादनकारकम् ।
वेदवृक्षोद्भवं नित्यं तत्पुण्याहं ब्रुवन्तु नः ॥

**oṃ brahma puṇyamaharyacca**
**sṛṣṭyutpādanakārakam**
**vedavṛkṣodbhavaṃ nityaṃ**
**tatpuṇyāhaṃ bruvantu naḥ**

Oṃ The Creative Capacity with the greatest merit, the Cause of the Birth of Creation, eternally has its being in the tree of Wisdom. May His blessing of merit be bestowed upon us.

भो ब्राह्मणाः ! मया क्रियमाणस्य दुर्गापूजनाख्यस्य कर्मणः
पुण्याहं भवन्तो ब्रुवन्तु ॥

**bho brāhmaṇāḥ ! mayā kriyamāṇasya**
**durgāpūjanākhyasya karmaṇaḥ**
**puṇyāhaṃ bhavanto bruvantu**

Oh Brahmiṇs! My sincere effort is to perform the worship of Durgā. Let these activities yield merit.

ॐ पुण्याहं ॐ पुण्याहं ॐ पुण्याहं ॥

**oṃ puṇyāhaṃ oṃ puṇyāhaṃ oṃ puṇyāhaṃ**

Oṃ Let these activities yield merit.

ॐ अस्य कर्मणः पुण्याहं भवन्तो ब्रुवन्तु ॥

**oṃ asya karmaṇaḥ puṇyāhaṃ bhavanto bruvantu**

Oṃ Let these activities yield merit.

ॐ पुण्याहं ॐ पुण्याहं ॐ पुण्याहं ॥

**oṃ puṇyāhaṃ oṃ puṇyāhaṃ oṃ puṇyāhaṃ**

Oṃ Let these activities yield merit (three times).

पृथिव्यामुद्धृतायां तु यत्कल्याणं पुरा कृतम् ।
ऋषिभिः सिद्धगन्धर्वैस्तत्कल्याणं ब्रुवन्तु नः ॥

**pṛthivyāmuddhṛtāyāṃ tu yatkalyāṇaṃ purā kṛtam**
**ṛṣibhiḥ siddha gandharvaistatkalyāṇaṃ bruvantu naḥ**

As solid as the earth, let supreme welfare be. May the Ṛṣis, the attained ones and the celestial singers bestow welfare upon us.

भो ब्राह्मणाः ! मया क्रियमाणस्य दुर्गापूजनाख्यस्य कर्मणः
कल्याणं भवन्तो ब्रुवन्तु ॥

**bho brāhmaṇāḥ ! mayā kriyamāṇasya**
**durgāpūjanākhyasya karmaṇaḥ**
**kalyāṇaṃ bhavanto bruvantu**

Oh Brahmiṇs! My sincere effort is to perform the worship of Durgā. Let these activities bestow welfare.

ॐ कल्याणं ॐ कल्याणं ॐ कल्याणं

**oṃ kalyāṇaṃ oṃ kalyāṇaṃ oṃ kalyāṇaṃ**

Oṃ Let these activities bestow welfare (three times).

सागरस्य तु या ऋद्धिर्महालक्ष्म्यादिभिः कृता ।
सम्पूर्णा सुप्रभावा च तामृद्धिं प्रब्रुवन्तु नः ॥

**sāgarasya tu yā ṛddhirmahālakṣmyādibhiḥ kṛtā**
**sampūrṇā suprabhāvā ca tāmṛddhiṃ prabruvantu naḥ**

May the ocean yield Prosperity, as it did when the Great Goddess of True Wealth and others were produced. Fully and completely giving forth excellent lustre, may Prosperity be unto us.

भो ब्राह्मणाः ! मया क्रियमाणस्य दुर्गापूजनाख्यस्य कर्मणः
ऋद्धिं भवन्तो ब्रुवन्तु ॥

**bho brāhmaṇāḥ ! mayā kriyamāṇasya**
**durgāpūjanākhyasya karmaṇaḥ**
**ṛddhiṃ bhavanto bruvantu**

Oh Brahmiṇs! My sincere effort is to perform the worship of Durgā. Let these activities bestow Prosperity.

ॐ कर्म ऋध्यताम् ॐ कर्म ऋध्यताम् ॐ कर्म ऋध्यताम्

**oṃ karma ṛdhyatām oṃ karma ṛdhyatām oṃ karma ṛdhyatām**

Oṃ Let these activities bestow Prosperity (three times).

स्वस्तिरस्तु याविनाशाख्या पुण्यकल्याणवृद्धिदा ।
विनायकप्रिया नित्यं तां च स्वस्तिं ब्रुवन्तु नः ॥

**svastirastu yā vināśākhyā puṇya kalyāṇa vṛddhidā**
**vināyakapriyā nityaṃ tāṃ ca svastiṃ bruvantu naḥ**

Let the Eternal Blessings that grant changes of indestructible merit and welfare be with us. May the Lord who removes all obstacles be pleased and grant to us Eternal Blessings.

भो ब्राह्मणाः ! मया क्रियमाणस्य दुर्गापूजनाख्यस्य कर्मणः

स्वस्तिं भवन्तो ब्रुवन्तु ॥

**bho brāhmaṇāḥ ! mayā kriyamāṇasya**
**durgāpūjanākhyasya karmaṇaḥ**
**svastiṃ bhavanto bruvantu**

Oh Brahmiṇs! My sincere effort is to perform the worship of Durgā. Let these activities bestow Eternal Blessings.

ॐ आयुष्मते स्वस्ति ॐ आयुष्मते स्वस्ति

ॐ आयुष्मते स्वस्ति

**oṃ āyuṣmate svasti oṃ āyuṣmate svasti**
**oṃ āyuṣmate svasti**

Oṃ May life be filled with Eternal Blessings (three times).

ॐ स्वस्ति न इन्द्रो वृद्धश्रवाः स्वस्ति नः पूषा विश्ववेदाः ।

स्वस्ति नस्तार्क्ष्यो अरिष्टनेमिः स्वस्ति नो बृहस्पतिर्दधातु ॥

**oṃ svasti na indro vṛddhaśravāḥ**
**svasti naḥ pūṣā viśvavedāḥ**
**svasti nastārkṣyo ariṣṭanemiḥ**
**svasti no bṛhaspatirdadhātu**

Oṃ Eternal Blessings to us, Oh Rule of the Pure, who perceives all that changes; Eternal Blessings to us, Searchers for Truth, Knowers of the Universe; Eternal Blessings to us, Oh Divine Being of Light, keep us safe; Eternal Blessings to us, Oh Spirit of All-Pervading Delight, grant them to us.

समुद्रमथनाज्ज्ञाता जगदानन्दकारिका ।

हरिप्रिया च माङ्गल्या तां श्रियं च ब्रुवन्तु नः ॥

**samudramathanājjātā jagadānandakārikā**
**haripriyā ca māṅgalyā tāṃ śriyaṃ ca bruvantu naḥ**

Who was born from the churning of the ocean, the cause of bliss to the worlds, the beloved of Viṣṇu and Welfare Herself, may Śrī, the Highest Respect, be unto us.

भो ब्राह्मणाः ! मया क्रियमाणस्य दुर्गापूजनाख्यस्य कर्मणः श्रीरस्त्विति भवन्तो ब्रुवन्तु ॥

**bho brāhmaṇāḥ ! mayā kriyamāṇasya**
**durgāpūjanākhyasya karmaṇaḥ**
**śrīrastviti bhavanto bruvantu**

Oh Brahmiṇs! My sincere effort is to perform the worship of Durgā. Let these activities bestow the Highest Respect.

ॐ अस्तु श्रीः ॐ अस्तु श्रीः ॐ अस्तु श्रीः

**oṃ astu śrīḥ oṃ astu śrīḥ oṃ astu śrīḥ**

Oṃ Let these activities bestow the Highest Respect (three times).

ॐ श्रीश्च ते लक्ष्मीश्च पत्न्यावहोरात्रे पार्श्वे नक्षत्राणि रूपमश्विनौ व्यात्तम् । इष्णन्निषाणामुं म इषाण सर्वलोकं म इषाण ॥

**oṃ śrīśca te lakṣmīśca patnyāvahorātre pārśve**
**nakṣatrāṇi rūpamaśvinau vyāttam**
**iṣṇanniṣāṇāmuṃ ma iṣāṇa sarvalokaṃ ma iṣāṇa**

Oṃ the Highest Respect to you, Goal of all Existence, wife of the full and complete night (the Unknowable One), at whose sides are the stars, and who has the form of the relentless search for Truth. Oh Supreme Divinity, Supreme Divinity, my Supreme Divinity, all existence is my Supreme Divinity.

मृकण्डसूनोरायुर्यद्ध्रुवलोमशयोस्तथा ।
आयुषा तेन संयुक्ता जीवेम शरदः शतम् ॥

**mṛkaṇḍasūnorāyuryaddhruvalomaśayostathā**
**āyuṣā tena saṃyuktā jīvema śaradaḥ śatam**

As the son of Mṛkaṇḍa, Mārkaṇḍeya, found imperishable life, may we be united with life and blessed with a hundred autumns.

शतं जीवन्तु भवन्तः

**śataṃ jīvantu bhavantaḥ**

May a hundred autumns be unto you.

शिवगौरीविवाहे या या श्रीरामे नृपात्मजे ।
धनदस्य गृहे या श्रीरस्माकं साऽस्तु सद्मनि ॥

**śiva gaurī vivāhe yā yā śrīrāme nṛpātmaje**
**dhanadasya gṛhe yā śrīrasmākaṃ sā-stu sadmani**

As the imperishable union of Śiva and Gaurī, as the soul of kings manifested in the respected Rāma, so may the Goddess of Respect forever be united with us and always dwell in our house.

ॐ अस्तु श्रीः ॐ अस्तु श्रीः ॐ अस्तु श्रीः

**oṃ astu śrīḥ oṃ astu śrīḥ oṃ astu śrīḥ**

Oṃ May Respect be unto you (three times).

प्रजापतिर्लोकपालो धाता ब्रह्मा च देवराट् ।
भगवाञ्छाश्वतो नित्यं नो वै रक्षन्तु सर्वतः ॥

**prajāpatirlokapālo dhātā brahmā ca devarāṭ**
**bhagavāñchāśvato nityaṃ no vai rakṣantu sarvataḥ**

The Lord of all beings, Protector of the worlds, Creator, Brahmā, Support of the Gods; may the Supreme Lord be gracious eternally and always protect us.

ॐ भगवान् प्रजापतिः प्रियताम्

**oṃ bhagavān prajāpatiḥ priyatām**

Oṃ May the Supreme Lord, the Lord of all beings, be pleased.

आयुष्मते स्वस्तिमते यजमानाय दाशुषे ।
श्रिये दत्ताशिषः सन्तु ऋत्विग्भिर्वेदपारगैः ॥

**āyuṣmate svastimate yajamānāya dāśuṣe**
**śriye dattāśiṣaḥ santu ṛtvigbhirvedapāragaiḥ**

May life and eternal blessings be granted to those who perform this worship and to those who assist. May respect be given to the priests who impart this wisdom.

ॐ स्वस्तिवाचनसमृद्धिरस्तु

**oṃ svastivācanasamṛddhirastu**

Oṃ May this invocation for eternal blessings find excellent prosperity.

## gāyatrī viddhi
## system of worship with gāyatrī

ॐ प्रजापतिर्ऋषिर्गायत्रीछन्दोऽग्निर्देवता व्याहृति होमे विनियोगः ।

**oṃ prajāptirṛṣirgāyatrī chando-gnirdevatā vyāhṛti home viniyogaḥ**

Oṃ The Lord of Creation is the Seer, Gāyatrī is the meter (24 syllables to the verse), Purification is the Divinity, the Proclamations of Delight are applied in offering.

ॐ भूः स्वाहा ॥

**oṃ bhūḥ svāhā**

Oṃ Gross Perception.

ॐ प्रजापतिर्ऋषिरुष्णिक्छन्दोवायुर्देवता व्याहृति होमे विनियोगः ।

**oṃ prajāpatirṛṣiruṣṇik chando vāyurdevatā vyāhṛti home viniyogaḥ**

The Lord of Creation is the Seer, Uṣṇik is the meter (28 syllables to the verse), Emancipation is the Divinity, the Proclamations of Delight are applied in offering.

ॐ भुवः स्वाहा ॥

**oṃ bhuvaḥ svāhā**

Oṃ Subtle Perception.

ॐ प्रजापतिर्ऋषिरनुष्टुप्छन्दः सूर्योदेवता व्याहृति होमे विनियोगः ।

**oṃ prajāpitirṛṣiranuṣṭup chandaḥ sūryodevatā vyāhṛti home viniyogaḥ**

The Lord of Creation is the Seer, Anuṣṭup is the meter (32 syllables to the verse), The Light of Wisdom is the Divinity, the Proclamations of Delight are applied in offering.

ॐ स्वः स्वाहा ॥

**oṃ svaḥ svāhā**

Oṃ Intuitive Perception.

ॐ प्रजापतिर्ऋषिर्बृहती छन्दः प्रजापतिर्देवता महाव्याहृति होमे विनियोगः ।

**oṃ prajāpatirṛṣirbṛhatī chandaḥ prajāpatirdevatā mahāvyāhṛti home viniyogaḥ**

The Lord of Creation is the Seer, Bṛhatī is the meter (40 syllables to the verse), The Lord of Creation is the Divinity, the Great (full, complete) Proclamations of Delight are applied in offering.

ॐ भूर्भुवः स्वः स्वाहा ॥

**oṃ bhūrbhuvaḥ svaḥ svāhā**

Oṃ Gross Perception, oṃ Subtle Perception, oṃ Intuitive Perception.

ॐ गायत्र्या विश्वामित्रऋषिर्गायत्री छन्दः सवितादेवता गायत्री जपे विनियोगः ॥

**oṃ gāyatryā viśvāmitraṛṣirgāyatrī chandaḥ savitādevatā gāyatrī jape viniyogaḥ**

The Gāyatrī (Mantra), The Friend of the Universe is the Seer, Gāyatrī is the meter (24 syllables to the verse), The Daughter of Light is the Divinity, the Gāyatrī (mantra) is applied in recitation.

*Holding tattva mudrā, touch head:*

विश्वामित्र ऋषये नमः

**viśvāmitra ṛṣaye namaḥ** *touch head*

To the Seer, Friend of the Universe, I bow.

गायत्री छन्दःसे नमः

**gāyatrī chandaḥse namaḥ** *touch mouth*

To the Meter, Gāyatrī (24 syllables to the verse), I bow.

सवित्रीदेवतायै नमः

**savitrīdevatāyai namaḥ** *touch heart*

To the Divinity, the Daughter of the Light, I bow.

ॐ हृदयाय नमः

**oṃ hṛdayāya namaḥ** *touch heart*

Oṃ in the heart, I bow.

ॐ भूः शिरसे स्वाहा

**oṃ bhūḥ śirase svāhā** *top of head*

Oṃ Gross Perception on the top of the head, I am One with God!

ॐ भुवः शिखायै वषट्

**oṃ bhuvaḥ śikhāyai vaṣaṭ** *back of head*

Oṃ Subtle Perception on the back of the head, Purify!

ॐ स्वः कवचाय हुं

**oṃ svaḥ kavacāya huṃ** *cross both arms*

Oṃ Intuitive Perception crossing both arms, Cut the Ego!

ॐ भूर्भुवः स्वः नेत्रत्रयाय वौषट्

**oṃ bhūrbhuvaḥ svaḥ netratrayāya vauṣaṭ** *touch three eyes*

Oṃ Gross Perception, Subtle Perception, Intuitive Perception in the three eyes, Ultimate Purity!

ॐ भूर्भुवः स्वः करतल कर पृष्ठाभ्यां अस्त्राय फट्

**oṃ bhūrbhuvaḥ svaḥ karatal kar pṛṣṭābhyāṃ astrāya phaṭ**

Oṃ I bow to Gross Perception, Subtle Perception, Intuitive Perception with the weapon of Virtue.

*roll hand over hand front and back and clap*

ॐ भूः हृदयाय नमः

**oṃ bhūḥ hṛdayāya namaḥ** *touch heart*

Oṃ Gross Perception in the heart, I bow.

ॐ भुवः शिरसे स्वाहा

**oṃ bhuvaḥ śirase svāhā** *top of head*

Oṃ Subtle Perception on the top of the head, I am One with God!

ॐ स्वः शिखायै वषट्

**oṃ svaḥ śikhāyai vaṣaṭ** *back of head*

Oṃ Intuitive Perception on the back of the head, Purify!

ॐ तत् सवितुर्वरेण्यम् कवचाय हुं

**oṃ tat saviturvareṇyam kavacāya huṃ** *cross both arms*
Oṃ That Light of Wisdom that is the Supreme crossing both arms, Cut the Ego!

ॐ भर्गो देवस्य धीमहि नेत्रत्रयाय वौषट्

**oṃ bhargo devasya dhīmahi netratrayāya vauṣaṭ**

*touch three eyes*

Oṃ Wealth of the Gods, we meditate in the three eyes, Ultimate Purify!

ॐ धियो यो नः प्रचोदयात् ॐ करतल कर पृष्ठाभ्यां अस्त्राय फट्

**oṃ dhiyo yo naḥ pracodayāt oṃ karatal kar pṛṣṭābhyāṃ astrāya phaṭ**
Oṃ May it grant to us increase in our meditations with the weapon of Virtue.

*roll hand over hand front and back and clap*

ॐ तत् सवितुर्हृदयाय नमः

**oṃ tat saviturhṛdayāya namaḥ** *touch heart*
Oṃ That Light of Wisdom in the heart, I bow.

ॐ वरेण्यम् शिरसे स्वाहा

**oṃ vareṇyam śirase svāhā** *top of head*
Oṃ That is the Supreme on the top of the head, I am One with God!

ॐ भर्गो देवस्य शिखायै वषट्

**oṃ bhargo devasya śikhāyai vaṣaṭ** *back of head*
Oṃ Wealth of the Gods on the back of the head, Purify!

ॐ धीमहि कवचाय हुं

**oṃ dhīmahi kavacāya huṃ** *cross both arms*
Oṃ We meditate crossing both arms, Cut the Ego!

ॐ धियो योनः नेत्रत्रयाय वौषट्

**oṃ dhiyo yo naḥ netratrayāya vauṣaṭ** *touch three eyes*
Oṃ May it grant to us increase in Ultimate Purity in the three eyes

ॐ प्रचोदयात् ॐ करतलकरपृष्ठाभ्यां अस्त्राय फट्

**oṃ pracodayāt oṃ karatal kar pṛṣṭhābhyāṃ astrāya phaṭ**
Oṃ Increase in our meditations with the weapon of Virtue.
*roll hand over hand front and back and clap*

ॐ भूर्भुवः स्वः । तत् सवितुर्वरेण्यम् भर्गो देवस्य धीमहि
धियो योनः प्रचोदयात् ॐ ॥

**oṃ bhūrbhuvaḥ svaḥ**
**tat saviturvareṇyam bhargo devasya dhīmahi**
**dhiyo yo naḥ pracodayāt oṃ**
Oṃ the Infinite Beyond Conception, the gross body, the subtle body and the causal body; we meditate on that Light of Wisdom that is the Supreme Wealth of the Gods. May it grant to us increase in our meditations.

महेश-वदनोत्पन्ना विष्णोर्हृदय सम्भवा ।

ब्रह्मणा समनुज्ञाता गच्छ देवि यथेच्छया ॥

**maheśa-vadanotpannā viṣṇorhṛdaya sambhavā**
**brahmaṇā samanujñātā gaccha devi yathecchayā**

Arisen from Maheśvara, The Great Seer of All, residing in the heart of the Consciousness that Pervades All, equally in the Wisdom of the Creative Capacity, the Goddess moves according to Her desire.

## ātmarakṣa

protection of the soul

ॐ जातवेदस इत्यस्य काश्यप ऋषिस्त्रिष्टुप्

छन्दोऽग्निर्देवता आत्मरक्षायां जपे विनियोगः ।

**oṃ jātavedasa ītyasya kāśyapa ṛṣistriṣṭup chandognirdevatā ātmarakṣāyāṃ jape viniyogaḥ**

Oṃ the mantra beginning, "The Knower of All," etc., Kaśyapa is the Seer, Triṣṭup is the meter (44 syllables to the verse), Agni is the divinity, for the protection of the soul these mantras are applied in recitation.

ॐ जातवेदसे सुनवाम सोममरातीयतोनि दहाति वेदः ।

स नः पर्षदति दुर्गाणि विश्वा नावेव सिन्धुं दुरितात्यग्निः ॥

**oṃ jātavedase sunavāma somam**
**arātīyatoni dahāti vedaḥ**
**sa naḥ parṣadati durgāṇi viśvā**
**nāveva sindhuṃ duritātyagniḥ**

Oṃ We worship the Knower of All with the offering of Love and Devotion. May the God of Purity reduce all enmity in the universe to ashes, and as an excellent oarsman, may he steer our ship across the sea of pain and confusion to the shores of Liberation.

ॐ दुर्गे दुर्गे रक्षाणि हुं फट् स्वाहा ॥

**oṃ durge durge rakṣāṇi huṃ phaṭ svāhā**

Oṃ Reliever of Difficulties, Reliever of Difficulties, Protect us, Cut the Ego! Purify! I am One with God!

ॐ अं हुं फट् स्वाहा ॥

**oṃ aṃ huṃ phaṭ svāhā**

Oṃ Aṃ (Creation, Beginning) Cut the Ego! Purity! I am One with God!

## rudropasthāna

the establishment of the reliever of sufferings

ॐ ऋतमित्यस्य कालाग्निरुद्र ऋषिरनुष्टुप् छन्दोरुद्रो देवता रुद्रोपस्थाने विनियोगः ।

**oṃ ṛtamityasya kālāgnirudra ṛṣiranuṣṭup chandorudro devatā rudropasthāne viniyogaḥ**

Oṃ "Whose sole form is the Entire Universe," the Reliever of Sufferings, Purifier of Time (or Purifier in Time) is the Seer, Anuṣṭup is the meter (32 syllables to the verse), the establishment of the Reliever of Sufferings is the application.

ॐ ऋतं सत्यं परं ब्रह्मा पुरुषं कृष्णपिङ्गलम् ।

ऊर्द्ध्वरेतं विरूपाक्षं विश्वरूपं नमो नमः ॥

**oṃ ṛtaṃ satyaṃ paraṃ brahmā**
**puruṣaṃ kṛṣṇapiṅgalam**
**ūrdvaretaṃ virūpākṣaṃ viśvarūpaṃ namo namaḥ**

Oṃ The Supreme Consciousness whose sole form is the Entire Universe, and Infinite Wisdom and Truth, who, for the advancement of Devotion, assumes the form of Consciousness both male and female (Umā, Maheśvara: Consciousness and Nature); whose one half is dark and the other half light, whose semen rises up, and who is the form of the universe, with three eyes, to that Universal Form, again and again we bow down in devotion.

एते गन्धपुष्पे ॐ ब्रह्मणे नमः

**ete gandhapuṣpe oṃ brahmaṇe namaḥ**

With these scented flowers oṃ we bow to Creative Consciousness.

एते गन्धपुष्पे ॐ ब्राह्मणेभ्यो नमः

**ete gandhapuṣpe oṃ brāhmaṇebhyo namaḥ**

With these scented flowers oṃ we bow to the Knowers of Divine Wisdom.

एते गन्धपुष्पे ॐ आचार्येभ्यो नमः

**ete gandhapuṣpe oṃ ācāryebhyo namaḥ**

With these scented flowers oṃ we bow to the Teachers of Divine Wisdom.

एते गन्धपुष्पे ॐ ऋषिभ्यो नमः

**ete gandhapuṣpe oṃ ṛṣibhyo namaḥ**

With these scented flowers oṃ we bow to the Seers of Divine Wisdom.

एते गन्धपुष्पे ॐ देवेभ्यो नमः

**ete gandhapuṣpe oṃ devebhyo namaḥ**

With these scented flowers oṃ we bow to the Exemplifiers of Divine Wisdom.

एते गन्धपुष्पे ॐ वेदेभ्यो नमः

**ete gandhapuṣpe oṃ vedebhyo namaḥ**

With these scented flowers oṃ we bow to the Wisdom of Divine Wisdom.

एते गन्धपुष्पे ॐ वायवे नमः

**ete gandhapuṣpe oṃ vāyave namaḥ**

With these scented flowers oṃ we bow to Emancipation.

एते गन्धपुष्पे ॐ मृत्यवे नमः

**ete gandhapuṣpe oṃ mṛtyave namaḥ**

With these scented flowers oṃ we bow to Transformation (moving beyond, death).

एते गन्धपुष्पे ॐ विष्णवे नमः

**ete gandhapuṣpe oṃ viṣṇave namaḥ**

With these scented flowers oṃ we bow to That which Pervades All.

एते गन्धपुष्पे ॐ वैश्रवणाय नमः

**ete gandhapuṣpe oṃ vaiśravaṇāya namaḥ**

With these scented flowers oṃ we bow to the Universal Being.

एते गन्धपुष्पे ॐ ऊपजाय नमः

**ete gandhapuṣpe oṃ ūpajāya namaḥ**

With these scented flowers oṃ we bow to The Cause of All.

ॐ भूर्भुवः स्वः । तत् सवितुर्वरेण्यम् भर्गो देवस्य धीमहि ।
धियो यो नः प्रचोदयात् ॐ ॥

**oṃ bhūrbhuvaḥ svaḥ tat saviturvareṇyam bhargo devasya dhīmahi dhiyo yo naḥ pracodayāt oṃ**

Oṃ the Infinite Beyond Conception, the gross body, the subtle body and the causal body; we meditate on that Light of Wisdom that is the Supreme Wealth of the Gods. May it grant to us increase in our meditations.

### kumārī pūjā

worship of the ever pure one

ॐ कुमारीमृग्वेदयुतां ब्रह्मरूपां विचिन्तायेत् ।
हंसस्थितां कुशहस्तां सूर्यमण्डल संस्थितां ॥

**oṃ kumārīmṛgvedayutāṃ brahmarūpāṃ vicintāyet haṃsasthitāṃ kuśahastāṃ sūryamaṇḍala saṃsthitāṃ**

Oṃ We contemplate the Goddess of Purity, embodiment of the Ṛg Veda, the form of Supreme Divinity. Situated upon the swan, with kuśa grass in Her hand, She is situated in the regions of the sun.

ॐ कौमारिं कमलरुढं त्रिनेत्रम् चन्द्रा सेकारम् ।
तप्तकाञ्चण वर्नव्यां नानालङ्कार भूषितम् ॥

**oṃ kaumāriṃ kamalaruḍhaṃ**
**trinetram candrā sekāram**
**taptakāñcaṇa varnavyāṃ nānālaṅkāra bhūṣitam**

Oṃ Kumāri has an orange color with three eyes and the Moon on Her head. Of the color of melted gold, She displays various ornaments.

रक्तम् बार परीधणम् रक्त माल्यण् लेपानम् ।
बामे नः आवयें धाये दाक्षिणेन वरा प्रदम् ॥

**raktam bāra parīdhaṇam rakta mālyaṇ lepānam**
**bāme naḥ āvayeṃ dhāye dākṣiṇena varā pradam**

She wears a red cloth and a red mālā or garland. With Her left hand She gives us freedom from fear, and with Her right hand She grants boons.

ॐ सर्वविस्त प्रधे देवि सर्वापदं विनिवाहिनि ।
सर्वशान्ति करी देवि नमोऽस्तु ते कुमारि के ॥

**oṃ sarvavista pradhe devi sarvāpadaṃ vinivāhini**
**sarvaśānti karī devi namo-stu te kumāri ke**

Oṃ Grant fulfillment of all desires, oh Goddess. Remove all obstacles. Cause all Peace, oh Goddess. We bow to you, to Kumāri.

ब्रह्मी महेश्वरि रौद्रि रूप त्रिताय धारिणि ।
आवायं वरं देहि नारायणि नमोऽस्तु ते ॥

**brahmī maheśvari raudri rūpa tritāya dhāriṇi**
**āvāyaṃ varaṃ dehi nārāyaṇi namo-stu te**

Creative Energy, the Energy of the Great Seer of All, the Energy of the Terrible One; She wears three forms. Give freedom from fear and boons; Exposer of Consciousness, we bow to you.

ॐ कौं कौमार्यै नमः

**oṃ kauṃ kaumaryai namaḥ**

Oṃ kauṃ we bow to the Goddess of Purity.

ॐ सावित्री विष्णुरूपाञ्च तार्क्ष्यस्थां पीतवाससिं ।

युवतीञ्च यजुर्वेद सूर्यमण्डल संस्थितां ॥

**oṃ sāvitrī viṣṇurūpāñca tārkṣyasthāṃ pītavāsasiṃ yuvatīñca yajurveda sūryamaṇḍala saṃsthitāṃ**

Oṃ Goddess of Light in the form of Viṣṇu, radiating light of yellow color; appearing in a youthful form as the Yājur Veda, She is situated in the regions of the sun.

ॐ सरस्वती शिवरूपाञ्च वृद्ध वृषभ वहिनीं ।

सूर्यमण्डल मध्यस्थां सामवेद समायुतां ॥

**oṃ sarasvatī śivarūpāñca vṛddhā vṛṣabha vahinīṃ sūryamaṇḍala madhyasthāṃ sāmaveda samāyutāṃ**

Oṃ Sarasvati is in the form of Śiva, appearing as an old woman riding upon a bull. Situated in the middle of the regions of the sun, She is united with the Sāma Veda.

**gāyatrī sampūṭ**

gāyatrī with oṃ before and after

ॐ भूर्भुवः स्वः ॐ तत् सवितुर्वरेण्यम् ॐ भर्गो देवस्य

धीमहि ॐ धियो यो नः प्रचोदयात् ॐ ॥

**oṃ bhūrbhuvaḥ svaḥ oṃ tat saviturvareṇyam oṃ bhargo devasya dhīmahi oṃ dhiyo yo naḥ pracodayāt oṃ**

Oṃ the Infinite Beyond Conception, the gross body, the subtle body and the causal body; oṃ we meditate on that Light of

Wisdom oṃ that is the Supreme Wealth of the Gods. Oṃ may it grant to us increase in our meditations.

ॐ भूर्भुवः स्वः तत् सवितुर्वरेण्यम् ॐ भर्गो देवस्य धीमहि ॐ धियो यो नः प्रचोदयात् ॐ ॥

**oṃ bhūrbhuvaḥ svaḥ tat saviturvareṇyam oṃ bhargo devasya dhīmahi oṃ dhiyo yo naḥ pracodayāt oṃ**

Oṃ the Infinite Beyond Conception, the gross body, the subtle body and the causal body; we meditate on that Light of Wisdom oṃ that is the Supreme Wealth of the Gods. Oṃ may it grant to us increase in our meditations oṃ.

ॐ भूर्भुवः स्वः तत् सवितुर्वरेण्यम् भर्गो देवस्य धीमहि ॐ धियो यो नः प्रचोदयात् ॐ ॥

**oṃ bhūrbhuvaḥ svaḥ tat saviturvareṇyam bhargo devasya dhīmahi oṃ dhiyo yo naḥ pracodayāt oṃ**

Oṃ the Infinite Beyond Conception, the gross body, the subtle body and the causal body; we meditate on that Light of Wisdom that is the Supreme Wealth of the Gods. Oṃ may it grant to us increase in our meditations oṃ.

ॐ भूर्भुवः स्वः तत् सवितुर्वरेण्यम् भर्गो देवस्य धीमहि
धियो यो नः प्रचोदयात् ॐ ॥

**oṃ bhūrbhuvaḥ svaḥ**
**tat saviturvareṇyam bhargo devasya dhīmahi**
**dhiyo yo naḥ pracodayāt oṃ**

Oṃ the Infinite Beyond Conception, the gross body, the subtle body and the causal body; aie meditate upon that Light of Wisdom that is the Supreme Wealth of the Gods. May it grant to us increase in our meditations oṃ.

आगच्छ वरदे देवि जप्ये मे सन्निधा भव ।
गायन्तं त्रायसे यस्माद् गायत्री त्वमतः स्मृता ॥

**āgaccha varade devi japye me sannidhā bhava**
**gāyaṇtaṃ trāyase yasmād gāyatrī tvamataḥ smṛtā**

Come, granting boons, oh Goddess, and be situated in me while I continue meditation and prayer. The three forms of wisdom are remembered in you, Gāyatrī.

आयाहि वरदे देवि त्र्यक्षरे ब्रह्मवादिनि ।
गायत्री छन्दसां मातर्ब्रह्मयोनि नमोऽस्तु ते ॥

**āyāhi varade devi tryakṣare brahmavādini**
**gāyatrī chandasāṃ mātarbrahmayoni namo-stu te**

Come, granting boons, oh Goddess, the three letters of the word of the Supreme Divinity. Oh Mother, in the rhythm of Gāyatrī (24 syllables to the verse) we bow to you as the womb of creation.

### sāmānyārghya

purification of water

Draw the following yantra on the plate or space for worship with sandal paste and/or water. Offer rice on the yantra for each of the four mantras:

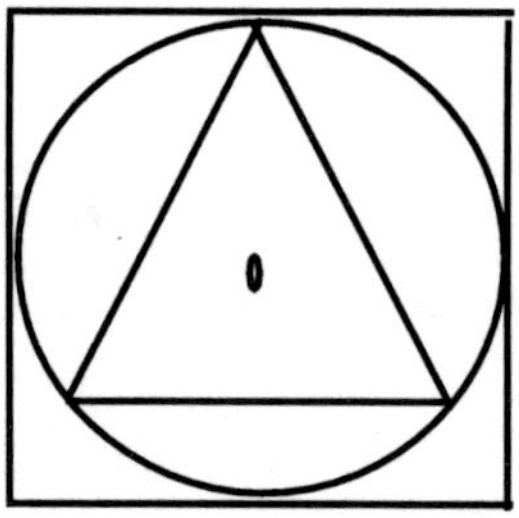

ॐ आधारशक्तये नमः

**oṃ ādhāra śaktaye namaḥ**
Oṃ we bow to the Primal Energy

ॐ कूर्म्माय नमः

**oṃ kūrmmāya namaḥ**
Oṃ we bow to the Support of the Earth

ॐ अनन्ताय नमः

**oṃ anantāya namaḥ**
Oṃ we bow to Infinity

ॐ पृथिव्यै नमः

**oṃ pṛthivyai namaḥ**
Oṃ we bow to the Earth

Place an empty water pot on the bindu in the center of the yantra while saying Phaṭ in this mantra:

स्थां स्थीं स्थिरो भव फट्

**sthāṃ sthīṃ sthiro bhava phaṭ**
Be Still in the Gross Body! Be Still in the Subtle Body! Be Still in the Causal Body! Purify!

Fill the pot with water while chanting the mantra:

ॐ गङ्गे च जमुने चैव गोदावरि सरस्वति ।
नर्मदे सिन्धु कावेरि जलेऽस्मिन् सन्निधिं कुरु ॥

**oṃ gaṅge ca jamune caiva godāvari sarasvati**
**narmade sindhu kāveri jale-smin sannidhiṃ kuru**

Oṃ the Ganges, Jamunā, Godāvarī, Sarasvatī, Narmadā, Sindhu, Kāverī, these waters are mingled together.

The Ganges is the Iḍā, the Jamunā is the Piṅgalā, the other five rivers are the five senses. The land of the seven rivers is within the body as well as outside.

Offer Tulasī leaves into the water

ॐ ऐं ह्रीं क्लीं श्रीं वृन्दावनवासिन्यै स्वाहा

**oṃ aiṃ hrīṃ klīṃ śrīṃ vṛndāvanavāsinyai svāhā**

Oṃ Wisdom, Māyā, Increase, to She who resides in Vṛndāvana, I am One with God!

Offer three flowers into the water pot with these mantras:

एते गन्धपुष्पे ॐ अं अर्कमण्डलाय द्वादशकलात्मने नमः

**ete gandhapuṣpe oṃ aṃ arkamaṇḍalāya dvādaśakalātmane namaḥ**

With these scented flowers oṃ "A" we bow to the twelve aspects of the realm of the sun: Tapinī, Tāpinī, Dhūmrā, Marīci, Jvālinī, Ruci, Sudhūmrā, Bhoga-dā, Viśvā, Bodhinī, Dhārinī, Kṣamā; Containing Heat, Emanating Heat, Smoky, Ray-producing, Burning, Lustrous, Purple or Smoky-Red, Granting Enjoyment, Universal, Which makes known, Productive of Consciousness, Which Supports, Which Forgives.

एते गन्धपुष्पे ॐ उं सोममण्डलाय षोडशकलात्मने नमः

**ete gandhapuṣpe oṃ uṃ somamaṇḍalāya ṣoḍaśakalātmane namaḥ**

With these scented flowers oṃ "U" we bow to the sixteen aspects of the realm of the moon: Amṛtā, Prāṇadā, Puṣā, Tuṣṭi, Puṣṭi, Rati, Dhṛti, Śaśinī, Candrikā, Kānti, Jyotsnā, Śrī, Prīti, Aṅgadā, Pūrṇā, Pūrṇāmṛtā; Nectar, Which Sustains life, Which

Supports, Satisfying, Nourishing, Playful, Constant, Unfailing, Producer of Joy, Beauty Enhanced by Love, Light, Grantor of Prosperity, Affectionate, Purifying the Body, Complete, Full of Bliss.

## एते गन्धपुष्पे ॐ मं वह्निमण्डलाय दशकलात्मने नमः

**ete gandhapuṣpe oṃ maṃ vahnimaṇḍalāya daśakalātmane namaḥ**

With these scented flowers oṃ "M" we bow to the ten aspects of the realm of fire: Dhūmrā, Arciḥ, Jvalinī, Śūkṣmā, Jvālinī, Visphuliṅginī, Suśrī, Surūpā, Kapilā, Havya-Kavya-Vahā; Smoky-Red, Flaming, Shining, Subtle, Burning, Sparkling, Beautiful, Well-Formed, Tawny, the Messenger to Gods and the Ancestors.

Wave hands in matsyā, dhenu and aṅkuśa mudrās while chanting this mantra:

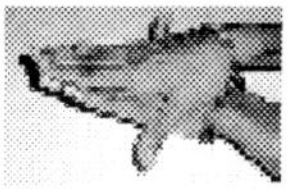

## ॐ गङ्गे च जमुने चैव गोदावरि सरस्वति ।
## नर्मदे सिन्धु कावेरि जलेऽस्मिन् सन्निधिं कुरु ॥

**oṃ gaṅge ca jamune caiva godāvari sarasvati narmade sindhu kāveri jale-smin sannidhiṃ kuru**

Oṃ the Ganges, Jamunā, Godāvarī, Sarasvatī, Narmadā, Sindhu, Kāverī, these waters are mingled together.

## ॐ ऐं ह्रीं क्लीं चामुण्डायै विच्चे

**oṃ aiṃ hrīṃ klīṃ cāmuṇḍāyai vicce**

Oṃ aiṃ hrīṃ klīṃ cāmuṇḍāyai vicce

Sprinkle water over all the articles to be offered, then throw some drops of water over your shoulders while repeating the mantra:

अमृताम् कुरु स्वाहा

**amṛtām kuru svāhā**

Make this immortal nectar! I am One with God!

## puṣpa śuddhi

purification of the flowers

Wave hands over flowers with prārthanā mudrā while chanting the first line and with dhenu mudrā while chanting the second line of this mantra:

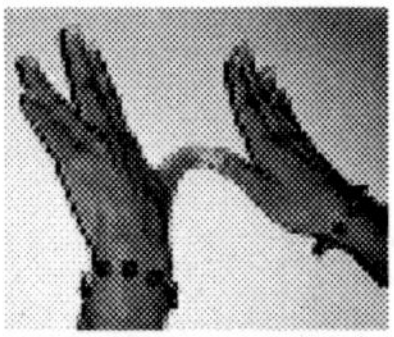

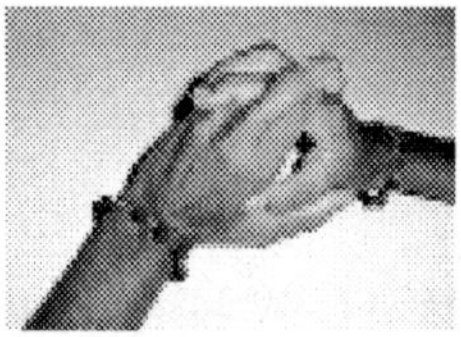

ॐ पुष्प पुष्प महापुष्प सुपुष्प पुष्पसम्भवे ।

पुष्पचयावकीर्णे च हुं फट् स्वाहा ॥

**oṃ puṣpa puṣpa mahāpuṣpa**
**supuṣpa puṣpa sambhave**
**puṣpa cayāvakīrṇe ca huṃ phaṭ svāhā**

Oṃ Flowers, flowers, oh Great Flowers, excellent flowers; flowers in heaps and scattered about, cut the ego, purify, I am One with God!

## kara śuddhi

purification of the hands

ॐ ऐं रं अस्त्राय फट्

**oṃ aiṃ raṃ astrāya phaṭ**

Oṃ Wisdom, the divine fire, with the weapon, Purify !

## kalaśa sthāpana

establishment of the pot

touch the earth

ॐ भूरसि भूमिरस्यदितिरसि विश्वधारा

विश्वस्य भुवनस्य धर्त्री ।

पृथिवीं यच्छ पृथिवीं दृंह पृथिवीं मा हिंसीः ॥

**oṃ bhūrasi bhūmirasyaditirasi viśvadhārā**
**viśvasya bhuvanasya dhartrī**
**pṛthivīṃ yaccha pṛthivīṃ dṛṃha pṛthivīṃ mā hiṃsīḥ**

Oṃ You are the object of sensory perception; you are the Goddess who distributes the forms of the earth. You are the Producer of the Universe, the Support of all existing things in the universe. Control (or sustain) the earth, firmly establish the earth, make the earth efficient in its motion.

offer rice where you touched earth

ॐ धान्यमसि धिनुहि देवान् धिनुहि यज्ञं ।

धिनुहि यज्ञपतिं धिनुहि मां यज्ञन्यम् ॥

**oṃ dhānyamasi dhinuhi devān dhinuhi yajñaṃ**
**dhinuhi yajñapatiṃ dhinuhi māṃ yajñanyam**

Oṃ You are the grains that satisfy and gladden the Gods, gladden the sacrifice, gladden the Lord of Sacrifice. Bring satisfaction to us through sacrifice.

place the pot on the rice

ॐ आजिग्घ्र कलशं मह्या त्वा विशन्त्विन्दवः ।

पुनरूर्ज्जा निवर्तस्व सा नः सहस्रं धुक्क्ष्वोरुधारा पयस्वती

पुनर्म्माविशताद्द्रयिः ॥

**oṃ ājigghra kalaśaṃ mahyā tvā viśantvindavaḥ punarūrjjā nivartasva sā naḥ sahasraṃ dhukkṣvorudhārā payasvatī punarmmāviśatāddrayiḥ**

Oṃ Cause the effulgent fire of perception to enter into your highly honored container for renewed nourishment. Remaining there, let it increase in thousands, so that upon removal, abounding in spotlessly pure strength, it may come flowing into us.

pour water into the pot

ॐ वरुणस्योत्तम्भनमसि वरुणस्य स्कम्भसर्ज्जनी स्थो ।

वरुणस्य ऋतसदन्न्यसि । वरुणस्य ऋतसदनमसि ।

वरुणस्य ऋतसदनमासीद ॥

**oṃ varuṇasyottambhanamasi varuṇasya skambhasarjjanī stho varuṇasya ṛtasadannyasi varuṇasya ṛtasadanamasi varuṇasya ṛtasadanamāsīda**

Oṃ You, Waters, are declared the Ultimate of waters established in all creation begotten, abiding in waters as the eternal law of truth; always abiding in waters as the eternal law of truth, and forever abiding in waters as the eternal law of truth.

place wealth into the pot

ॐ धन्वना गा धन्वनाजिं जयेम

धन्वना तीव्राः समद्रो जयेम ।

धनुः शत्रोरपकामं कृणोति धन्वना सर्वाः प्रदिशो जयेम ॥

**oṃ dhanvanā gā dhanvanājiṃ jayema**
**dhanvanā tīvrāḥ samadro jayema**
**dhanuḥ śatrorapakāmaṃ kṛṇoti**
**dhanvanā sarvāḥ pradiśo jayema**

Oṃ Let wealth, even abundance, be victorious. Let wealth be sufficient as to be victorious over the severe ocean of existence. Like a bow to keep us safe from the enemies of desire, let that wealth be victorious to illuminate all.

place fruit on top of the pot

ॐ याः फलिनीर्याऽफलाऽअपुष्पाऽयाश्च पुष्पिणीः ।
बृहस्पतिप्रसूतास्ता नो मुञ्चन्त्वंहसः ॥

**oṃ yāḥ phalinīryā-phalā-apuṣpā-yāśca puṣpiṇīḥ**
**bṛhaspatiprasūtāstā no muñcantvaṃhasaḥ**

Oṃ That which bears fruit and that which bears no fruit; that without flowers and that with flowers as well. To we who exist born of the Lord of the Vast, set us FREE! ALL THIS IS GOD!

put red powder on the fruit

ॐ सिन्धोरिव प्राध्वने शूघनासो वातप्रमियः पतयन्ति
यह्वाः । घृतस्य धारा अरुषो न वाजी काष्ठा भिन्दन्नर्म्मिभिः
पिन्वमानः ॥

**oṃ sindhoriva prādhvane śūghanāso**
**vātapramiyaḥ patayanti yahvāḥ**
**ghṛtasya dhārā aruṣo na vājī kāṣṭhā**
**bhindannarmmibhiḥ pinvamānaḥ**

Oṃ The pious mark of red vermilion, symbolizing the ocean of love, placed prominently upon the head above the nose bursting forth, allows the vibrance of youth to fly. As the stream of ghee pours into the flames, those spirited steeds of the Divine

Fire consume the logs of wood, increasing the will and self-reliance of the worshipper.

ॐ सिन्दूरमरुणाभासं जपाकुसुमसन्निभम् ।
पूजिताऽसि मया देवि प्रसीद परमेश्वरि ॥
ॐ ऐं ह्रीं क्लीं चामुण्डायै विच्चे सिन्दूरं समर्पयामि

**oṃ sindūramaruṇābhāsaṃ japākusumasannibham**
**pūjitā-si mayā devi prasīda parameśvari**
**oṃ aiṃ hrīṃ klīṃ cāmuṇḍāyai vicce sindūraṃ samarpayāmi**

Oṃ This red colored powder symbolizes Love, who drives the chariot of the Light of Wisdom, with which we are worshipping our Lord. Please be pleased, Oh Great Seer of All. With this offering of red-colored powder oṃ aiṃ hrīṃ klīṃ cāmuṇḍāyai vicce.

kuṅkum

ॐ कुङ्कुमं कान्तिदं दिव्यं कामिनीकामसम्भवम् ।
कुङ्कुमेनाऽर्चिते देवि प्रसीद परमेश्वरि ॥
ॐ ऐं ह्रीं क्लीं चामुण्डायै विच्चे कुङ्कुमं समर्पयामि

**oṃ kuṅkumaṃ kāntidaṃ divyaṃ**
**kāminī kāmasambhavam**
**kuṅkumenā-rcite devi prasīda parameśvari**
**oṃ aiṃ hrīṃ klīṃ cāmuṇḍāyai vicce kuṅkumaṃ samarpayāmi**

Oṃ You are being adorned with this divine red powder, which is made more beautiful by the love we share with you, and is so pleasing. Oh Goddess, when we present this red powder be pleased, Oh Supreme Ruler of All. With this offering of red colored powder oṃ aiṃ hrīṃ klīṃ cāmuṇḍāyai vicce.

sandal paste

ॐ श्रीखण्डचन्दनं दिव्यं गन्धाढ्यं सुमनोहरम् ।

विलेपनं च देवेशि चन्दनं प्रतिगृह्यताम् ॥

ॐ ऐं ह्रीं क्लीं चामुण्डायै विच्चे चन्दनं समर्पयामि

**oṃ śrīkhaṇḍacandanaṃ divyaṃ**
**gandhāḍhyaṃ sumano haram**
**vilepanaṃ ca deveśi candanaṃ pratigṛhyatām**
**oṃ aiṃ hrīṃ klīṃ cāmuṇḍāyai vicce candanaṃ samarpayāmi**

Oṃ You are being adorned with this beautiful divine piece of sandal wood, ground to a paste that is so pleasing. Please accept this offering of sandal paste, Oh Supreme Sovereign of all the Gods. With this offering of sandal paste oṃ aiṃ hrīṃ klīṃ cāmuṇḍāyai vicce.

turmeric

ॐ हरिद्रारञ्जिता देवि सुख-सौभाग्यदायिनि ।

तस्मात्त्वं पूजयाम्यत्र दुःखशान्तिं प्रयच्छ मे ॥

ॐ ऐं ह्रीं क्लीं चामुण्डायै विच्चे हरिद्रां समर्पयामि

**oṃ haridrārañjitā devi**
**sukha saubhāgyadāyini**
**tasmāttvaṃ pūjayāmyatra**
**duḥkha śāntiṃ prayaccha me**
**oṃ aiṃ hrīṃ klīṃ cāmuṇḍāyai vicce haridrāṃ samarpayāmi**

Oṃ Oh Goddess, you are being gratified by this turmeric, the giver of comfort and beauty. When you are worshipped like this, then you must bestow upon us the greatest peace. With the offering of turmeric oṃ aiṃ hrīṃ klīṃ cāmuṇḍāyai vicce.

milk bath

ॐ कामधेनुसमुद्भूतं सर्वेषां जीवनं परम् ।

पावनं यज्ञहेतुश्च स्नानार्थं प्रतिगृह्यताम् ॥

ॐ ऐं ह्रीं क्लीं चामुण्डायै विच्चे पयस्नानं समर्पयामि

**oṃ kāmadhenu samudbhūtaṃ**
**sarveṣāṃ jīvanaṃ param**
**pāvanaṃ yajña hetuśca snānārthaṃ pratigṛhyatām**
**oṃ aiṃ hrīṃ klīṃ cāmuṇḍāyai vicce paya snānaṃ samarpayāmi**

Oṃ Coming from the ocean of being, the Fulfiller of all Desires, the Grantor of Supreme Bliss to all souls. For the motive of purifying or sanctifying this holy union, we request you to accept this bath. With this offering of milk for your bath oṃ aiṃ hrīṃ klīṃ cāmuṇḍāyai vicce.

yogurt bath

ॐ पयसस्तु समुद्भूतं मधुराम्लं शशिप्रभम् ।

दध्यानितं मया दत्तं स्नानार्थं प्रतिगृह्यताम् ॥

ॐ ऐं ह्रीं क्लीं चामुण्डायै विच्चे दधिस्नानं समर्पयामि

**oṃ payasastu samudbhūtaṃ**
**madhurāmlaṃ śaśiprabham**
**dadhyānitaṃ mayā dattaṃ**
**snānārthaṃ pratigṛhyatām**

**oṃ aiṃ hrīṃ klīṃ cāmuṇḍāyai vicce dadhi snānaṃ samarpayāmi**

Oṃ Derived from the milk of the ocean of being, sweet and pleasing like the glow of the moon, let these curds eternally be our ambassador, as we request you to accept this bath. With this offering of yogurt for your bath oṃ aiṃ hrīṃ klīṃ cāmuṇḍāyai vicce.

ghee bath

ॐ नवनीतसमुत्पन्नं सर्वसन्तोषकारकम् ।

घृतं तुभ्यं प्रदास्यामि स्नानार्थं प्रतिगृह्यताम् ॥

ॐ ऐं ह्रीं क्लीं चामुण्डायै विच्चे घृतस्नानं समर्पयामि

**oṃ navanīta samutpannaṃ sarvasantoṣakārakam**
**ghṛtaṃ tubhyaṃ pradāsyāmi**
**snānārthaṃ pratigṛhyatām**
**oṃ aiṃ hrīṃ klīṃ cāmuṇḍāyai vicce ghṛta snānaṃ samarpayāmi**

Oṃ Freshly prepared from the ocean of being, causing all fulfillment, we offer this delightful ghee (clarified butter) and request you to accept this bath. With this offering of ghee for your bath oṃ aiṃ hrīṃ klīṃ cāmuṇḍāyai vicce.

honey bath

ॐ तरुपुष्पसमुद्भूतं सुस्वादु मधुरं मधु ।

तेजोपुष्टिकरं दिव्यं स्नानार्थं प्रतिगृह्यताम् ॥

ॐ ऐं ह्रीं क्लीं चामुण्डायै विच्चे मधुस्नानं समर्पयामि

**oṃ tarupuṣpa samudbhūtam**
**susvādu madhuraṃ madhu**
**tejo puṣṭikaraṃ divyaṃ snānārtham pratigṛhyatām**
**oṃ aiṃ hrīṃ klīṃ cāmuṇḍāyai vicce madhu snānaṃ samarpayāmi**

Oṃ Prepared from flowers of the ocean of being, enjoyable as the sweetest of the sweet, causing the fire of divine nourishment to burn swiftly, we request you to accept this bath. With this offering of honey for your bath oṃ aiṃ hrīṃ klīṃ cāmuṇḍāyai vicce.

sugar bath

ॐ इक्षुसारसमुद्भूता शर्करा पुष्टिकारिका ।
मलापहारिका दिव्या स्नानार्थं प्रतिगृह्यताम् ॥
ॐ ऐं ह्रीं क्लीं चामुण्डायै विच्चे शर्करास्नानं समर्पयामि

**oṃ ikṣusāra samudbhūtā śarkarā puṣṭikārikā**
**malāpahārikā divyā snānārthaṃ pratigṛhyatām**
**oṃ aiṃ hrīṃ klīṃ cāmuṇḍāyai vicce śarkarā snānaṃ samarpayāmi**

Oṃ From the lake of sugar-cane, from the ocean of being, which causes the nourishment of sugar to give divine protection from all impurity, we request you to accept this bath. With this offering of sugar for your bath oṃ aiṃ hrīṃ klīṃ cāmuṇḍāyai vicce.

five nectars bath

ॐ पयो दधि घृतं चैव मधु च शर्करायुतम् ।
पञ्चामृतं मयाऽऽनीतं स्नानार्थं प्रतिगृह्यताम् ॥
ॐ ऐं ह्रीं क्लीं चामुण्डायै विच्चे पञ्चामृतस्नानं समर्पयामि

**oṃ payo dadhi ghṛtaṃ caiva**
**madhu ca śarkarāyutam**
**pañcāmṛtaṃ mayā--nītaṃ**
**snānārthaṃ pratigṛhyatām**
**oṃ aiṃ hrīṃ klīṃ cāmuṇḍāyai vicce pañcāmṛta snānaṃ samarpayāmi**

Oṃ Milk, curd, ghee and then honey and sugar mixed together; these five nectars are our ambassador as we request you to accept this bath. With this offering of five nectars for your bath oṃ aiṃ hrīṃ klīṃ cāmuṇḍāyai vicce.

scented oil

ॐ नानासुगन्धिद्रव्यं च चन्दनं रजनीयुतम् ।
उद्वर्तनं मया दत्तं स्नानार्थं प्रतिगृह्यताम् ॥
ॐ ऐं ह्रीं क्लीं चामुण्डायै विच्चे उद्वर्तनस्नानं समर्पयामि

**oṃ nānāsugandhidravyaṃ ca**
**candanaṃ rajanīyutam**
**udvartanaṃ mayā dattaṃ**
**snānārthaṃ pratigṛhyatām**
**oṃ aiṃ hrīṃ klīṃ cāmuṇḍāyai vicce udvartana snānaṃ samarpayāmi**

Oṃ With various beautifully smelling ingredients, as well as the scent of sandal, we offer you this scented oil, Oh Goddess. With this offering of scented oil oṃ aiṃ hrīṃ klīṃ cāmuṇḍāyai vicce.

scent bath

गन्धद्वारां दुराधर्षां नित्यपुष्टां करीषिणीम् ।
ईश्वरीं सर्वभूतानां तामिहोपह्वये श्रियम् ॥

ॐ ऐं ह्रीं क्लीं चामुण्डायै विच्चे गन्धस्नानं समर्पयामि

**gandhadvārāṃ durādharṣāṃ nityapuṣṭāṃ karīṣiṇīm**
**īśvarīṃ sarvabhūtānāṃ tāmihopahvaye śriyam**
**oṃ aiṃ hrīṃ klīṃ cāmuṇḍāyai vicce gandha snānaṃ samarpayāmi**

She is the cause of the scent that is the door to religious ecstasy, unconquerable (never-failing), continually nurturing for all time. May we never tire from calling that manifestation of the Highest Respect, the Supreme Goddess of all existence. With this offering of scented bath oṃ aiṃ hrīṃ klīṃ cāmuṇḍāyai vicce.

water bath

ॐ गङ्गे च जमुने चैव गोदावरि सरस्वति ।
नर्मदे सिन्धु कावेरि स्नानार्थं प्रतिगृह्यताम् ॥
ॐ ऐं ह्रीं क्लीं चामुण्डायै विच्चे गङ्गास्नानं समर्पयामि

**oṃ gaṅge ca jamune caiva godāvari sarasvati**
**narmade sindhu kāveri snānārthaṃ pratigṛhyatām**
**oṃ aiṃ hrīṃ klīṃ cāmuṇḍāyai vicce gaṅgā snānaṃ samarpayāmi**

Oṃ Please accept the waters from the Gaṅges, the Jamunā, Godāvarī, Sarasvatī, Narmadā, Sindhu and Kāverī, which have been provided for your bath. With this offering of Ganges bath waters oṃ aiṃ hrīṃ klīṃ cāmuṇḍāyai vicce.

cloth

ॐ शीतवातोष्णसंत्राणं लज्जायै रक्षणं परं ।
देहालंकरणं वस्त्रं अथ शान्तिं प्रयच्छ मे ॥
ॐ ऐं ह्रीं क्लीं चामुण्डायै विच्चे वस्त्रं समर्पयामि

**oṃ śīta vātoṣṇa saṃ trāṇaṃ**
**lajjāyai rakṣaṇaṃ paraṃ**
**dehālaṅkaraṇaṃ vastraṃ**
**atha śāntiṃ prayaccha me**
**oṃ aiṃ hrīṃ klīṃ cāmuṇḍāyai vicce vastraṃ samarpayāmi**

Oṃ To take away the cold and the wind, and to fully protect your modesty, we adorn your body with this cloth, and thereby find the greatest Peace. With this offering of wearing apparel oṃ aiṃ hrīṃ klīṃ cāmuṇḍāyai vicce.

sacred thread

ॐ यज्ञोपवीतं परमं पवित्रं प्रजापतेर्यत् सहजं पुरस्तात् ।
आयुष्यमग्रं प्रतिमुञ्च शुभ्रं यज्ञोपवीतं बलमस्तु तेजः ॥

**oṃ yajñopavītaṃ paramaṃ pavitraṃ**
**prajāpateryat sahajaṃ purastāt**
**āyuṣyamagraṃ pratimuñca śubhraṃ**
**yajñopavītaṃ balamastu tejaḥ**

Oṃ the sacred thread of the highest purity is given by Prajāpati, the Lord of Creation, for the greatest facility. You bring life and illuminate the greatness of liberation. Oh sacred thread, let your strength be of radiant light.

शमो दमस्तपः शौचं क्षान्तिरार्जवमेव च ।
ज्ञानं विज्ञानमास्तिक्यं ब्रह्मकर्म स्वभावजम् ॥

**śamo damastapaḥ śaucaṃ kṣāntirārjavameva ca**
**jñānaṃ vijñānamāstikyaṃ**
**brahmakarma svabhāvajam**

Peacefulness, self-control, austerity, purity of mind and body, patience and forgiveness, sincerity and honesty, wisdom, knowledge and self-realization are the natural activities of a Brahmaṇa.

नवभिस्तन्तुभिर्युक्तं त्रिगुणं देवतामयं ।
उपवीतं मया दत्तं गृहाण त्वं सुरेश्वरि ॥
ॐ ऐं ह्रीं क्लीं चामुण्डायै विच्चे यज्ञोपवीतं समर्पयामि

**navamiṣṭantubhiryuktaṃ triguṇaṃ devatā mayaṃ**
**upavītaṃ mayā dattaṃ gṛhāṇa tvaṃ sureśvari**
**oṃ aiṃ hrīṃ klīṃ cāmuṇḍāyai vicce yajñopavītaṃ samarpayāmi**

With nine desirable threads all united together, exemplifying the three guṇas (the three qualities of harmony of our deity), this sacred thread will be our ambassador. Oh Ruler of the Gods, please accept this. With this offering of a sacred thread oṃ aiṃ hrīṃ klīṃ cāmuṇḍāyai vicce.

rudrākṣa

त्र्यम्बकं यजामहे सुगन्धिं पुष्टिवर्द्धनम् ।
उर्व्वारुकमिव बन्धनान्मृत्योर्म्मुक्षीयमामृतात् ॥
ॐ ऐं ह्रीं क्लीं चामुण्डायै विच्चे रुद्राक्षं समर्पयामि

**tryambakaṃ yajāmahe**
**sugandhiṃ puṣṭivarddhanam**
**urvvārukamiva bandhanānmṛtyormmukṣīyamāmṛtāt**
**oṃ aiṃ hrīṃ klīṃ cāmuṇḍāyai vicce rudrākṣaṃ samarpayāmi**

We worship the Father of the three worlds, of excellent fame, Grantor of Increase. As a cucumber is released from its bondage to the stem, so may we be freed from Death to dwell in immortality. With this offering of rudrākṣa oṃ aiṃ hrīṃ klīṃ cāmuṇḍāyai vicce.

mālā

ॐ मां माले महामाये सर्वशक्तिस्वरूपिणि ।
चतुर्वर्गस्त्वयि न्यस्तस्तस्मान्मे सिद्धिदा भव ॥
ॐ ऐं ह्रीं क्लीं चामुण्डायै विच्चे मालां समर्पयामि

**oṃ māṃ māle mahāmāye sarvaśaktisvarūpiṇi**
**caturvargastvayi nyastastasmānme siddhidā bhava**
**oṃ aiṃ hrīṃ klīṃ cāmuṇḍāyai vicce mālāṃ samarpayāmi**

Oṃ my rosary, the Great Limitation of Consciousness, containing all energy within as your intrinsic nature, fulfilling the four desires of men, give us the attainment of your perfection. With this offering of a mālā oṃ aiṃ hrīṃ klīṃ cāmuṇḍāyai vicce.

rice

अक्षतान् निर्मलान् शुद्धान् मुक्ताफलसमन्वितान् ।
गृहाणेमान महादेव देहि मे निर्मलां धियम् ॥
ॐ ऐं ह्रीं क्लीं चामुण्डायै विच्चे अक्षतान् समर्पयामि

**akṣatān nirmalān śuddhān muktāphalasamanvitān**
**gṛhāṇemān mahādeva dehi me nirmalāṃ dhiyam**
**oṃ aiṃ hrīṃ klīṃ cāmuṇḍāyai vicce akṣatān samarpayāmi**

Oh Great Goddess, please accept these grains of rice, spotlessly clean, bestowing the fruit of liberation, and give us a spotlessly clean mind. With the offering of grains of rice oṃ aiṃ hrīṃ klīṃ cāmuṇḍāyai vicce.

flower garland

शङ्ख-पद्मजपुष्पादि शतपत्रैर्विचित्रताम् ।

पुष्पमालां प्रयच्छामि गृहाण त्वं सुरेश्वरि ॥

ॐ ऐं ह्रीं क्लीं चामुण्डायै विच्चे पुष्पमालां समर्पयामि

**śaṅkha-padma japuṣpādi śatapatrairvicitratām**
**puṣpamālāṃ prayacchāmi gṛhāṇa tvaṃ sureśvari**
**oṃ aiṃ hrīṃ klīṃ cāmuṇḍāyai vicce puṣpamālāṃ samarpayāmi**

We offer you this garland of flowers with spiraling lotuses, other flowers and leaves. Be pleased to accept it, Oh Ruler of All the Gods. With this offering of a garland of flowers oṃ aiṃ hrīṃ klīṃ cāmuṇḍāyai vicce.

flower

मल्लिकादि सुगन्धीनि मालित्यादीनि वै प्रभो ।

मयाऽहृतानि पूजार्थं पुष्पाणि प्रतिगृह्यताम् ॥

ॐ ऐं ह्रीं क्लीं चामुण्डायै विच्चे पुष्पम् समर्पयामि

**mallikādi sugandhīni mālityādīni vai prabho**
**mayā-hṛtāni pūjārthaṃ puṣpāṇi pratigṛhyatām**
**oṃ aiṃ hrīṃ klīṃ cāmuṇḍāyai vicce puṣpam samarpayāmi**

Various flowers, such as mallikā and others of excellent scent, are being offered to you, Our Lord. All these flowers have come from the devotion of our hearts for your worship. Please accept them. With this offering of a flower oṃ aiṃ hrīṃ klīṃ cāmuṇḍāyai vicce.

### sthirī karaṇa

establishment of stillness in the pot

ॐ सर्वतीर्थमयं वारि सर्वदेवसमन्वितम् ।

इमं घटं समागच्छ तिष्ठ देवगणैः सह ॥

**oṃ sarvatīrthamayaṃ vāri sarvadevasamanvitam**
**imaṃ ghaṭaṃ samāgaccha tiṣṭha devagaṇaiḥ saha**

All the places of pilgrimage as well as all of the Gods, all are placed within this container. Oh Multitude of Gods, be established within!

### lelihānā mudrā

(literally, sticking out or pointing)

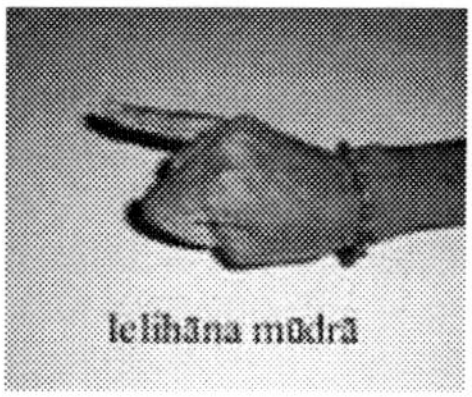

lelihāna mūdrā

स्थां स्थीं स्थिरो भव

विड्वङ्ग आशुर्भव वाज्यर्व्वन् ।

पृथुर्भव शुषदस्त्वमग्नेः पुरीषवाहनः ॥

**sthāṃ sthīṃ sthiro bhava**
**viḍvaṅga āśurbhava vājyarvvan**
**pṛthurbhava śuṣadastvamagneḥ purīṣavāhanaḥ**

Be Still in the Gross Body! Be Still in the Subtle Body! Be Still in the Causal Body! Quickly taking in this energy and shining forth as the Holder of Wealth, oh Divine Fire, becoming abundant, destroy the current of negativity from the face of this earth.

## prāṇa pratiṣṭhā

establishment of life

ॐ अं आं ह्रीं क्रों यं रं लं वं शं षं सं हों हं सः

**oṃ aṃ āṃ hrīṃ kroṃ yaṃ raṃ laṃ vaṃ śaṃ ṣaṃ saṃ hoṃ haṃ saḥ**

Oṃ The Infinite Beyond Conception, Creation (the first letter), Consciousness, Māyā, the cause of the movement of the subtle body to perfection and beyond; the path of fulfillment: control, subtle illumination, one with the earth, emancipation, the soul of peace, the soul of delight, the soul of unity (all this is I), perfection, Infinite Consciousness, I am this.

ॐ ऐं ह्रीं क्लीं चामुण्डायै विच्चे प्राणा इह प्राणाः

**oṃ aiṃ hrīṃ klīṃ cāmuṇḍāyai vicce prāṇā iha prāṇāḥ**

Oṃ aiṃ hrīṃ klīṃ cāmuṇḍāyai vicce You are the life of this life!

ॐ अं आं ह्रीं क्रों यं रं लं वं शं षं सं हों हं सः

**oṃ aṃ āṃ hrīṃ kroṃ yaṃ raṃ laṃ vaṃ śaṃ ṣaṃ saṃ hoṃ haṃ saḥ**

Oṃ The Infinite Beyond Conception, Creation (the first letter), Consciousness, Māyā, the cause of the movement of the subtle body to perfection and beyond; the path of fulfillment: control, subtle illumination, one with the earth, emancipation, the soul of peace, the soul of delight, the soul of unity (all this is I), perfection, Infinite Consciousness, I am this.

ॐ ऐं ह्रीं क्लीं चामुण्डायै विच्चे जीव इह स्थितः

**oṃ aiṃ hrīṃ klīṃ cāmuṇḍāyai vicce jīva iha sthitaḥ**

Oṃ aiṃ hrīṃ klīṃ cāmuṇḍāyai vicce You are situated in this life (or individual consciousness).

ॐ अं आं ह्रीं क्रों यं रं लं वं शं षं सं हों हं सः

**oṃ aṃ āṃ hrīṃ kroṃ yaṃ raṃ laṃ vaṃ śaṃ ṣaṃ saṃ hoṃ haṃ saḥ**

Oṃ The Infinite Beyond Conception, Creation (the first letter), Consciousness, Māyā, the cause of the movement of the subtle body to perfection and beyond; the path of fulfillment: control, subtle illumination, one with the earth, emancipation, the soul of peace, the soul of delight, the soul of unity (all this is I), perfection, Infinite Consciousness, I am this.

ॐ ऐं ह्रीं क्लीं चामुण्डायै विच्चे सर्वेन्द्रियाणि

**oṃ aiṃ hrīṃ klīṃ cāmuṇḍāyai vicce sarvendriyāṇi**

Oṃ aiṃ hrīṃ klīṃ cāmuṇḍāyai vicce You are all these organs (of action and knowledge).

ॐ अं आं ह्रीं क्रों यं रं लं वं शं षं सं हों हं सः

**oṃ aṃ āṃ hrīṃ kroṃ yaṃ raṃ laṃ vaṃ śaṃ ṣaṃ saṃ hoṃ haṃ saḥ**

Oṃ The Infinite Beyond Conception, Creation (the first letter), Consciousness, Māyā, the cause of the movement of the subtle body to perfection and beyond; the path of fulfillment: control, subtle illumination, one with the earth, emancipation, the soul of peace, the soul of delight, the soul of unity (all this is I), perfection, Infinite Consciousness, I am this.

ॐ ऐं ह्रीं क्लीं चामुण्डायै विच्चे वाग् मनस्त्वक्चक्षुः-श्रोत्र-घ्राण-प्राणा इहागत्य सुखं चिरं तिष्ठन्तु स्वाहा

**oṃ aiṃ hrīṃ klīṃ cāmuṇḍāyai vicce vāg manast-vakcakṣuḥ śrotra ghrāṇa prāṇā ihāgatya sukhaṃ ciraṃ tiṣṭhantu svāhā**

Oṃ aiṃ hrīṃ klīṃ cāmuṇḍāyai vicce You are all these vibrations, mind, sound, eyes, ears, tongue, nose and life force. Bring forth infinite peace and establish it forever, I am One with God!

## kara nyāsa

establishment in the hands

ॐ ह्रां अंगुष्ठाभ्यां नमः

**oṃ hrāṃ aṇguṣṭhābhyāṃ namaḥ** *thumb forefinger*

Oṃ hrāṃ in the thumb I bow.

ॐ ह्रीं तर्जनीभ्यां स्वाहा

**oṃ hrīṃ tarjanībhyāṃ svāhā** *thumb forefinger*

Oṃ hrīṃ in the forefinger, I am One with God!

ॐ ह्रूं मध्यमाभ्यां वषट्

**oṃ hrūṃ madhyamābhyāṃ vaṣaṭ** *thumb middlefinger*

Oṃ hrūṃ in the middle finger, Purify!

ॐ ह्रैं अनामिकाभ्यां हुं

**oṃ hraiṃ anāmikābhyāṃ huṃ** *thumb ring finger*

Oṃ hraiṃ in the ring finger, Cut the Ego!

ॐ ह्रौं कनिष्ठिकाभ्यां बौषट्

**oṃ hrauṃ kaniṣṭhikābhyāṃ vauṣaṭ** *thumb little finger*

Oṃ hrauṃ in the little finger, Ultimate Purity!

*Roll hand over hand forwards while reciting* karatal kar,
*and backwards while chanting* pṛṣṭhābhyāṃ,
*then clap hands when chanting* astrāya phaṭ.

ॐ हः करतल कर पृष्ठाभ्यां अस्त्राय फट् ॥

**oṃ hraḥ karatal kar pṛṣṭhābhyāṃ astrāya phaṭ**

Oṃ hraḥ I bow with the weapon of Virtue.

ॐ ऐं ह्रीं क्लीं चामुण्डायै विच्चे

**oṃ aiṃ hrīṃ klīṃ cāmuṇḍāyai vicce**

Oṃ aiṃ hrīṃ klīṃ cāmuṇḍāyai vicce.

**aṅga nyāsa**

establishment in the body

*Holding tattva mudrā, touch heart.*

ॐ ह्रां हृदयाय नमः

**oṃ hrāṃ hṛdayāya namaḥ** *touch heart*

Oṃ hrāṃ in the heart, I bow.

*Holding tattva mudrā, touch top of head.*

ॐ ह्रीं शिरसे स्वाहा

**oṃ hrīṃ śirase svāhā** *top of head*

Oṃ hrīṃ on the top of the head, I am One with God!

*With thumb extended, touch back of head.*

ॐ ह्रूं शिखायै वषट्

**oṃ hrūṃ śikhāyai vaṣaṭ** *back of head*

Oṃ hrūṃ on the back of the head, Purify!

*Holding tattva mudrā, cross both arms.*

ॐ हैं कवचाय हुं

**oṃ hraiṃ kavacāya huṃ**

Oṃ hraiṃ crossing both arms, Cut the Ego!

*Holding tattva mudrā, touch two eyes and in between at once with three middle fingers.*

ॐ हौं नेत्रत्रयाय वौषट्

**oṃ hrauṃ netratrayāya vauṣaṭ** *touch three eyes*

Oṃ hrauṃ in the three eyes, Ultimate Purity!

Roll hand over hand forwards while reciting *karatal kar*, and backwards while chanting *pṛṣṭhābhyāṃ*, then clap hands when chanting *astrāya phaṭ*.

ॐ हः करतल कर पृष्ठाभ्यां अस्त्राय फट् ॥

**oṃ hraḥ karatal kar pṛṣṭhābhyāṃ astrāya phaṭ**

Oṃ hraḥ I bow with the weapon of Virtue.

ॐ ऐं ह्रीं क्लीं चामुण्डायै विच्चे

**oṃ aiṃ hrīṃ klīṃ cāmuṇḍāyai vicce**

Oṃ aiṃ hrīṃ klīṃ cāmuṇḍāyai vicce

## japa

## prāṇa pratiṣṭhā sūkta

hymn of the establishment of life

ॐ अस्यै प्राणाः प्रतिष्ठन्तु अस्यै प्राणाः क्षरन्तु च ।
अस्यै देवत्वमर्चायै मामहेति कश्चन ॥

**oṃ asyai prāṇāḥ pratiṣṭhantu**
**asyai prāṇāḥ kṣarantu ca**
**asyai devatvamārcāyai māmaheti kaścana**

Oṃ Thus has the life force been established in you, and thus the life force has flowed into you. Thus to you, God, offering is made, and in this way make us shine.

कलाकला हि देवानां दानवानां कलाकलाः ।
संगृह्य निर्मितो यस्मात् कलशस्तेन कथ्यते ॥

**kalākalā hi devānāṃ dānavānāṃ kalākalāḥ**
**saṃgṛhya nirmito yasmāt kalaśastena kathyate**

All the Gods are Fragments of the Cosmic Whole. Also all the asuras are Fragments of the Cosmic Whole. Thus we make a house to contain all these energies.

कलशस्य मुखे विष्णुः कण्ठे रुद्रः समाश्रितः ।
मूले त्वस्य स्थितो ब्रह्मा मध्ये मातृगणाः स्मृताः ॥

**kalaśasya mukhe viṣṇuḥ kaṅṭhe rudraḥ samāśritaḥ**
**mūle tvasya sthito brahmā madhye mātṛgaṇāḥ smṛtāḥ**

In the mouth of the pot is Viṣṇu, in the neck resides Rudra. At the base is situated Brahmā and in the middle we remember the multitude of mothers.

कुक्षौ तु सागराः सप्त सप्तद्वीपा च मेदिनी ।
अर्जुनी गोमती चैव चन्द्रभागा सरस्वती ॥

**kukṣau tu sāgarāḥ sapta saptadvīpā ca medinī**
**arjunī gomatī caiva candrabhāgā sarasvatī**

In the belly are the seven seas and the seven islands of the earth. The rivers Arjunī, Gomatī, Candrabhāgā, Sarasvatī;

कावेरी कृष्णवेणा च गङ्गा चैव महानदी ।
ताप्ती गोदावरी चैव माहेन्द्री नर्मदा तथा ॥

**kāverī kṛṣṇaveṇā ca gaṅgā caiva mahānadī**
**tāptī godāvarī caiva māhendrī narmadā tathā**

Kāverī, Kṛṣṇaveṇā and the Gaṅges and other great rivers; the Tāptī, Godāvarī, Māhendrī and Narmadā.

नदाश्च विविधा जाता नद्यः सर्वास्तथापराः ।
पृथिव्यां यानि तीर्थानि कलशस्थानि तानि वै ॥

**nadāśca vividhā jātā nadyaḥ sarvāstathāparāḥ**
**pṛthivyāṃ yāni tīrthāni kalaśasthāni tāni vai**

The various rivers and the greatest of beings born, and all the respected places of pilgrimage on the earth, are established within this pot.

सर्वे समुद्राः सरितस्तीर्थानि जलदा नदाः ।
आयान्तु मम शान्त्यर्थं दुरितक्षयकारकाः ॥

**sarve samudrāḥ saritastīrthāni jaladā nadāḥ**
**āyāntu mama śāntyartham duritakṣayakārakāḥ**

All of the seas, rivers and waters from all the respected places of pilgrimage have been brought for the peace of that which is bad or wicked.

ऋग्वेदोऽथ यजुर्वेदः सामवेदो ह्यथर्वणः ।
अङ्गैश्च सहिताः सर्वे कलशं तु समाश्रिताः ॥

**ṛgvedo-tha yajurvedaḥ sāmavedo hyatharvaṇaḥ**
**aṅgaiśca sahitāḥ sarve kalaśaṃ tu samāśritāḥ**

The Ṛg Veda, Yajur Veda, Sāma Veda and Atharva Veda, along with all of their limbs, are assembled together in this pot.

अत्र गायत्री सावित्री शान्तिः पुष्टिकरी तथा ।
आयान्तु मम शान्त्यर्थं दुरितक्षयकारकाः ॥

**atra gāyatrī sāvitrī śāntiḥ puṣṭikarī tathā**
**āyāntu mama śāntyartham duritakṣayakārakāḥ**

Here Gāyatrī, Sāvitrī, Peace and Increase have been brought for the peace of that which is bad or wicked.

देवदानवसंवादे मथ्यमाने महोदधौ ।
उत्पन्नोऽसि तदा कुम्भ विधृतो विष्णुना स्वयम् ॥

**deva dānava saṃvāde mathyamāne mahodadhau**
**utpanno-si tadā kumbha vidhṛto viṣṇunā svayam**

The Gods and asuras, speaking together, are the great givers of churning to the mind. Rise to the top of this pot to separate them from what is actually Viṣṇu, Himself.

त्वत्तोये सर्वतीर्थानि देवाः सर्वे त्वयि स्थिताः ।
त्वयि तिष्ठन्ति भूतानि त्वयि प्राणाः प्रतिष्ठिताः ॥

**tvattoye sarvatīrthāni devāḥ sarve tvayi sthitāḥ**
**tvayi tiṣṭhanti bhūtāni tvayi prāṇāḥ pratiṣṭhitāḥ**

Within you are all the pilgrimage places. All the Gods are situated within you. All existence is established within you. All life is established within you.

शिवः स्वयं त्वमेवासि विष्णुस्त्वं च प्रजापतिः ।
आदित्या वसवो रुद्रा विश्वेदेवाः सपैतृकाः ॥

**śivaḥ svayaṃ tvamevāsi viṣṇustvaṃ ca prajāpatiḥ**
**ādityā vasavo rudrā viśvedevāḥ sapaitṛkāḥ**

You alone are Śiva; you are Brahmā and Viṣṇu, the sons of Āditi, Finders of the Wealth, Rudra, the Universal Deities and the ancestors.

त्वयि तिष्ठन्ति सर्वेऽपि यतः कामफलप्रदाः ।
त्वत्प्रसादादिमं यज्ञं कर्तुमीहे जलोद्भव ।
सान्निध्यं कुरु मे देव प्रसन्नो भव सर्वदा ॥

**tvayi tiṣṭhanti sarve-pi yataḥ kāmaphalapradāḥ**
**tvatprasādādimaṃ yajñaṃ kartumīhe jalodbhava**
**sānnidhyaṃ kuru me deva prasanno bhava sarvadā**

All and everything has been established in you, from whence you grant the fruits of desires. From you comes the blessed fruit of the sacrifice performed with excellence. May those riches increase. Manifest your presence within us, Lord. Always be pleased.

नमो नमस्ते स्फटिकप्रभाय सुश्वेतहाराय सुमङ्गलाय ।
सुपाशहस्ताय झषासनाय जलाधिनाथाय नमो नमस्ते ॥

**namo namaste sphaṭikaprabhāya**
**suśvetahārāya sumaṅgalāya**
**supāśahastāya jhaṣāsanāya**
**jalādhināthāya namo namaste**

We bow, we bow to He who shines like crystal, to He who emits excellent clarity and excellent welfare. With the net of unity in his hand, who takes the form of a fish, to the Lord of all waters and that which dwells within, we bow, we bow!

पाशपाणे नमस्तुभ्यं पद्मिनीजीवनायक ।
पुण्याहवाचनं यावत् तावत्त्वं सन्निधौ भव ॥

**pāśapāṇe namastubhyaṃ padminījīvanāyaka**
**puṇyāhavācanaṃ yāvat tāvattvaṃ sannidhau bhava**

We bow to Him with the net of unity in his hand, Seer of the Life of the Lotus One. With this meritorious invocation, please make your presence manifest.

## viśeṣārghya

establishment of the conch shell offering
Draw the following yantra on the plate or space
for worship with sandal paste and/or water.
Offer rice on the yantra for each of the four mantras:

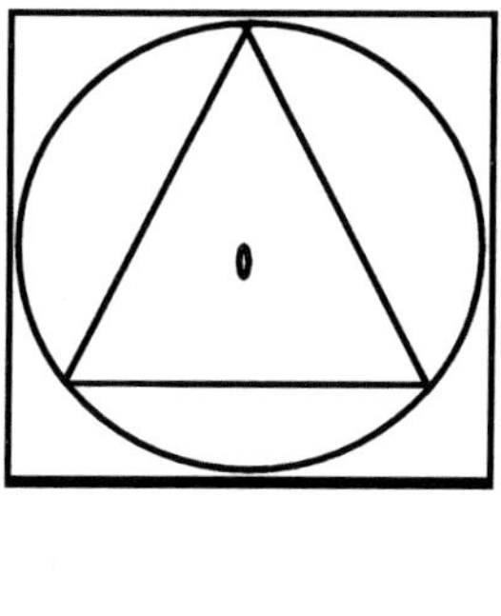

ॐ आधारशक्तये नमः

**oṃ ādhāraśaktaye namaḥ**
Oṃ we bow to the Primal Energy

ॐ कूर्म्माय नमः

**oṃ kūrmmāya namaḥ**
Oṃ we bow to the Support of the Earth

ॐ अनन्ताय नमः

**oṃ anantāya namaḥ**
Oṃ we bow to Infinity

ॐ पृथिव्यै नमः

**oṃ pṛthivyai namaḥ**
Oṃ we bow to the Earth

Place a conch shell on the bindu in the center of the yantra while saying this mantra:

स्थां स्थीं स्थिरो भव फट्

**sthāṃ sthīṃ sthiro bhava phaṭ**
Be Still in the Gross Body! Be Still in the Subtle Body! Be Still in the Causal Body! Purify!

Fill the conch shell with water while chanting this mantra.

ॐ गङ्गे च जमुने चैव गोदावरि सरस्वति ।
नर्मदे सिन्धु कावेरि जलेऽस्मिन् सन्निधिं कुरु ॥

**oṃ gaṅge ca jamune caiva godāvari sarasvati**
**narmade sindhu kāveri jale-smin sannidhiṃ kuru**

Oṃ the Ganges, Jamunā, Godāvarī, Sarasvatī, Narmadā, Sindhu, Kāverī, these waters are mingled together.

Offer Tulasī leaves into the water

ॐ ऐं ह्रीं क्लीं श्रीं वृन्दावनवासिन्यै स्वाहा

**oṃ aiṃ hrīṃ klīṃ śrīṃ vṛndāvanavāsinyai svāhā**

Oṃ Wisdom, Māyā, Increase, to She who resides in Vṛndāvana, I am One with God!

Offer three flowers into the water pot with the mantra:

एते गन्धपुष्पे ॐ अं अर्कमण्डलाय द्वादशकलात्मने नमः

**ete gandhapuṣpe oṃ aṃ arkamaṇḍalāya dvādaśakalātmane namaḥ**

With these scented flowers oṃ "A" we bow to the twelve aspects of the realm of the sun. Tapinī, Tāpinī, Dhūmrā, Marīci, Jvālinī, Ruci, Sudhūmrā, Bhoga-dā, Viśvā, Bodhinī, Dhārinī, Kṣamā; Containing Heat, Emanating Heat, Smoky, Ray-producing, Burning, Lustrous, Purple or Smoky-Red, Granting Enjoyment, Universal, Which Makes known, Productive of Consciousness, Which Supports, Which Forgives.

एते गन्धपुष्पे ॐ उं सोममण्डलाय षोडशकलात्मने नमः

**ete gandhapuṣpe oṃ uṃ somamaṇḍalāya ṣoḍaśakalātmane namaḥ**

With these scented flowers oṃ "U" we bow to the sixteen aspects of the realm of the moon: Amṛtā, Prāṇadā, Puṣā, Tuṣṭi, Puṣṭi, Rati, Dhṛti, Śaśinī, Caṇḍrikā, Kānti, Jyotsnā, Śrī, Prīti, Aṅgadā, Pūrṇā, Pūrṇāmṛta; Nectar, Which Sustains Life, Which Supports, Satisfying, Nourishing, Playful, Constant, Unfailing, Producer of Joy, Beauty Enhanced by Love, Light, Grantor of Prosperity, Affectionate, Purifying the Body, Complete, Full of Bliss.

एते गन्धपुष्पे ॐ मं वह्निमण्डलाय दशकलात्मने नमः

**ete gandhapuṣpe oṃ maṃ vahnimaṇḍalāya daśakalātmane namaḥ**

With these scented flowers oṃ "M" we bow to the ten aspects of the realm of fire: Dhūmrā, Arciḥ, Jvalinī, Śūkṣmā, Jvālinī, Visphūliṅginī, Suśrī, Surūpā, Kapilā, Havya-Kavya-Vahā; Smoky-Red, Flaming, Shining, Subtle, Burning, Sparkling, Beautiful, Well-formed, Tawny, the Messenger to the Gods and Ancestors.

एते गन्धपुष्पे हुं

**ete gandhapuṣpe huṃ**

With these scented flowers huṃ

Wave hands in matsyā, dhenu and aṅkuśa mudrās while chanting this mantra:

ॐ गङ्गे च जमुने चैव गोदावरि सरस्वति ।

नर्मदे सिन्धु कावेरि जलेऽस्मिन् सन्निधिं कुरु ॥

**oṃ gaṅge ca jamune caiva godāvari sarasvati narmade sindhu kāveri jale-smin sannidhiṃ kuru**

Oṃ the Ganges, Jamunā, Godāvarī, Sarasvatī, Narmadā, Sindhu, Kāverī, these waters are mingled together.

ॐ ऐं ह्रीं क्लीं चामुण्डायै विच्चे

**oṃ aiṃ hrīṃ klīṃ cāmuṇḍāyai vicce**

Oṃ aiṃ hrīṃ klīṃ cāmuṇḍāyai vicce

Sprinkle water over all the articles to be offered, then throw some drops of water over your shoulders while repeating the mantra:

अमृतम् कुरु स्वाहा

**amṛtam kuru svāhā**

Make this immortal nectar! I am One with God!

## bhūta śuddhi

purification of the elements

Pronounce each Bījā sixteen times in its proper location:

| | | | | | |
|---|---|---|---|---|---|
| लं | Mulādhāra | (1st Cakra) | **Laṃ** | Indra | Earth |
| वं | Swādiṣṭhana | (2nd Cakra) | **Vaṃ** | Varuṇa | Water |
| रं | Maṇipura | (3rd Cakra) | **Raṃ** | Agni | Fire |
| यं | Anahata | (4th Cakra) | **Yaṃ** | Vāyu | Air |
| हं | Viśuddha | (5th Cakra) | **Haṃ** | Soma | Ether |
| ॐ | Āgnyā | (6th Cakra) | **Oṃ** | Īśvara | The Ultimate |

Then move up and down the Suṣumṇa through the cakras, pronouncing each Bījā once, and feeling its presence in its proper location.

ॐ लं वं रं यं हं ॐ

**oṃ laṃ vaṃ raṃ yaṃ haṃ oṃ**

Oṃ Earth, Water, Fire, Air, Ether, The Ultimate.

ॐ हं यं रं वं लं ॐ

**oṃ haṃ yaṃ raṃ vaṃ laṃ oṃ**
Oṃ The Ultimate, Ether, Air, Fire, Water, Earth.

ॐ मूलशृङ्गाटाच्छिरः सुषुम्नापथेन जीवशिवं परमशिवपदे षोजयामि स्वाहा ॥

**oṃ mūlaśṛṅgāṭācchiraḥ suṣumnāpathena jīvaśivaṃ paramaśivapade ṣojayāmi svāhā**
Oṃ Piercing the triangular junction (yantra) situated in the Mulādhāra, the center of energy between the genitals and the rectum, I direct the auspicious life force upwards by way of the Suṣumna, the subtle canal that transmits nerve impulses along the spinal column, to unite in Supreme Bliss, I am One with God!

ॐ यं लिङ्गशरीरं शोषय शोषय स्वाहा ॥

**oṃ yaṃ liṅgaśarīraṃ śoṣaya śoṣaya svāhā**
Oṃ Yaṃ (Vāyu, Air, the Spirit of Emancipation) in the subtle body, purify, purify, I am One with God!

ॐ रं सङ्कोचशरीरं दह दह स्वाहा ॥

**oṃ raṃ saṅkocaśarīraṃ daha daha svāhā**
Oṃ Raṃ (Agni, Fire, the Purifying Light of Wisdom) in the limited body, burn, burn, I am One with God!

ॐ परमशिव सुषुम्नापथेन मूलशृङ्गाटमुल्लसोल्लस ज्वल ज्वल प्रज्वल प्रज्वल सोऽहं हंसः स्वाहा ॥

**oṃ paramaśiva suṣumnāpathena**
**mūlaśṛṅgāṭamullasollasa**
**jvala jvala prajvala prajvala so-haṃ haṃsaḥ svāhā**
Oṃ Oh Supreme Bliss, filling the path of the Suṣumna from the triangular junction in the Mulādhāra, dancing brilliantly, shine, shine, radiate, radiate, That is I, I am That, I am One with God!

## kara śuddhi

wipe your hands with a flower

ॐ ऐं रं अस्त्राय फट्

**oṃ aiṃ raṃ astrāya phaṭ**
Oṃ Wisdom, the Subtle Body of Light, with this weapon, Purify!

Tap ground three times with fist or heel

फट् फट् फट्

**phaṭ phaṭ phaṭ**
Purify! Purify! Purify!

## bhūtāpsāraṇa

dispersion of inimical energies

Bhūta has a number of meanings, which makes a play on the words in the following verses, switching meanings even while using the same word. Its noun forms mean. variously: purified being, good being; created thing, world; uncanny being, spirit, ghost, goblin; past, fact, reality, actual occurrence; welfare; elements, especially as applied to the five gross elements of earth, water, fire, air and ether (see bhūta śuddhi). Here we are calling on the friendly or good Bhūtas to destroy obstacles created by unfriendly or bad Bhūtas.

ॐ अपसर्पन्तु ते भूता ये भूता भुवि संस्थिताः ।
ये भूता विघ्नकर्त्तारस्ते नश्यन्तु शिवज्ञया ॥

**oṃ apasarpantu te bhūtā ya bhūtā bhuvi saṃsthitāḥ ye bhūtā vighnakarttāraste naśyantu śivajñayā**

Oṃ We consign to you friendly spirits, friendly spirits that are situated on this earth plane, the activity of destroying any obstacles placed by unfriendly spirits, by order of the Wisdom of Infinite Goodness.

ॐ भूतप्रेतपिशाचाश्च दानवा राक्षसाश्च ये ।
शान्तिं कुर्वन्तु ते सर्वे ईमं गृह्वतु मद्बलिम् ॥

**oṃ bhūtapretapiśācāśca dānavā rākṣasāśca ye śāntiṃ kurvantu te sarve īmaṃ gṛhvatu madbalim**

Oṃ Hey ghosts, goblins, demons, unfriendly spirits and various forms of negativity projecting egos: You have been made entirely at peace. Please accept this offering from me.

ॐ वेतालाश्च पिशाचाश्च राक्षसाश्च सरीसुपाः ।
अपसर्पन्तु ते सर्वे नारसिंहेन ताढिताः ॥

**oṃ vetālāśca piśācāśca rākṣasāśca sarīsupāḥ apasarpantu te sarve nārasiṃhena tāḍhitāḥ**

Oṃ Other demons, goblins, various forms of negativity-projecting egos, creeping and crawling things: I consign to you completely the striking blows of Nārasiṃha, Viṣṇu in His incarnation of man-lion.

**aghamārṣaṇa**

internal cleaning

Perform Jāl Neti by taking water from the Samanyārghya, the purified water, into the left palm. Inhale it through the Iḍa or left nostril, and bring it all the way up into the Āgnyā Cakra, then expel it through the Piṅgalā or right nostril. Blow out the nasal passages so that they are clean.

ॐ ऋतमित्यस्य ऋक्त्रयस्याघमर्षण

ऋषिरनष्टुप्छन्दोभाववृत्तं देवतामश्वमेधावभृथे विनियोगः ।

**oṃ ṛtamityasya ṛktrayasyāghamarṣaṇa ṛṣiranaṣṭupchandobhāvavṛttaṃ devatāmaśvamedhāvabhṛthe viniyogaḥ**

Oṃ Introducing the three Mantras that begin with "From Truth...", etc., Internal Cleaning is the Seer, Anuṣṭup is the meter (32 syllables to the verse), Who Changes the Intensity of Reality is the divinity. Equal in merit to the horse sacrifice, this practice is being offered in application.

ॐ ऋतं च सत्यं चाभीद्धात्तपसोऽध्यजायत ।

ततो रत्र्यजायत ततः समुद्रोऽर्णवः ॥

**oṃ ṛtaṃ ca satyaṃ cābhīddhāttapaso-dhyajāyata tato ratryajāyata tataḥ samudro-rṇavaḥ**

Oṃ From truth, from the Imperishable Truth, the Performers of Tapasya, or strict spiritual discipline, have come. Then came forth the night, and then the sea of objects and relationships, with the multitude of its waves.

समुद्रार्णवादधि संवत्सरो अजायत ।

अहोरात्राणिविदधदिश्वस्य भिषतो वशी ॥

**samudrārṇavādadhi saṃvatsaro ajāyata**
**ahorātrāṇividadhadiśvasya bhiṣato vaśī**

From the fluctuations of the waves on the sea, the years came forth. The night transformed into day, and the universe took birth.

सूर्या चन्द्रमसौ धाता यथापूर्वमकल्पयत् ।

दिवं च पृथिवीं चान्तरिक्षमथो स्वः ॥

**sūryā candramasau dhātā yathāpūrvamakalpayat**
**divaṃ ca pṛthivīṃ cāntarikṣamatho svaḥ**

The Sun and the Moon gave forth their lights in accordance with the command of the Creator. And the earth, the atmosphere and the heavens were His Own.

**jāl netī, prāṇāyāma**

cleaning of the sinuses, control of breath

**agni prajvālitaṃ**

enkindling the sacred fire

**agni gāyatrī**

ॐ वैश्वानराय विद्महे लालिलय धीमहे ।

तन्नो अग्निः प्रचोदयात् ॐ ॥

**oṃ vaisvānarāya vidmahe lālilaya dhīmahe**
**tanno agniḥ pracodayāt oṃ**

Oṃ We meditate upon the All-Pervading Being, we contemplate the Luminous One who is the final resting place of all. May that Divine Fire, the Light of Meditation, grant us increase.

upasaṃhara mudrā

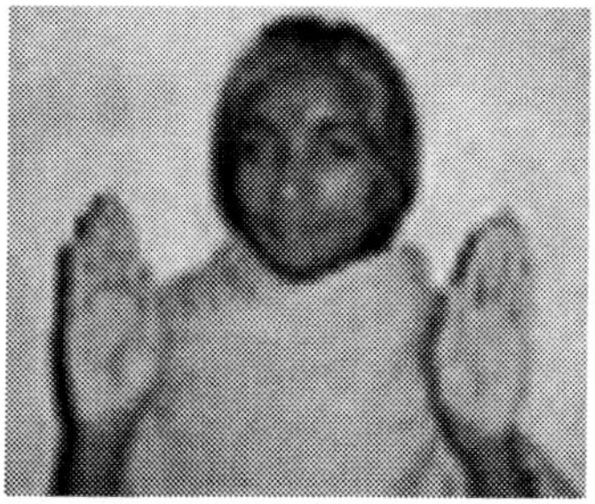

ह्वयाम्यग्निं प्रथमं स्वस्तये ।

ह्वयामि मित्रावरुणाविहावसे ।

ह्वयामि रात्रीं जगतो निवेशनीं ।

ह्वयामिदेवं सवितारमूतये ॥

**hvayāmyagniṃ prathamaṃ svastaye**
**hvayāmi mitrā varuṇā vihāvase**
**hvayāmi rātrīṃ jagato niveṣanīṃ**
**hvayāmi devaṃ savitāramūtaye**

I am calling you, Agni, the Divine Fire, the Light of Meditation, first to grant success. I am calling you Friendship and the Continuous Flow of Equilibrium also to receive this offering. I am calling the Night of Duality who covers the universe. I am calling the Light of Wisdom, the Divine Being, to rise up within us.

हिरण्यगर्भः समवर्ततागे्र भूतस्य जातः पतिरेक आसीत् ।
स दाधार पृथिवीं द्यामुतेमां कस्मै देवाय हविषा विधेम ॥

**hiranyagarbhaḥ samavartatāgre bhūtasya jātaḥ patireka āsīt**
**sa dādhāra pṛthivīṃ dyāmutemāṃ kasmai devāya haviṣā vidhema**

Oh Golden Womb, You are the One Eternal Existence from which all beings born on the earth have come forth. You always bear the earth and all that rises upon it. (You tell us) to which God shall we offer our knowledge and attention?

यथा विद्वां अरंकरद् विश्वेभ्यो यजतेभ्यः ।
अयमग्ने त्वे अपि यं यज्ञं चकृमा वयम् ॥

**yathā vidvāṃ araṃkarad viśvebhyoḥ yajatebhyaḥ**
**ayamagne tve api yaṃ yajñaṃ cakṛmā vayam**

Through knowledge of this Eternal Cause, all beings born in the universe have come forth. It is in you, Oh Agni, Oh Light of Meditation, in the flame of sacrifice, that this constant movement will find rest.

त्वमग्ने प्रथमो अङ्गिरा ऋषिर्देवो देवानामभवः शिवः सखा ।
तव व्रते कवयो विद्मनापसोऽजायन्त मरुतो भ्राजदृष्टयः ॥

**tvamagne prathamo aṅgirā ṛṣirdevo**
**devānāmabhavaḥ śivaḥ sakhā**
**tava vrate kavayo vidmanāpaso-**
**jāyanta maruto bhrājadṛṣṭayaḥ**

You, Oh Divine Light of Meditation, are the first among the performers of spiritual discipline, a Seer, a God; your name became one with all the Gods. You are the friend of Śiva, the

Consciousness of Infinite Goodness. Through devotion to you, all the inspired poets (Ṛṣis who propound Vedic Knowledge, or Wisdom of Universality) come to Divine Knowledge, as did the Maruts (the 49 Gods of severe penance) come forth from your worship.

त्वं मुखं सर्वदेवनां सप्तचिर्हविद्मते ।
आगच्छ भगवनग्ने यज्ञेऽस्मिन् सन्निधा भव ॥

**tvaṃ mukhaṃ sarvadevanāṃ saptacirhavidmate**
**āgaccha bhagavanagne yajñe-smin sannidhā bhava**

You are the mouth of all the Gods; with your seven tongues you accept the offerings. Come here, Oh Lord Divine Fire, and take your seat in the midst of our sacrifice.

ॐ वैश्वानर जातवेद इहावह लोहिताक्ष सर्व कर्माणि साधय स्वाहा ॥

**oṃ vaiśvānara jātaveda ihāvaha lohitākṣa sarva karmāṇi sādhaya svāhā**

Oṃ Oh Universal Being, Knower of All, come here with your red eyes. All of our Karma burn it! I AM ONE WITH GOD!

ॐ अग्नीमिळे पुरोहितं यज्ञस्य देवमृत्विजम् ।
होतारं रत्न धातमम् ॥

**oṃ agnīmiḷe purohitaṃ yajñasya devamṛtvijam**
**hotāraṃ ratna dhātamam**

Oṃ Oh Agni, Light of Meditation, you are the Priest of Sacrifice, serving the offering of the divine nectar of Immortality. You give jewels to those who offer.

ॐ अग्निं प्रज्वलितं वन्दे जातवेदं हुताशनम् ।
सुवर्णवर्णममलं समिद्धं विश्वतो मुखम्

**oṃ agni prajvalitaṃ vande jātavedaṃ hutāśanam suvarṇavarṇamamalaṃ samiddhaṃ viśvato mukham**

Oṃ We lovingly adore the Divine Fire, the Light of Meditation, sparkling, flaming brightly, knower of all, recipient of our offerings. With His excellent golden color, everywhere His omnipresent mouths are devouring oblations.

ॐ अग्नये नमः

**oṃ agnaye namaḥ**

Oṃ We bow to the Divine Fire.

अग्ने त्वं चण्डिकानामसि

**agne tvaṃ caṇḍikānāmasi**

Oh Divine Fire, we are now calling you by the name Caṇḍi, She who Tears Apart Thoughts.

ॐ वागीश्वरी मृतुस्नातां नीलेन्दीवरलोचनाम् ।
वागीश्वरेण संयुक्तां कृराभव समन्वितम्

**oṃ vāgīśvarī mṛtu-snātāṃ nīlendīvaralocanām vāgīśvareṇa saṃyuktāṃ kṛrābhava samanvitam**

Oṃ The Supreme Goddess of Speech, dear Mother Saraswati, has just completed Her bath following Her monthly course of menstruation. With eyes of blue, bestowing boons, She moves into union with Vāgīṣvara, Brahma, the Lord of All Vibrations, and together they create the intensity of reality, the attitude that unites all.

एते गन्धपुष्पे ॐ ह्रीं वागीश्वर्यै नमः

**ete gandhapuṣpe oṃ hrīṃ vāgīśvaryai namaḥ**

With these scented flowers oṃ we bow to the Supreme Goddess of Speech, or all Vibrations.

एते गन्धपुष्पे ॐ ह्रीं वागीश्वराय नमः

**ete gandhapuṣpe oṃ hrīṃ vāgīśvarāya namaḥ**

With these scented flowers oṃ we bow to the Supreme Lord of Speech, or all Vibrations.

एते गन्धपुष्पे ॐ अग्नेर्हिरण्यादि सप्तजिह्वाभ्यो नमः

**ete gandhapuṣpe oṃ agnerhiraṇyādi saptajihvābhyo namaḥ**

With these scented flowers oṃ we bow to the seven tongues of the Divine Fire, such as golden, etc.

| | |
|---|---|
| 1. Kālī | Black |
| 2. Karālī | Increasing, formidable |
| 3. Mano-javā | Swift as thought |
| 4. Su-Lohitā | Excellent shine |
| 5. Sudhūmra-Varnā | Purple |
| 6. Ugrā or Sphulingīnī | Fearful |
| 7. Pradīptā | Giving light |

एते गन्धपुष्पे ॐ सहस्रार्चिषे हृदयाय नमः

**ete gandhapuṣpe oṃ sahasrārciṣe hṛdayāya namaḥ**

With these scented flowers oṃ we bow to the heart from which emanates a thousand rays.

इत्याद्यग्ने षदङ्गेभ्यो नमः

**ityādyagne ṣadaṅgebhyo namaḥ**

In this way establish the Divine Fire in the six centers of the body.

एते गन्धपुष्पे ॐ अग्नये जातवेदसे इत्यद्याष्टमूर्त्तिभ्यो नमः

**ete gandhapuṣpe oṃ agnaye jātavedase ityadyaṣṭa mūrttibhyo namaḥ**

With these scented flowers oṃ we bow to the Divine Fire, the Knower of All, etc., in His eight forms for worship.

| | |
|---|---|
| 1. Jāta-Veda | Knower of All |
| 2. Sapta-Jihva | Seven tongued |
| 3. Vaiśvānara | Universal Being |
| 4. Havyā-Vāhana | Carrier of Oblations |
| 5. Aśwodara-Ja | Fire of Stomach, lower areas |
| 6. Kaumāra Tejaḥ | From which the son of Śiva is born |
| 7. Viśva-Mukha | Which can devour the universe |
| 8. Deva-Mukha | The mouth of the Gods |

एते गन्धपुष्पे ॐ ब्राह्म्यद्याष्टशक्तिभ्यो नमः

**ete gandhapuṣpe oṃ brāhmyadyaṣṭaśaktibhyo namaḥ**

With these scented flowers oṃ we bow to the eight Śaktis or Energies, such as Brāhmī, etc.

| | |
|---|---|
| 1. Brāhmī | Creative Energy |
| 2. Nārāyaṇī | Exposer of Consciousness |
| 3. Māheśvarī | Energy of the Seer of All |
| 4. Cāmuṇḍā | Slayer of Passion and Meanness |
| 5. Kaumārī | The Ever Pure One |
| 6. Aparājitā | The Unconquerable |
| 7. Vārāhī | The Boar of Sacrifice |
| 8. Nārasiṃhī | The Man-Lion of Courage |

एते गन्धपुष्पे ॐ पद्माद्यष्टनिधिभ्यो नमः

**ete gandhapuṣpe oṃ padmādyaṣṭa nidhibhyo namaḥ**

With these scented flowers oṃ we bow to the eight Treasures of the Lord of Wealth, such as Padma, etc.

| | |
|---|---|
| 1. Padma | The lotus of Peace |
| 2. Mahā-Padma | The great lotus of universal Peace |
| 3. Śaṅkha | The conch of all vibrations |
| 4. Makara | The emblem of Love |
| 5. Kacchapa | Tortoise, the emblem of support |
| 6. Mukunda | The Crest Jewel |
| 7. Nanda | Bliss |
| 8. Nīla | The blue light within like a Sapphire |

एते गन्धपुष्पे ॐ इन्द्रादि लोकपालेभ्यो नमः

**ete gandhapuṣpe oṃ indrādi lokapālebhyo namaḥ**

With these scented flowers oṃ we bow to Indra and the Protectors of the Ten Directions.

| | |
|---|---|
| 1. Indra | East |
| 2. Agni | South-East |
| 3. Yama | South |
| 4. Nairrita | South-West |
| 5. Varuṇa | West |
| 6. Vāyu | North-West |
| 7. Kuvera (Soma) | North |
| 8. Īśāna | North-East |
| 9. Brahmā | Above |
| 10. Viṣṇu (Ananta) | Below |

एते गन्धपुष्पे ॐ वज्राद्यस्त्रेभ्यो नमः

**ete gandhapuṣpe oṃ vajrādyastrebhyo namaḥ**

With these scented flowers oṃ we bow to the Thunderbolt and other weapons.

| | |
|---|---|
| 1. Vajra | Indra's thunderbolt |
| 2. Śakti | Agni's spear, dart, energy |
| 3. Daṇḍa | Yama's staff |
| 4. Khaḍga | Nairrita's sword |
| 5. Pāśa | Varuṇa's net or noose |
| 6. Aṅkuśa | Vāyu's hook |
| 7. Gadā | Kuvera's mace |
| 8. Triśūla | Īśāna's trident |
| 9. Padma or Kamaṇḍelu | Brahma's lotus or begging bowl |
| 10. Cakra | Viṣṇu's discus |

एते गन्धपुष्पे ॐ वह्निर्चैतन्याय नमः

**ete gandhapuṣpe oṃ vahnir caitanyāya namaḥ**

With these scented flowers oṃ we bow to the Consciousness of the Divine Fire.

एते गन्धपुष्पे ॐ अग्नि मूर्त्तये नमः

**ete gandhapuṣpe oṃ agni mūrttaye namaḥ**

With these scented flowers oṃ we bow to the Image of the Divine Fire, the Light of Meditation.

ॐ अग्नये नमः

**oṃ agnaye namaḥ**

Oṃ we bow to the Divine Fire.

रं रं रं रं रं

**raṃ raṃ raṃ raṃ raṃ**

**R** The Subtle Body; **a** Consciousness; **ṃ** Perfection

**Raṃ**: the manifestation of Perfection in the Subtle Body of Consciousness.

## mātṛkā pūjā

worship of gaṇeśa and the sixteen mothers

समीपे मातृवर्गस्य सर्वविघ्नहरं सदा ।

त्रैलोक्य वन्दितं देवं गणेशं स्थापयाम्यहम् ॥

**samīpe mātṛvargasya sarvavighnaharaṃ sadā trailokya vanditaṃ devaṃ gaṇeśaṃ sthāpayāmyaham**

Situated before the group of Mothers, He always removes all obstacles. He is the God praised by all the Three worlds; I establish Gaṇeśa, the Lord of Wisdom.

ॐ भूर्भुवः स्वः गणपतये नमः । गणपतिमावाहयामि स्थापयामि ॥

**oṃ bhūrbhuvaḥ svaḥ gaṇapataye namaḥ gaṇapatimāvāhayāmi sthāpayāmi**

Oṃ the Infinite Beyond Conception, the gross body, the subtle body and the causal body. I bow to Gaṇeśa. I invite Gaṇeśa and establish Him within.

हेमाद्रितनयां देवीं वरदां शङ्करप्रियाम् ।

लम्बोदरस्य जननीं गौरीमावाहयाम्यहम् ॥

**hemādritanayāṃ devīṃ varadāṃ śaṅkarapriyām lambodarasya jananīṃ gaurīmāvāhayāmyaham**

The Goddess is the daughter of the snowy mountain, She gives boons and is the beloved of Śiva. With a big stomach, She is the Mother (of existence). I invite Gaurī, She who is Rays of Light.

ॐ भूर्भुवः स्वः गौर्यै नमः । गौरीमावाहयामि स्थापयामि ॥

**oṃ bhūrbhuvaḥ svaḥ gauryai namaḥ**
**gaurīmāvāhayāmi sthāpayāmi**

Oṃ the Infinite Beyond Conception, the gross body, the subtle body and the causal body. I bow to Gaurī. I invite Gaurī and establish Her within.

पद्मावं पद्मवदनां पद्मनाभोरुसंस्थिताम् ।
जगत्प्रियां पद्मवासां पद्मामावाहयाम्यहम् ॥

**padmāvaṃ padmavadanāṃ**
**padmanābhorusaṃsthitām**
**jagatpriyāṃ padmavāsāṃ padmāmāvāhayāmyaham**

Favorable as a lotus, with a lotus-like mouth, situated in the navel of a lotus. She is beloved of the universe, resident of the lotus. I invite Padma, She who is the Lotus (the wealth of Peace and Love).

ॐ पद्मायै नमः पद्मामावाहयामि स्थापयामि ॥

**oṃ padmāyai namaḥ padmāmāvāhayāmi**
**sthāpayāmi**

Oṃ I bow to Padma. I invite Padma and establish Her within.

दिव्यरूपां विशालाक्षीं शुचि कुण्डल धारिणीम् ।
रक्तमुक्ताद्यलङ्कारां शचीमावाहयाम्यहम् ॥

**divyarūpāṃ viśālākṣīṃ śuci kuṇḍala dhāriṇīm**
**raktamuktādyalaṅkārāṃ śacīmāvāhayāmyaham**

The form of divinity, the goal of the universe, She wears earrings, which shine with purity. Her ornaments are of red pearls. I invite Śacī, the Goddess of Purity.

ॐ शच्ये नमः शचीमावाहयामि स्थापयामि ॥

**oṃ śacye namaḥ śacīmāvāhayāmi sthāpayāmi**

Oṃ I bow to Śacī. I invite Śacī and establish Her within.

विश्वेऽस्मिन् भूरिवरदां जरां निर्जरसेविताम् ।

बुद्धिप्रबोधिनीं सौम्यां मेधामावाहयाम्यहम् ॥

**viśve-smin bhūrivaradāṃ jarāṃ nirjarasevitām**
**buddhiprabodhinīṃ saumyāṃ**
**medhāmāvāhayāmyaham**

She gives boons to the aged of this universe, to the aged She gives the service of freedom from wasting away. To the Intellect She is known as the Beautiful. I invite Medhā, the Intellect of Love.

ॐ मेधायै नमः मेधामावाहयामि स्थापयामि ॥

**oṃ medhāyai namaḥ medhāmāvāhayāmi**
**sthāpayāmi**

Oṃ I bow to Medhā. I invite Medhā and establish Her within.

जगत्सृष्टिकरीं धात्रीं देवीं पणवमातृकाम् ।

वेदगर्भां यज्ञमयीं सावित्रीं स्थापयाम्यहम् ॥

**jagatsṛṣṭikarīṃ dhātrīṃ devīṃ paṇavamātṛkām**
**vedagarbhāṃ yajñamayīṃ sāvitrīṃ**
**sthāpayāmyaham**

She is the Goddess who is the Cause, the Giver of Birth to the perceivable universe, the Mother of the Praṇava, oṃ. The Vedas came from Her womb. She is sacrifice incarnate. I establish Sāvitrī, the Goddess of the Light.

ॐ सावित्र्यै नमः सावित्रीमावाहयामि स्थापयामि ॥

**oṃ sāvitryai namaḥ sāvitrīmāvāhayāmi sthāpayāmi**

Oṃ I bow to Sāvitrī. I invite Sāvitrī and establish Her within.

सर्वास्त्रधारिणीं देवीं सर्वाभरणभूषिताम् ।

सर्वदेवस्तुतां वन्द्यां विजयां स्थापयाम्यहम् ॥

**sarvāstradhāriṇīṃ devīṃ sarvābharaṇabhūṣitām**
**sarvadevastutāṃ vandyāṃ vijayāṃ**
**sthāpayāmyaham**

She is the Goddess who holds all weapons, and She shines with all ornaments. All the Gods sing Her praises and hymns. I establish Vijayā, the Goddess of Victory.

ॐ विजयायै नमः विजयामावाहयामि स्थापयामि ॥

**oṃ vijayāyai namaḥ vijayāmāvāhayāmi sthāpayāmi**

Oṃ I bow to Vijayā. I invite Vijayā and establish Her within.

सुरारिमथिनीं देवीं देवानामभयप्रदाम् ।

त्रैलोक्य वन्दितां शुभ्रां जयामावाहयाम्यहम् ॥

**surārimathinīṃ devīṃ devānāmabhayapradām**
**trailokya vanditāṃ śubhrāṃ jayāmāvāhayāmyaham**

She is the Goddess who is the staff of the Gods, whose name removes fear from the Gods. She is the manifestation of excellence who is praised in the three worlds. I invite Jayā, Conquest.

ॐ जयायै नमः जयामावाहयामि स्थापयामि ॥

**oṃ jayāyai namaḥ jayāmāvāhayāmi sthāpayāmi**

Oṃ I bow to Jayā. I invite Jayā and establish Her within.

मयूरवाहनां देवीं कड्ग-शक्ति-धनुर्धराम् ।
आवाहयेद् देवसेनां तारकासुरमर्दिनीम् ॥

**mayūravāhanāṃ devīṃ kaḍga-śakti-dhanurdharām**
**āvāhayed devasenāṃ tārakāsuramardinīm**

She is the Goddess who rides upon a peacock, holding aloft a sword, energy and a bow. I invite the Commander of the forces of the Gods, the Slayer of Tārakāsura, the Illuminator of Duality.

ॐ देवसेनायै नमः देवसेनामावाहयामि स्थापयामि ॥

**oṃ devasenāyai namaḥ devasenāmāvāhayāmi sthāpayāmi**

Oṃ I bow to the Commander of the forces of the Gods. I invite the commander of the forces of the Gods and establish Her within.

अग्रजा सर्वदेवानां कव्यार्थं या प्रतिष्ठिता ।
पितॄणां तृप्तिदां देवीं स्वधामावाहयाम्यहम् ॥

**agrajā sarvadevānāṃ kavyārthaṃ yā pratiṣṭitā**
**pitṝṇāṃ tṛptidāṃ devīṃ svadhāmāvāhayāmyaham**

She is the first born of all the Gods, and was established first by the ancient poets. She is the Goddess who gives pleasure to the ancestors. I invite Svadhā, One's own Giving.

ॐ स्वधायै नमः स्वधामावाहयामि स्थापयामि ॥

**oṃ svadhāyai namaḥ svadhāmāvāhayāmi sthāpayāmi**

Oṃ I bow to Svadhā. I invite Svadhā and establish Her within.

हविर्गृत्वा महादत्ता देवेभ्यो या प्रयच्छति ।
तां दिव्यरूपां वरदां स्वाहामावाहयाम्यहम् ॥

**havirgṛtvā mahādattā devebhyo yā prayacchati**
**tāṃ divyarūpāṃ varadāṃ svāhāmāvāhayāmyaham**

The Great Giver of oblations with ghee, which are essential for the Gods. You give blessings in the form of divinity. I invite Svāhā, I am One with God!

ॐ स्वाहायै नमः स्वाहामावाहयामि स्थापयामि ॥

**oṃ svāhāyai namaḥ svāhāmāvāhayāmi sthāpayāmi**

Oṃ I bow to Svāhā. I invite Svāhā and establish Her within.

आवाहयाम्यहम् मातॄः सकलाः लोकपूजिताः ।
सर्वकल्याणरूपिण्यो वरदा दिव्यभूषणाः ॥

**āvāhayāmyaham mātṝḥ sakalāḥ lokapūjitāḥ**
**sarvakalyāṇarūpiṇyo varadā divyabhūṣaṇāḥ**

I invite the Mother who is worshipped throughout the three worlds. She is the form of all welfare, and She gives blessings that shine with divinity.

ॐ मातृभ्यो नमः मातॄः आवाहयामि स्थापयामि ॥

**oṃ mātṛbhyo namaḥ mātṝḥ āvāhayāmi sthāpayāmi**

Oṃ I bow to the Mothers. I invite the Mothers and establish them within.

आवाहयेल्लोकमातॄर्जयन्तीप्रमुखाः शुभाः ।
नानाऽभीष्टप्रदाः शान्ताः सर्वलोकहितावहाः ॥

**āvāhayellokamātṝrjayantīpramukhāḥ śubhāḥ**
**nānā-bhīṣṭapradāḥ śāntāḥ sarvalokahitāvahāḥ**

I invite the Mothers of the Universe, who shine before every Victory! They give various kinds of supremacy and peace, and invite the joy of all the worlds.

ॐ लोकमातृभ्यो नमः लोकमातृः आवाहयामि

स्थापयामि ॥

**oṃ lokamātṛbhyo namaḥ lokamātṝḥ āvāhayāmi sthāpayāmi**

Oṃ I bow to the Mothers of the Universe. I invite the Mothers of the Universe and establish them within.

सर्वहर्षकरीं देवीं भाक्तानामभयप्रदाम् ।

हर्षोत्फुल्लास्यकमलां धृतिमावाहयाम्यहम् ॥

**sarvaharṣakarīṃ devīṃ bhāktānāmabhayapradām**
**harṣotphullāsyakamalāṃ dhṛtimāvāhayāmyaham**

The Goddess is the Cause of all gladness. To devotees who take Her name She grants freedom from fear. She is the blossom of the lotus of Gladness. I invite Dhṛti, Constancy.

ॐ धृत्यै नमः धृतिमावाहयामि स्थापयामि ॥

**oṃ dhṛtyai namaḥ dhṛtimāvāhayāmi sthāpayāmi**

Oṃ I bow to Dhṛti. I invite Dhṛti and establish Her within.

पोषयन्तीं जगत्सर्वं स्वदेहप्रभवैर्नवैः ।

शाकैः फलैर्जलैरत्नैः पुष्टिमावाहयाम्यहम् ॥

**poṣayantīṃ jagatsarvaṃ svadehaprabhavairnavaiḥ**
**śākaiḥ phalairjalairatnaiḥ puṣṭimāvāhayāmyaham**

She who gives prosperity (abundance) to the entire universe, bringing forth from Her own body vegetables, fruits, water and gems. I invite Puṣṭi, Increase.

ॐ पुष्ट्यै नमः पुष्टिमावाहयामि स्थापयामि ॥

**oṃ puṣṭyai namaḥ puṣṭimāvāhayāmi sthāpayāmi**

Oṃ I bow to Puṣṭi. I invite Puṣṭi and establish Her within.

देवैराराधितां देवीं सदा सन्तोषकारिणीम् ।

प्रसादसुमुखीं देवीं तुष्टिमावाहयाम्यहम् ॥

**devairārādhitāṃ devīṃ sadā santoṣakāriṇīm**
**prasādasumukhīṃ devīṃ tuṣṭimāvāhayāmyaham**

She is the Goddess who pleases the Gods, always the cause of satisfaction. From the excellent face of the Goddess comes blessings. I invite Tuṣṭi, Satisfaction.

ॐ तुष्ट्यै नमः तुष्टिमावाहयामि स्थापयामि ॥

**oṃ tuṣṭyai namaḥ tuṣṭimāvāhayāmi sthāpayāmi**

Oṃ I bow to Tuṣṭi. I invite Tuṣṭi and establish Her within.

पत्तने नगरे ग्रामे विपिने पर्वते गृहे ।

नानाजातिकुलेशानीं दुर्गामावाहयाम्यहम् ॥

**pattane nagare grāme vipine parvate gṛhe**
**nānājātikuleśānīṃ durgāmāvāhayāmyaham**

In the air, in the city, in the village, in the woods, on the mountains, in a house, She is the Supreme Ruler of the family in various forms of birth. I invite Durgā, the Reliver of Difficulties.

ॐ आत्मनः कुलदेवतायै नमः आत्मनः
कुलदेवतामावाहयामि स्थापयामि ॥

**oṃ ātmanaḥ kuladevatāyai namaḥ ātmanaḥ kuladevatāmāvāhayāmi sthāpayāmi**

Oṃ I bow to the soul who is the Goddess of the Family. I invite the soul who is the Goddess of the Family and establish Her within.

ॐ गौरी पद्मा शची मेधा सावित्री विजया जया ।
देवसेना स्वधा स्वाहा मातरो लोकमातरः ॥

**oṃ gaurī padmā śacī medhā sāvitrī vijayā jayā devasenā svadhā svāhā mātaro lokamātaraḥ**

Oṃ Gaurī, Padmā, Śacī, Medhā, Sāvitrī, Vijayā, Jayā; Devasenā, Svadhā, Svāhā, Mātaro, Lokamātaraḥ,

धृतिः पुष्टिस्तथा तुष्टिः आत्मनः कुलदेवताः ।
गणेशेनाधिका ह्येता वृद्धौ पूज्यास्तु षौडश ॥

**dhṛtiḥ puṣṭistathā tuṣṭiḥ ātmanaḥ kuladevatāḥ gaṇeśenādhikā hyetā vṛddhau pūjyāstu ṣauḍaśa**

Dhṛti, Puṣṭi and then Tuṣṭi, and the soul who is the Goddess of the Family; with Gaṇeśa situated before, we make worship of the sixteen.

आयुरारोग्यमैश्वर्यं ददध्वं मातरो मम ।
निर्विघ्नं सर्वकार्येषु कुरुध्वं सगणाधिपाः ॥

**āyurārogyamaiśvaryaṃ dadadhvaṃ mātaro mama nirvighnaṃ sarvakāryeṣu kurudhvaṃ sagaṇādhipāḥ**

Give us life and freedom from disease, imperishable qualities, oh my Mothers. Make all desired effects free from obstacles with your multitudes.

ॐ गणपत्यादि कुलदेवतान्त मातृभ्यो नमः ॥

**oṃ gaṇapatyādi kuladevatānta mātṛbhyo namaḥ**

Oṃ I bow to Gaṇeśa and the other members of the family of Goddesses and Mothers.

## nava durgā pūjā (1)

worship of the nine forms of durgā (1)

ॐ भूर्भुवः स्वः शैलपुत्रि इहा गच्छ इहतिष्ठ शैलपुत्र्यै नमः ।

शैलपुत्रीमावाहयामि स्थापयामि नमः । पाध्यादिभिः

पूजनम्बिधाय ॥

**oṃ bhūrbhuvaḥ svaḥ śailaputri ihā gaccha ihatiṣṭa śailaputryai namaḥ śailputrīmāvāhayāmi sthāpayāmi namaḥ pādhyādibhiḥ pūjanambidhāya**

Oṃ the Infinite Beyond Conception, the gross body, the subtle body and the causal body. Goddess of Inspiration, come here, stay here. I bow to the Goddess of Inspiration. I invite the Goddess of Inspiration and establish Her within. You are being worshipped with water for washing your feet.

ॐ जगत्पूज्ये जगद्वन्ध्ये सर्वशक्ति स्वरूपिणि ।

पूजां गृहाण कौमारि जगन्मातर्नमोऽस्तु ते ॥

**oṃ jagatpūjye jagadvandhye sarvaśakti svarūpiṇi pūjāṃ gṛhāṇa kaumāri jaganmātarnamo-stu te**

Oṃ You are worshipped in the world, praised in the world, as the intrinsic nature of all energy. Oh Ever Pure One, please accept this worship. We bow to you, oh Mother of the universe.

ॐ भूर्भुवः स्वः ब्रह्मचारिणि इहा गच्छ इहतिष्ट ब्रह्मचारिण्यै नमः । ब्रह्मचारिणीमावाहयामि स्थापयामि नमः । पाध्यादिभिः पूजनम्बिधाय ॥

**oṃ bhūrbhuvaḥ svaḥ brahmacāriṇi ihā gaccha ihatiṣṭa brahmacāriṇyai namaḥ brahmacāriṇīmāvāhayāmi sthāpayāmi namaḥ pādhyādibhiḥ pūjanambidhāya**

Oṃ the Infinite Beyond Conception, the gross body, the subtle body and the causal body. Goddess of Learning, come here, stay here. I bow to the Goddess of Learning. I invite the Goddess of Learning and establish Her within. You are being worshipped with water for washing your feet.

ॐ त्रिपुरां त्रिगुणाधारां मार्गज्ञान स्वरूपिणीम् ।
त्रैलोक्य वन्दितां देवीं त्रिमुर्तिं पूजयाम्यहम् ॥

**oṃ tripurāṃ triguṇādhārāṃ mārgajñāna svarūpiṇīm**
**trailokya vanditāṃ devīṃ trimurtiṃ pūjayāmyaham**

Oṃ You are the residence of the three cities, the support of the three guṇas, the intrinsic nature of the road to Wisdom. The Goddess who is praised in the three worlds, oh Image of the Three, I am worshipping you.

ॐ भूर्भुवः स्वः चन्द्रघंटे इहा गच्छ इहतिष्ट चन्द्रघंटायै नमः । चन्द्रघंटामावाहयामि स्थापयामि नमः । पाध्यादिभिः पूजनम्बिधाय ॥

**oṃ bhūrbhuvaḥ svaḥ caṇdraghaṇṭe ihā gaccha ihatiṣṭa candraghaṇṭāyai namaḥ candraghaṇṭāmāvāhayāmi sthāpayāmi namaḥ pādhyādibhiḥ pūjanambidhāya**

Oṃ the Infinite Beyond Conception, the gross body, the subtle body and the causal body. Goddess of Practice, come here, stay here. I bow to the Goddess of Practice. I invite the Goddess of Practice and establish Her within. You are being worshipped with water for washing your feet.

ॐ कालिकां तु कलातीतां कल्याण ह्रिदयां शिवाम् ।
कल्याण जननीं नित्यं कल्याणीं पूजयाम्यहम् ॥

**oṃ kālikāṃ tu kalātītāṃ kalyāṇa hridayāṃ śivām kalyāṇa jananīṃ nityaṃ kalyāṇīṃ pūjayāmyaham**

Oṃ You divide Time, but remain beyond division, Welfare in the heart of Lord Śiva. Always grant Welfare, oh Divine Mother, I worship the Goddess of Welfare.

ॐ भूर्भुवः स्वः कुष्माण्ड इहा गच्छ इहतिष्ट कुष्माण्डायै नमः । कुष्माण्डामावाहयामि स्थापयामि नमः । पाध्यादिभिः पूजनम्बिधाय ॥

**oṃ bhūrbhuvaḥ svaḥ kuṣmāṇḍa ihā gaccha ihatiṣṭa kuṣmāṇḍāyai namaḥ kuṣmāṇḍāmāvāhayāmi sthāpayāmi namaḥ pādhyādibhiḥ pūjanambidhāya**

Oṃ the Infinite Beyond Conception, the gross body, the subtle body and the causal body. Goddess of Refinement, come here, stay here. I bow to the Goddess of Refinement. I invite the Goddess of Refinement and establish Her within. You are being worshipped with water for washing your feet.

ॐ अणिमादि गुणोदारां मकराकार चक्षुसम् ।
अनन्त शक्ति भेदां तां कामाक्षीं पूजयाम्यहम् ॥

**oṃ aṇimādi guṇodārāṃ makarākāra cakṣusam**
**ananta śakti bhedāṃ tāṃ kāmākṣīṃ pūjayāmyaham**

Oṃ You give rise to the qualities of every atom, the eyes that perceive all form. You distinguish the infinite energy, oh Eyes of Desire, I am worshipping you.

ॐ भूर्भुवः स्वः स्कन्दमातः इहा गच्छ इहतिष्ठ स्कन्दमात्रे
नमः । स्कन्दमातरमावाहयामि स्थापयामि नमः ।
पाध्यादिभिः पूजनम्बिधाय ॥

**oṃ bhūrbhuvaḥ svaḥ skandamātaḥ ihā gaccha**
**ihatiṣṭa skandamātre namaḥ**
**skandamātaramāvāhayāmi sthāpayāmi namaḥ**
**pādhyādibhiḥ pūjanambidhāya**

Oṃ the Infinite Beyond Conception, the gross body, the subtle body and the causal body. Goddess who Nurtures Divinity, come here, stay here. I bow to the Goddess who Nurtures Divinity. I invite the Goddess who Nurtures Divinity and establish Her within. You are being worshipped with water for washing your feet.

ॐ चण्डवीरां चण्डमायां चण्डमुण्ड प्रभञ्जनीम् ।
तां नमामि च देवेशीं चण्डिकां पूजयाम्यहम् ॥

**oṃ caṇḍavīrāṃ caṇḍamāyāṃ**
**caṇḍamuṇḍa prabhañjanīm**
**tāṃ namāmi ca deveśīṃ caṇḍikāṃ pūjayāmyaham**

Oṃ you are the warrior against anger, the limitation of anger, the stupidity of anger you cut asunder. I bow to Her, the Supreme Goddess, I worship She who Tears Apart Thoughts.

ॐ भूर्भुवः स्वः कात्यायनि इहा गच्छ इहतिष्ट कात्यायन्यै
नमः । कात्यायनीमावाहयामि स्थापयामि नमः ।
पाध्यादिभिः पूजनम्बिधाय ॥

**oṃ bhūrbhuvaḥ svaḥ kātyāyani ihā gaccha ihatiṣṭa**
**kātyāyanyai namaḥ kātyāyanīmāvāhayāmi**
**sthāpayāmi namaḥ pādhyādibhiḥ pūjanambidhāya**

Oṃ the Infinite Beyond Conception, the gross body, the subtle body and the causal body. Goddess who is Ever Pure, come here, stay here. I bow to the Goddess who is Ever Pure. I invite the Goddess who is Ever Pure and establish Her within. You are being worshipped with water for washing your feet.

ॐ सुखानन्द करीं शान्तां सर्व देवैर्नमस्कृताम् ।
सर्व भूतात्मिकां देवीं शाम्भवीं पूजयाम्यहम् ॥

**oṃ sukhānanda karīṃ śāntāṃ**
**sarva devairnamaskṛtām**
**sarva bhūtātmikāṃ devīṃ**
**śāmbhavīṃ pūjayāmyaham**

Oṃ the Bliss of happiness, Cause of Peace, all the Gods continually bow to you. You are the soul of all existence, oh Goddess, you who belong to Śiva, I worship you.

ॐ भूर्भुवः स्वः कालरात्रि इहा गच्छ इहतिष्ट कालरात्र्यै
नमः । कालरात्रीमावाहयामि स्थापयामि नमः ।
पाध्यादिभिः पूजनम्बिधाय ॥

**oṃ bhūrbhuvaḥ svaḥ kālarātri ihā gaccha ihatiṣṭa kālarātryai namaḥ kālarātrīmāvāhayāmi sthāpayāmi namaḥ pādhyādibhiḥ pūjanambidhāya**

Oṃ the Infinite Beyond Conception, the gross body, the subtle body and the causal body. Dark Night (surrendering the ego), come here, stay here. I bow to the Dark Night. I invite the Dark Night and establish Her within. You are being worshipped with water for washing your feet.

ॐ चण्डवीरां चण्डमायां रक्तबीज प्रभञ्जनीम् ।

तां नमामि च देवेशीं गायत्रीं पूजयाम्यहम् ॥

**oṃ caṇḍavīrāṃ caṇḍamāyāṃ**
**raktabīja prabhañjanīm**
**tāṃ namāmi ca deveśīṃ gāyatrīṃ pūjayāmyaham**

Oṃ you are the warrior against anger, the limitation of anger, you cut asunder the Seed of Desire. I bow to Her, the Supreme Goddess. I worship Gāyatrī, the three forms of wisdom.

ॐ भूर्भुवः स्वः महागौरि इहा गच्छ इहतिष्ट महागौर्यै नमः ।

महागौरीमावाहयामि स्थापयामि नमः । पाध्यादिभिः

पूजनम्बिधाय ॥

**oṃ bhūrbhuvaḥ svaḥ mahāgauri ihā gaccha ihatiṣṭa mahāgauryai namaḥ mahāgaurīmāvāhayāmi sthāpayāmi namaḥ pādhyādibhiḥ pūjanambidhāya**

Oṃ the Infinite Beyond Conception, the gross body, the subtle body and the causal body. The Great Radiant Light, come here, stay here. I bow to the Great Radiant Light. I invite the Great Radiant Light and establish Her within. You are being worshipped with water for washing your feet.

ॐ सुन्दरीं स्वर्णवर्णाङ्गीं सुख सौभाग्यदायिनीम् ।
सन्तोष जननीं देवीं सुभद्रां पूजयाम्यहम् ॥

**oṃ sundarīṃ svarṇavarṇāṅgīṃ**
**sukha saubhāgyadāyinīm**
**santoṣa jananīṃ devīṃ subhadrāṃ pūjayāmyaham**

Oṃ Beautiful with a golden-colored body, bestower of happiness and beauty. Oh Mother of the Universe, the Goddess of Contentment, I worship the Excellent of excellence.

ॐ भूर्भुवः स्वः सिद्धिदे इहा गच्छ इहतिष्ठ सिद्धिदायै नमः ।
सिद्धिदामावाहयामि स्थापयामि नमः । पाध्यादिभिः
पूजनम्बिधाय ॥

**oṃ bhūrbhuvaḥ svaḥ siddhide ihā gaccha ihatiṣṭa siddhidāyai namaḥ siddhidāmāvāhayāmi sthāpayāmi namaḥ pādhyādibhiḥ pūjanambidhāya**

Oṃ the Infinite Beyond Conception, the gross body, the subtle body and the causal body. The Grantor of Perfection, come here, stay here. I bow to the Grantor of Perfection. I invite the Grantor of Perfection and establish Her within. You are being worshipped with water for washing your feet.

ॐ दुर्गमे दुस्तरेकार्ये भयदुर्ग विनाशिनि ।
पूजयामि सदा भक्त्या दुर्गां दुर्गतिनाशिनीम् ॥

**oṃ durgame dustarekārye bhayadurga vināśini**
**pūjayāmi sadā bhaktyā durgāṃ durgatināśinīm**

Oṃ You are the Destroyer of fear from difficulties for me, from the effects of wickedness. I always worship with devotion the Reliever of Difficulties, who destroys all difficulties.

ॐ प्रथमं शैलपुत्री च द्वितीयं ब्रह्मचारिणी ।
तृतीयं चन्द्रघण्टेति कूष्माण्डेति चतुर्थकम् ॥

**oṃ prathamaṃ śailaputrī ca dvitīyaṃ brahmacāriṇī**
**tṛtīyaṃ candraghaṇṭeti kūṣmāṇḍeti caturthakam**

Oṃ First is the Goddess of Inspiration, and second the Goddess of Learning; third is the Goddess of Practice, the Goddess of Refinement is fourth.

पञ्चमं स्कन्दमातेति षष्ठं कात्यायनीति च ।
सप्तमं कालरात्रीति महागौरीति चाष्टमम् ॥

**pañcamaṃ skandamāteti ṣaṣṭhaṃ kātyāyanīti ca**
**saptamaṃ kālarātrīti mahāgaurīti cāṣṭamam**

Fifth is the Goddess who Nurtures Divinity, sixth is the One Who is Ever Pure; seventh is the Goddess of the Dark Night of Surrendering the Ego, the Goddess of the Great Radiant Light is eighth.

नवमं सिद्धिदात्री च नवदुर्गाः प्रकीर्तिताः ।
उक्तान्येतानि नामानि ब्रह्मणैव महात्मना ॥

**navamaṃ siddhidātrī ca navadurgāḥ prakīrtitāḥ**
**uktānyetāni nāmāni brahmaṇaiva mahātmanā**

Ninth is the Goddess who Grants Perfection. The nine Durgās, Relievers of Difficulties, have been enumerated, and these names have been revealed by the great soul of the Supreme Himself.

श्री दुर्गायै नमः ॥

**śrī durgāyai namaḥ**

We bow to the Respected Reliever of Difficulties

**nava patrikā pūjā**

worship of the nine containers of divinity

ॐ दुर्गे देवि समागच्छ सान्निध्यमिह कल्पय ।
रम्भारूपेण सर्वत्र शान्तिं कुरु नमोऽस्तु ते ॥

**oṃ durge devi samāgaccha sānnidhyamiha kalpaya**
**rambhārūpeṇa sarvatra śāntiṃ kuru namo-stu te**

Oṃ Oh Goddess Durgā, come here and reside in my thoughts. In the form of beauty everywhere make peace. I bow to you.

ॐ रम्भाधिष्ठात्र्यै ब्रह्माण्यै नमः

**oṃ rambhādhiṣṭhātryai brahmāṇyai namaḥ**

Oṃ thus is sung a hymn to Beauty. I bow to the Creative Energy.

महिषासुरयुद्धेषु कच्वीभूतासि सुव्रते ।
मम चानुग्रहार्थाय आगतागि हरप्रिये ॥

**mahiṣāsurayuddheṣu kacvībhūtāsi suvrate**
**mama cānugrahārthāya āgatāgi harapriye**

In the battle with the Great Ego, you shined upon all existence, oh One of Excellent Vows. For the purpose of my advancement, come oh Beloved of Viṣṇu.

ॐ कच्व्यधिष्ठात्र्यै कालिकायै नमः

**oṃ kacvyadhiṣṭhātryai kālikāyai namaḥ**

Oṃ thus is sung a hymn to the Shining One. I bow to She who is Beyond Time.

हरिद्रे वरदे देवि उमारूपासि सुव्रते ।
मम विघ्नविनाशाय प्रसीद त्वं हरप्रिये ॥

**haridre varade devi umārūpāsi suvrate**
**mama vighnavināśāya prasīda tvaṃ harapriye**

Oh Goddess covered in tumeric, in the form of Umā you give boons, oh One of Excellent Vows. Destroy all of my obstacles. You be pleased, oh Beloved of Viṣṇu.

ॐ हरिद्राधिष्ठात्र्यै दुर्गायै नमः

**oṃ haridrādhiṣṭhātryai durgāyai namaḥ**

Oṃ thus is sung a hymn to the Goddess covered in tumeric. I bow to the Reliever of Difficulties.

निशुम्भशुम्भमथने सेन्द्रैर्दैवगणैः सह ।
जयन्ति पूजितासि त्वकस्माकं वरदा भव ॥

**niśumbhaśumbhamathane sendrairdaivagaṇaiḥ saha**
**jayanti pūjitāsi tvakasmākaṃvaradā bhava**

You destroy Self-Deprecation and Self-Conceit along with the multitude of the armies of the Gods. You are being worshipped along with those who are victorious. Give us boons.

ॐ जयन्त्याधिष्ठात्र्यै कौमार्यै नमः

**oṃ jayantyādhiṣṭhātryai kaumāryai namaḥ**

Oṃ thus is sung a hymn to the Goddess of Victory. I bow to the Ever Pure One.

महादेवप्रियकरो वासुदेवप्रियः सदा ।
उमाप्रीतिकरो वृक्षो बिल्वरूप नमोऽस्तु ते ॥

**mahādevapriyakaro vāsudevapriyaḥ sadā**
**umāprītikaro vṛkṣo bilvarūpa namo-stu te**

She is the beloved of Mahādeva (Śiva), and She is always beloved of Vāsudeva (Viṣṇu). Umā loves this tree. In the form of Bilva I bow to you.

ॐ बिल्वाधिष्ठात्र्यै शिवायै नमः

**bilvādhiṣṭātryai śivāyai namaḥ**

Oṃ thus is sung a hymn to the Bilva. I bow to Śivā (Divine Mother).

दाढिमि त्वः पुरा युद्धे रक्तबिजस्य सम्मुखे ।

उमाकार्ज्यं कृतं यस्मात्तस्मात्तं रक्ष मां सदा ॥

**dāḍhimi tvaḥ purā yuddhe raktabijasya sammukhe**
**umākārjyaṃ kṛtaṃ yasmāttasmāttaṃ rakṣa māṃ sadā**

You fought with the multitudes of Raktabijas facing you. In order to perform the work of Umā, always protect me.

ॐ दाढिम्यधिष्ठात्र्यै रक्तदन्तिकायै नमः

**oṃ dāḍhimyadhiṣṭhātryai raktadantikāyai namaḥ**

Oṃ thus is sung a hymn to the Multitudes. I bow to She with Red Teeth.

हरप्रीतिकरो वृक्षोह्यशोकः शोकनाशनः ।

दुर्गाप्रीतिकरो यस्मान्मामशोकं सदा कुरु ॥

**harapritikaro vṛkṣohyaśokaḥ śokanāśanaḥ**
**durgāpritikaro yasmānmāmaśokaṃ sadā kuru**

Hara (Śiva) loves this tree, yesterday's grief and all grief it destroys. Durgā especially loves this, so make me eternally free from grief.

ॐ अशोकाधिष्ठात्र्यै शोकरहितायै नमः

**oṃ aśokādhiṣṭhātryai śokarahitāyai namaḥ**

Oṃ thus is sung a hymn to Freedom from Grief. I bow to She who makes us free from grief.

यस्य पत्रे वसेद्देवी मानवृक्षः शचीप्रियः ।

मम चानुग्रहार्थाय पूजां गृह्व प्रसीद मे ॥

**yasya patre vasedevī mānavṛkṣaḥ śacīpriyaḥ**
**mama cānugrahārthāya pūjāṃ gṛhva prasīda me**

Upon this leaf from the tree of thought the Goddess sits, the beloved of Sacī (Indra's wife). For the purpose of my progress please accept my worship and be pleased with me.

ॐ मानाधिष्ठात्र्यै चामुण्डायै नमः

**oṃ mānādhiṣṭhātryai cāmuṇḍāyai namaḥ**

Oṃ thus is sung a hymn to Thoughts. I bow to She who moves in the paradigm of Consciousness.

जगतः प्राणरक्षार्थं ब्रह्मणा निर्मितं पुरा ।

उमाप्रीतिकरं धान्यं तस्मात्त्वं रक्ष मां सदा ॥

**jagataḥ prāṇarakṣārthaṃ brahmaṇā nirmitaṃ purā**
**umāprītikaraṃ dhānyaṃ tasmāttvaṃ rakṣa māṃ sadā**

This giving of wealth is beloved by Umā. It protects the life force of the perceivable universe and proves the validity of the Supreme Divinity. Please protect me always.

ॐ धान्याधिष्ठात्र्यै महालक्ष्म्यै नमः

**oṃ dhānyādhiṣṭhātryai mahālakṣmyai namaḥ**

Oṃ thus is sung a hymn to the Giving of Wealth. I bow to the Great Goddess of True Wealth.

**nava durgā pūjā (2)**

worship of the nine forms of durgā (2)

चथुर्मुखीं जगद्धात्रीं हंसरूढां वरप्रदाम् ।

सृष्टिरूपां महाभागां ब्रह्माणीं तां नमाम्यहम् ॥

**cathurmukhīṃ jagaddhātrīṃ**
**haṃsarūḍhāṃ varapradām**
**sṛṣṭirūpāṃ mahābhāgāṃ**
**brahmāṇīṃ tāṃ namāmyaham**

She has four faces, the Progenitress of the Universe who rides upon a swan and grants boons. She is the form of creation, of great parts. We bow to Her, to Brahmāṇī.

ॐ ह्रीं श्रीं ब्रह्माण्यै नमः

**oṃ hrīṃ śrīṃ brahmāṇyai namaḥ**

Oṃ Māyā, Increase, I bow to the Creative Energy.

वृषारूढां शुभां शुभ्रां त्रिनेत्रां वरदां शिवाम् ।

माहेश्वरीं नमाम्यद्य सृष्टिसंहारकारिणीम् ॥

**vṛṣārūḍhāṃ śubhāṃ śubhrāṃ**
**trinetrāṃ varadāṃ śivām**
**māheśvarīṃ namāmyadya sṛṣṭisaṃhārakāriṇīm**

She rides upon a buffalo, shining radiantly, She is Śivā with three eyes and She grants boons. We bow to Māheśvarī, the

Great Seer of All, who is the cause of the dissolution of the creation.

ॐ ह्रीं श्रीं माहेश्वर्यै नमः

**oṃ hrīṃ śrīṃ māheśvaryai namaḥ**

Oṃ Māyā, Increase, I bow to the Great Seer of All.

कौमारीं पीतवसनां मयूरवरवाहनाम् ।

शक्तिहस्तां महाभागां नमामि वरदां सदा ॥

**kaumārīṃ pītavasanāṃ mayūravaravāhanām**
**śaktihastāṃ mahābhāgāṃ namāmi varadāṃ sadā**

Kumārī, the Ever Pure One, is of a yellow color. She rides upon a peacock, with energy in Her hands, of great parts. I bow to She who always grants boons.

ॐ ह्रीं श्रीं कौमार्यै नमः

**oṃ hrīṃ śrīṃ kaumāryai namaḥ**

Oṃ Māyā, Increase, I bow to the Ever Pure One.

शङ्खचक्रगदापद्मधारिणीं कृष्णरूपिणीम् ।

स्थितिरूपां खगेन्द्रस्थां वैष्णवीं तां नमाम्यहम् ॥

**śaṅkacakragadāpadmadhāriṇīṃ kṛṣṇarūpiṇīm**
**sthitirūpāṃ khagendrasthāṃ vaiṣṇavīṃ tāṃ namāmyaham**

She holds the conch shell, discus, club and lotus. As the intrinsic nature of Kṛṣṇa, She is the form of Circumstances. Situated with the king of swords, She is Vaiṣṇavī, the Energy pervading all existence. We bow to Her.

ॐ ह्रीं श्रीं वैष्णव्यै नमः

**oṃ hrīṃ śrīṃ vaiṣṇavyai namaḥ**

Oṃ Māyā, Increase, I bow to the Energy pervading all existence.

वराहरूपिणीं देवीं दंष्ट्रोद्धृतवसुन्दराम् ।
शुभदां पीतवसनां वाराहीं तां नमाम्यहम् ॥

**varāharūpiṇīṃ devīṃ daṃṣṭroddhṛtavasundarām**
**śubhadāṃ pītavasanāṃ vārāhīṃ tāṃ namāmyaham**

She is the Goddess who appears as a boar. Her great teeth are beautiful. She is the Giver of Purity, of yellow color. We bow to Her, to Vārāhī, the Boar of Sacrifice.

ॐ ह्रीं श्रीं वाराह्यै नमः

**oṃ hrīṃ śrīṃ vārāhyai namaḥ**

Oṃ Māyā, Increase, I bow to the Boar of Sacrifice.

नृसिंहरूपिणीं देवीं दैत्यदानवदर्पहाम् ।
शुभां शुभप्रदां शुभ्रां नारसिंहीं नमाम्यहम् ॥

**nṛsiṃharūpiṇīṃ devīṃ daityadānavadarpahām**
**śubhāṃ śubhapradāṃ śubhrāṃ nārasiṃhīṃ namāmyaham**

She is the Goddess who appears as the man-lion, the reflection of the forces of duality and animalism. She shines and gives forth the radiance of Her shine. We bow to Nārasiṃhī, the man-lion of courage.

ॐ ह्रीं श्रीं नारसिंह्यै नमः

**oṃ hrīṃ śrīṃ nārasiṃhyai namaḥ**

Oṃ Māyā, Increase, I bow to Nārasiṃhī, the man-lion of courage.

इन्द्राणीं गजकूम्भस्थां सहस्रानयनोज्ज्वलाम् ।
नमामि वरदां देवीं सर्वदेवनमस्कृताम् ॥

**indrāṇīṃ gajakūmbhasthāṃ sahasrānayanojjalām**
**namāmi varadāṃ devīṃ sarvadevanamaskṛtām**

Indrāṇī, the Energy of the Rule of the Pure, sits upon the shoulders of an elephant, with a thousand eyes shining. I bow to the Goddess who gives boons, and to whom all the Gods also bow as well.

ॐ ह्रीं श्रीं इन्द्राण्यै नमः

**oṃ hrīṃ śrīṃ indrāṇyai namaḥ**

Oṃ Māyā, Increase, I bow to Indrāṇī, the Energy of the Rule of the Pure.

चामुण्डां चण्डमथनीं मुण्डमालोपशोभिताम् ।
अटटहासमूदितां नमाम्यात्मविभूतये ॥

**cāmuṇḍāṃ caṇḍamathanīṃ muṇḍamālopaśobhitām**
**aṭaṭahāsamūditāṃ namāmyātmavibhūtaye**

The Slayer of Passion and Meaness, who churns Passion, shines forth with a garland of skulls. She emits a loud laugh. I bow to the soul who manifests in existence.

ॐ ह्रीं श्रीं चामुण्डायै नमः

**oṃ hrīṃ śrīṃ cāmuṇḍāyai namaḥ**

Oṃ Māyā, Increase, I bow to the Slayer of Passion and Meaness.

कात्यायनीं दशभूजां महिषासुरमर्दिनीम् ।

प्रसन्नवदनां देवीं वरदां तां नमाम्यहम् ॥

**kātyāyanīṃ daśabhūjāṃ mahiṣāsuramardinīṃ prasannavadanāṃ devīṃ varadāṃ tāṃ namāmyaham**

The Ever Pure One has ten arms, the Slayer of the Great Ego. She is the Goddess with the pleased face. We bow to Her, the Giver of Boons.

ॐ ह्रीं श्रीं कात्यायन्यै नमः

**oṃ hrīṃ śrīṃ kātyāyanyai namaḥ**

Oṃ Māyā, Increase, I bow to the Ever Pure One.

चण्डिके नवदुर्गे त्वं महादेवमनोरमे ।

पूजां समस्तां संगृह्य रक्ष मां त्रिदशेश्वरि ॥

**caṇḍike navadurge tvaṃ mahādevamanorame pūjāṃ samastāṃ saṃgṛhya rakṣa māṃ tridaśeśvari**

You Who Tear Apart Thoughts and the other nine Durgās are the beauty of Śiva. Please accept this all-encompassing worship and protect me, oh Supreme among the three qualities.

ॐ ह्रीं श्रीं चण्डिकायै नमः

**oṃ hrīṃ śrīṃ caṇḍikāyai namaḥ**

Oṃ Māyā, Increase, I bow to She Who Tears Apart Thoughts.

ॐ ह्रीं श्रीं नवदुर्गायै नमः

**oṃ hrīṃ śrīṃ navadurgāyai namaḥ**

Oṃ Māyā, Increase, I bow to the Nine forms of Durgā.

## yantra pūjā

worship of the yantra

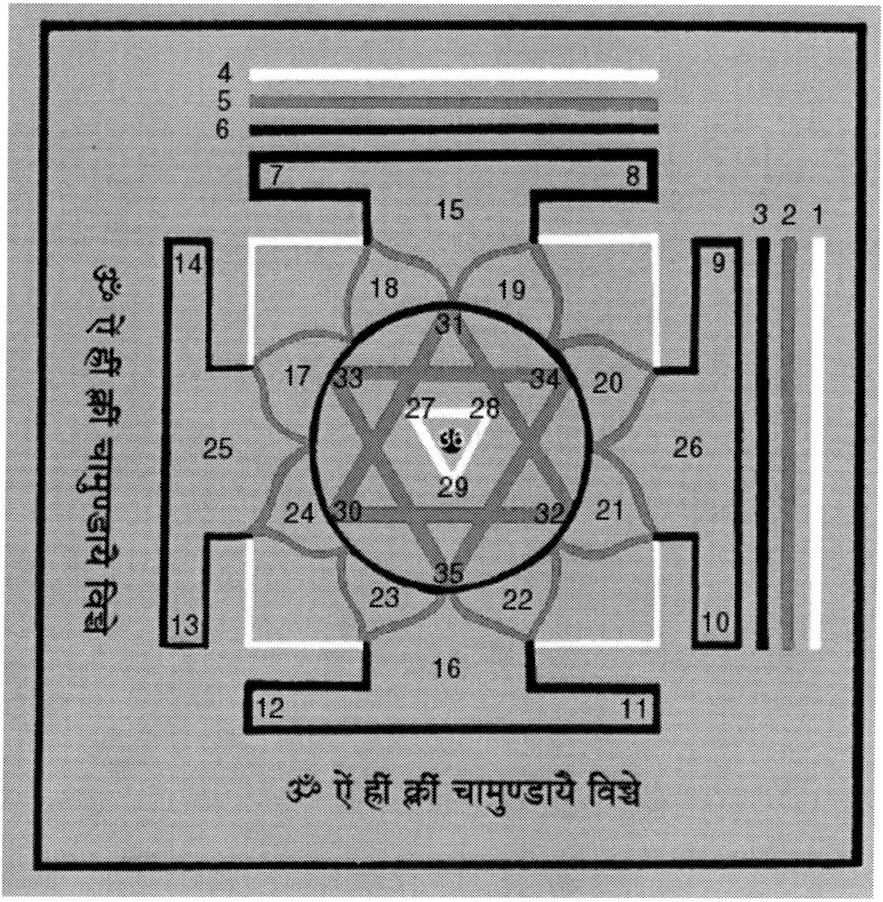

सोभयस्यास्य देवस्य विग्रहो यन्त्र कल्पणा ।
विना यन्त्रेण चेत्पूजा देवता न प्रसीदति ॥

**sobhayasyāsya devasya vigraho yantra kalpaṇā**
**vinā yantreṇa cetpūjā devatā na prasīdati**

We contemplate the form of the yantra that depicts the radiance of the Gods. Without using the yantra in the worship of consciousness the Gods are not as pleased.

यन्त्र मन्त्रमयं प्रहुर्देवता मन्त्ररूपिणी ।
यन्त्रेणापूजितो देवः सहसा न प्रसीदति ।
सर्वेषामपि मन्त्रणां यन्त्र पूजा प्रशस्यते ॥

**yantra mantramayaṃ prahurdevatā mantrarūpiṇī**
**yantreṇāpūjito devaḥ sahasā na prasīdati**
**sarveṣāmapi mantraṇāṃ yantra pūjā praśasyate**

The yantra conveys the objective meaning of the mantra, while the deity is the form of the mantra. By worshipping the deity by means of the yantra, the deity is completely satisfied. To attain all the bliss of the mantra, the worship of the yantra is highly recommended.

ततः स्थण्डिलमध्ये तु हसौःगर्भं त्रिकोणकम् ।
षट्कोणं तद्वहिर्वृत्तां ततोऽष्टदलपङ्कजम् ।
भूपुरं तद्वहिर्विद्वान् विलिखेद्यन्त्रमुत्तमम् ॥

**tataḥ sthaṇḍilamadhye tu**
**hasauḥgarbhaṃ trikoṇakam**
**ṣaṭkoṇaṃ tadvahirvṛttāṃ tato-ṣṭadalapaṅkajam**
**bhūpuraṃ tadvahirvidvān vilikhedhyantramuttamam**

In the center of the place of worship is the single point that contains ha and sauḥ, Śiva and Śakti without distinction. Thereafter comes the three-cornered equilateral triangle. Then six angles, outside of which is a circle, followed by eight lotus petals. The four doors are outside, and in this way the wise will draw the most excellent yantra.

ॐ यन्त्रराजाय विद्महे महायन्त्राय धीमहे ।

तन्नो यन्त्रः प्रचोदयात् ॥

**oṃ yantrarājāya vidmahe mahāyantrāya dhīmahe tanno yantraḥ pracodayāt**

Oṃ we meditate on the King of Yantras, we contemplate the greatest yantra. May that yantra grant us increase.

ॐ परमेश्वराय विद्महे परातत्त्वाय धीमहे ।

तन्नो ब्रह्माः प्रचोदयात् ॥

**oṃ parameśvarāya vidmahe parātattvāya dhīmahe tanno brahmāḥ pracodayāt**

Oṃ we meditate on the Highest Supreme Divinity, we contemplate the Highest Principle. May that Supreme Divinity grant us increase.

- 1 -

ॐ मुकुन्दाय नमः

**oṃ mukundāya namaḥ**

Oṃ I bow to the Giver of Liberation.

- 2 -

ॐ ईशनाय नमः

**oṃ īśanāya namaḥ**

Oṃ I bow to the Ruler of All.

- 3 -

ॐ पुरन्दराय नमः

**oṃ purandarāya namaḥ**

Oṃ I bow to the Giver of Completeness.

- 4 -

ॐ ब्रह्मणे नमः

**oṃ brahmaṇe namaḥ**

Oṃ I bow to the Creative Consciousness.

- 5 -

ॐ वैवस्वताय नमः

**oṃ vaivasvatāya namaḥ**

Oṃ I bow to the Universal Radiance.

- 6 -

ॐ इन्दवे नमः

**oṃ indave namaḥ**

Oṃ I bow to the Ruler of Devotion.

- 7 -

ॐ आधारशक्तये नमः

**oṃ ādhāraśaktaye namaḥ**

Oṃ I bow to the primal energy that sustains existence.

- 8 -

ॐ कुर्म्माय नमः

**oṃ kurmmāya namaḥ**

Oṃ I bow to the Tortoise that supports creation.

- 9 -

ॐ अनन्ताय नमः

**oṃ anantāya namaḥ**

Oṃ I bow to Infinity (personified as a thousand-hooded snake who stands upon the Tortoise, holding aloft the worlds).

- 10 -

ॐ पृथिव्यै नमः

**oṃ pṛthivyai namaḥ**

Oṃ I bow to the Earth.

- 11 -

ॐ क्षीरसमूद्राय नमः

**oṃ kṣīrasamūdrāya namaḥ**

Oṃ I bow to the milk ocean, or ocean of nectar, the infinite expanse of existence from which all manifested.

- 12 -

ॐ श्वेतद्वीपाय नमः

**oṃ śvetadvīpāya namaḥ**

Oṃ I bow to the Island of Purity, which is in the ocean.

- 13 -

ॐ मणिमन्दपाय नमः

**oṃ maṇimandapāya namaḥ**

Oṃ I bow to the Palace of Gems, which is on the island, the home of the Divine Mother.

- 14 -

ॐ कल्पवृक्षाय नमः

**oṃ kalpavṛkṣāya namaḥ**

Oṃ I bow to the Tree of Fulfillment, which satisfies all desires, growing in the palace courtyard.

- 15 -

ॐ मणिवेदिकायै नमः

**oṃ maṇivedikāyai namaḥ**

Oṃ I bow to the altar containing the gems of wisdom.

- 16 -

ॐ रत्नसिंहासनाय नमः

**oṃ ratnasiṃhāsanāya namaḥ**

Oṃ I bow to the throne of the jewel.

- 17 -

ॐ धर्म्माय नमः

**oṃ dharmmāya namaḥ**

Oṃ I bow to the Way of Truth and Harmony.

- 18 -

ॐ ज्ञानाय नमः

**oṃ jñānāya namaḥ**

Oṃ I bow to Wisdom.

- 19 -

ॐ वैराग्याय नमः

**oṃ vairāgyāya namaḥ**

Oṃ I bow to Detachment.

- 20 -

ॐ ईश्वर्ज्याय नमः

**oṃ īśvarjyāya namaḥ**

Oṃ I bow to the Imperishable Qualities.

- 21 -

ॐ अधर्म्माय नमः

**oṃ adharmmāya namaḥ**

Oṃ I bow to Disharmony.

- 22 -

ॐ अज्ञानाय नमः

**oṃ ajñānāya namaḥ**

Oṃ I bow to Ignorance.

- 23 -

ॐ अवैराग्याय नमः

**oṃ avairāgyāya namaḥ**

Oṃ I bow to Attachment.

- 24 -

ॐ अनीश्वर्ज्याय नमः

**oṃ anīśvarjyāya namaḥ**

Oṃ I bow to the Transient.

- 25 -

ॐ अनन्ताय नमः

**oṃ anantāya namaḥ**

Oṃ I bow to the Infinite.

- 26 -

ॐ पद्माय नमः

**oṃ padmāya namaḥ**

Oṃ I bow to the Lotus.

- 27 -

अं अर्कमण्डलाय द्वादशकलात्मने नमः

**aṃ arkamaṇḍalāya dvādaśakalātmane namaḥ**

"A" we bow to the twelve aspects of the realm of the sun. Tapinī, Tāpinī, Dhūmrā, Marīci, Jvālinī, Ruci, Sudhūmrā, Bhoga-dā, Viśvā, Bodhinī, Dhārinī, Kṣamā: Containing Heat, Emanating Heat, Smoky, Ray-pProducing, Burning, Lustrous, Purple or Smoky-Red, Granting enjoyment, Universal, Which Makes Known, Productive of Consciousness, Which supports, Which Forgives.

- 28 -

उं सोममण्डलाय षोडशकलात्मने नमः

**uṃ somamaṇḍalāya ṣoḍaśakalātmane namaḥ**

"U" we bow to the sixteen aspects of the realm of the moon. Amṛtā, Prāṇadā, Puṣā, Tuṣṭi, Puṣṭi, Rati, Dhṛti, Śaśinī, Candrikā, Kānti, Jyotsnā, Śrī, Prīti, Aṅgadā, Pūrṇā, Pūrṇāmṛtā: Nectar, Which Sustains Life, Which supports, Satisfying, Nourishing, Playful, Constant, Unfailing, Producer of Joy, Beauty Enhanced by Love, Light, Grantor of Prosperity, Affectionate, Purifying the Body, Complete, Full of Bliss.

- 29 -

मं वह्निमण्डलाय दशकलात्मने नमः

**maṃ vahnimaṇḍalāya daśakalātmane namaḥ**

"M" we bow to the ten aspects of the realm of fire: Dhūmrā, Arciḥ, Jvalinī, Śūkṣmā, Jvālinī, Visphuliṅginī, Suśrī, Surūpā, Kapilā, Havya-Kavya-Vahā: Smoky-Red, Flaming, Shining, Subtle, Burning, Sparkling, Beautiful, Well-Formed, Tawny, The Messenger to Gods and Ancestors.

- 30 -

ॐ सं सत्त्वाय नमः

**oṃ saṃ sattvāya namaḥ**

Oṃ I bow to activity, execution, light, knowledge, being.

- 31 -

ॐ रं रजसे नमः

**oṃ raṃ rajase namaḥ**

Oṃ I bow to desire, inspiration, becoming.

- 32 -

ॐ तं तमसे नमः

**oṃ taṃ tamase namaḥ**

Oṃ I bow to wisdom, to the darkness that exposes light, to rest.

- 33 -

ॐ आं आत्मने नमः

**oṃ āṃ ātmane namaḥ**

Oṃ I bow to the Soul.

- 34 -

ॐ अं अन्तरात्मने नमः

**oṃ aṃ antarātmane namaḥ**

Oṃ I bow to the Innermost Soul.

- 35 -

ॐ पं परमात्मने नमः

**oṃ paṃ paramātmane namaḥ**

Oṃ I bow to the Universal Soul, or the Consciousness that exceeds manifestation.

- 36 -

ॐ ह्रीं ज्ञानात्मने नमः

**oṃ hrīṃ jñānātmane namaḥ**

Oṃ I bow to the Soul of Infinite Wisdom.

# सर्वतो भद्रमण्डल देवता स्थापनम्

## sarvato bhadramaṇḍala devatā sthāpanam

Establishment of the Excellent Circle of Deities

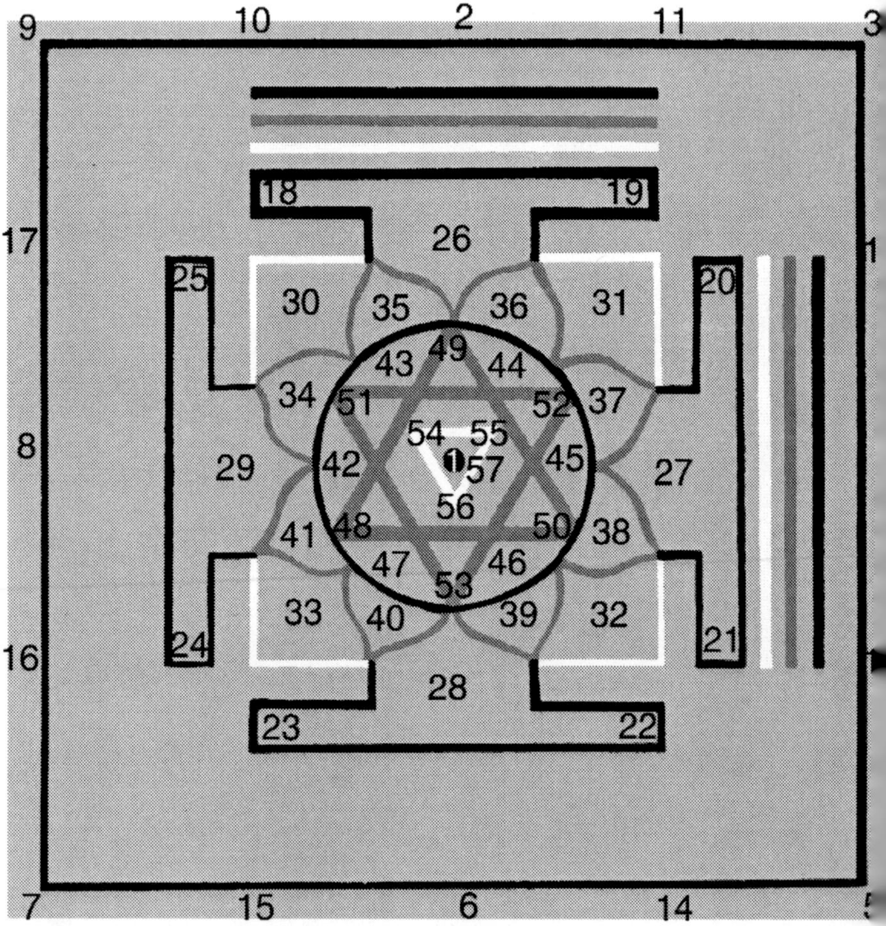

- 1 -

ॐ भूर्भुवः स्वः ब्रह्मणे नमः ब्रह्मणमावाहयामि स्थापयामि

**oṃ bhūrbhuvaḥ svaḥ brahmaṇe namaḥ brahmaṇamāvāhayāmi sthāpayāmi**

Oṃ the Infinite Beyond Conception, the gross body, the subtle body and the causal body, we bow to the Creative Consciousness (Center). We invoke you, invite you and establish your presence.

- 2 -

ॐ भूर्भुवः स्वः सोमाय नमः सोममावाहयामि स्थापयामि

**oṃ bhūrbhuvaḥ svaḥ somāya namaḥ somamāvāhayāmi sthāpayāmi**

Oṃ the Infinite Beyond Conception, the gross body, the subtle body and the causal body, we bow to the Lord of Devotion (N). We invoke you, invite you and establish your presence.

- 3 -

ॐ भूर्भुवः स्वः ईशानाय नमः ईशानमावाहयामि स्थापयामि

**oṃ bhūrbhuvaḥ svaḥ īśānāya namaḥ īśānamāvāhayāmi sthāpayāmi**

Oṃ the Infinite Beyond Conception, the gross body, the subtle body and the causal body, we bow to the Ruler of All (NE). We invoke you, invite you and establish your presence.

- 4 -

ॐ भूर्भुवः स्वः इन्द्राय नमः इन्द्रमावाहयामि स्थापयामि

**oṃ bhūrbhuvaḥ svaḥ indrāya namaḥ indramāvāhayāmi sthāpayāmi**

Oṃ the Infinite Beyond Conception, the gross body, the subtle body and the causal body, we bow to the Rule of the Pure (E). We invoke you, invite you and establish your presence.

- 5 -

ॐ भूर्भुवः स्वः अग्नये नमः अग्निमावाहयामि स्थापयामि

**oṃ bhūrbhuvaḥ svaḥ agnaye namaḥ agnimāvāhayāmi sthāpayāmi**

Oṃ the Infinite Beyond Conception, the gross body, the subtle body and the causal body, we bow to the Divine Fire (SE). We invoke you, invite you and establish your presence.

- 6 -

ॐ भूर्भुवः स्वः यमाय नमः यममावाहयामि स्थापयामि

**oṃ bhūrbhuvaḥ svaḥ yamāya namaḥ yamamāvāhayāmi sthāpayāmi**

Oṃ the Infinite Beyond Conception, the gross body, the subtle body and the causal body, we bow to the Supreme Controller (S). We invoke you, invite you and establish your presence.

- 7 -

ॐ भूर्भुवः स्वः निर्ऋतये नमः निर्ऋतिमावाहयामि स्थापयामि

**oṃ bhūrbhuvaḥ svaḥ nirṛtaye namaḥ nirṛtimāvāhayāmi sthāpayāmi**

Oṃ the Infinite Beyond Conception, the gross body, the subtle body and the causal body, we bow to the Destroyer (SW). We invoke you, invite you and establish your presence.

- 8 -

ॐ भूर्भुवः स्वः वरुणाय नमः वरुणमावाहयामि स्थापयामि

**oṃ bhūrbhuvaḥ svaḥ varuṇāya namaḥ varuṇamāvāhayāmi sthāpayāmi**

Oṃ the Infinite Beyond Conception, the gross body, the subtle body and the causal body, we bow to the Lord of Equilibrium (W). We invoke you, invite you and establish your presence.

- 9 -

ॐ भूर्भुवः स्वः वायवे नमः वायुमावाहयामि स्थापयामि

**oṃ bhūrbhuvaḥ svaḥ vāyave namaḥ vāyumāvāhayāmi sthāpayāmi**

Oṃ the Infinite Beyond Conception, the gross body, the subtle body and the causal body, we bow to the Lord of Liberation (NW). We invoke you, invite you and establish your presence.

- 10 -

ॐ भूर्भुवः स्वः अष्टवसुभ्यो नमः अष्टवसुन् आवाहयामि स्थापयामि

**oṃ bhūrbhuvaḥ svaḥ aṣṭavasubhyo namaḥ aṣṭavasun āvāhayāmi sthāpayāmi**

Oṃ the Infinite Beyond Conception, the gross body, the subtle body and the causal body, we bow to the Eight Lords of Benificence. We invoke you, invite you and establish your presence.

- 11 -

ॐ भूर्भुवः स्वः एकादशरुद्रेभ्यो नमः एकादशरुद्रानावाहयामि स्थापयामि

**oṃ bhūrbhuvaḥ svaḥ ekādaśarudrebhyo namaḥ ekādaśarudrānāvāhayāmi sthāpayāmi**

Oṃ the Infinite Beyond Conception, the gross body, the subtle body and the causal body, we bow to the Eleven Relievers from Sufferings. We invoke you, invite you and establish your presence.

- 12 -

ॐ भूर्भुवः स्वः द्वादशादित्येभ्यो नमः द्वादशादित्यानावाहयामि स्थापयामि

**oṃ bhūrbhuvaḥ svaḥ dvādaśādityebhyo namaḥ dvādaśādityānāvāhayāmi sthāpayāmi**

Oṃ the Infinite Beyond Conception, the gross body, the subtle body and the causal body, we bow to the Twelve Sons of Light. We invoke you, invite you and establish your presence.

- 13 -

ॐ भूर्भुवः स्वः अश्विभ्यां नमः अश्विनौ आवाहयामि स्थापयामि

**oṃ bhūrbhuvaḥ svaḥ aśvibhyāṃ namaḥ aśvinau āvāhayāmi sthāpayāmi**

Oṃ the Infinite Beyond Conception, the gross body, the subtle body and the causal body, we bow to the Two Horses of Pure Desire. We invoke you, invite you and establish your presence.

- 14 -

ॐ भूर्भुवः स्वः सपैतृकविश्वेभ्यो देवेभ्यो नमः सपैतृकविश्वान् देवानावाहयामि स्थापयामि

**oṃ bhūrbhuvaḥ svaḥ sapaitṛkaviśvebhyo devebhyo namaḥ sapaitṛkaviśvān devānāvāhayāmi sthāpayāmi**

Oṃ the Infinite Beyond Conception, the gross body, the subtle body and the causal body, we bow to the Ancestors along with the Shining Ones of the Universe. We invoke you, invite you and establish your presence.

- 15 -

ॐ भूर्भुवः स्वः सप्तयक्षेभ्यो नमः सप्तयक्षानावाहयामि स्थापयामि

**oṃ bhūrbhuvaḥ svaḥ saptayakṣebhyo namaḥ saptayakṣānāvāhayāmi sthāpayāmi**

Oṃ the Infinite Beyond Conception, the gross body, the subtle body and the causal body, we bow to the Energy that brings the good and bad of wealth. We invoke you, invite you and establish your presence.

- 16 -

ॐ भूर्भुवः स्वः अष्टकुलनागेभ्यो नमः

अष्टकुलनागानावाहयामि स्थापयामि

**oṃ bhūrbhuvaḥ svaḥ aṣṭakulanāgebhyo namaḥ aṣṭakulanāgānāvāhayāmi sthāpayāmi**

Oṃ the Infinite Beyond Conception, the gross body, the subtle body and the causal body, we bow to the Family of Eight Snakes. We invoke you, invite you and establish your presence.

- 17 -

ॐ भूर्भुवः स्वः गन्धर्वाऽप्सरोभ्यो नमः गन्धर्वाऽप्सरसः

आवाहयामि स्थापयामि

**oṃ bhūrbhuvaḥ svaḥ gandharvā-psarobhyo namaḥ gandharvā-psarasaḥ āvāhayāmi sthāpayāmi**

Oṃ the Infinite Beyond Conception, the gross body, the subtle body and the causal body, we bow to the celestial musicians and heavenly maidens. We invoke you, invite you and establish your presence.

- 18 -

ॐ भूर्भुवः स्वः स्कन्दाय नमः स्कन्दमावाहयामि स्थापयामि

**oṃ bhūrbhuvaḥ svaḥ skandāya namaḥ skandamāvāhayāmi sthāpayāmi**

Oṃ the Infinite Beyond Conception, the gross body, the subtle body and the causal body, we bow to the God of War. We invoke you, invite you and establish your presence.

- 19 -

ॐ भूर्भुवः स्वः वृषभाय नमः वृषभमावाहयामि स्थापयामि

**oṃ bhūrbhuvaḥ svaḥ vṛṣabhāya namaḥ vṛṣabhamāvāhayāmi sthāpayāmi**

Oṃ the Infinite Beyond Conception, the gross body, the subtle body and the causal body, we bow to the Bull of Discipline, Conveyance of Śiva, Nandi. We invoke you, invite you and establish your presence.

- 20 -

ॐ भूर्भुवः स्वः शूलाय नमः शूलमावाहयामि स्थापयामि

**oṃ bhūrbhuvaḥ svaḥ śūlāya namaḥ śūlamāvāhayāmi sthāpayāmi**

Oṃ the Infinite Beyond Conception, the gross body, the subtle body and the causal body, we bow to the Spear of Concentration. We invoke you, invite you and establish your presence.

- 21 -

ॐ भूर्भुवः स्वः महाकालाय नमः महाकालमावाहयामि स्थापयामि

**oṃ bhūrbhuvaḥ svaḥ mahākālāya namaḥ mahākālamāvāhayāmi sthāpayāmi**

Oṃ the Infinite Beyond Conception, the gross body, the subtle body and the causal body, we bow to the Great Time. We invoke you, invite you and establish your presence.

- 22 -

ॐ भूर्भुवः स्वः दक्षादि सप्तगणेभ्यो नमः दक्षादि सप्तगणानावाहयामि स्थापयामि

**oṃ bhūrbhuvaḥ svaḥ dakṣādi saptagaṇebhyo namaḥ dakṣādi saptagaṇānāvāhayāmi sthāpayāmi**

Oṃ the Infinite Beyond Conception, the gross body, the subtle body and the causal body, we bow to Ability and the other seven qualities. We invoke you, invite you and establish your presence.

- 23 -

ॐ भूर्भुवः स्वः दुर्गायै नमः दुर्गामावाहयामि स्थापयामि

**oṃ bhūrbhuvaḥ svaḥ durgāyai namaḥ durgāmāvāhayāmi sthāpayāmi**

Oṃ the Infinite Beyond Conception, the gross body, the subtle body and the causal body, we bow to the Reliever of Difficulties. We invoke you, invite you and establish your presence.

- 24 -

ॐ भूर्भुवः स्वः विष्णवे नमः विष्णुमावाहयामि स्थापयामि

**oṃ bhūrbhuvaḥ svaḥ viṣṇave namaḥ viṣṇumāvāhayāmi sthāpayāmi**

Oṃ the Infinite Beyond Conception, the gross body, the subtle body and the causal body, we bow to the All-Pervading Consciousness. We invoke you, invite you and establish your presence.

- 25 -

ॐ भूर्भुवः स्वः स्वधायै नमः स्वधामावाहयामि स्थापयामि

**oṃ bhūrbhuvaḥ svaḥ svadhāyai namaḥ svadhāmāvāhayāmi sthāpayāmi**

Oṃ the Infinite Beyond Conception, the gross body, the subtle body and the causal body, we bow to the Ancestors. We invoke you, invite you and establish your presence.

- 26 -

ॐ भूर्भुवः स्वः मृत्युरोगेभ्यो नमः मृत्युरोगानावाहयामि स्थापयामि

**oṃ bhūrbhuvaḥ svaḥ mṛtyurogebhyo namaḥ mṛtyurogānāvāhayāmi sthāpayāmi**

Oṃ the Infinite Beyond Conception, the gross body, the subtle body and the causal body, we bow to the Spirit of deadly illnesses. We invoke you, invite you and establish your presence.

- 27 -

ॐ भूर्भुवः स्वः गणपतये नमः गणपतिमावाहयामि स्थापयामि

**oṃ bhūrbhuvaḥ svaḥ gaṇapataye namaḥ gaṇapatimāvāhayāmi sthāpayāmi**

Oṃ the Infinite Beyond Conception, the gross body, the subtle body and the causal body, we bow to the Lord of the Multitudes. We invoke you, invite you and establish your presence.

- 28 -

ॐ भूर्भुवः स्वः अद्भ्यो नमः अपः आवाहयामि स्थापयामि

**oṃ bhūrbhuvaḥ svaḥ adbhyo namaḥ apaḥ āvāhayāmi sthāpayāmi**

Oṃ the Infinite Beyond Conception, the gross body, the subtle body and the causal body, we bow to Acts of Sacrifice. We invoke you, invite you and establish your presence.

- 29 -

ॐ भूर्भुवः स्वः मरुद्भ्यो नमः मरुतः आवाहयामि स्थापयामि

**oṃ bhūrbhuvaḥ svaḥ marudbhyo namaḥ marutaḥ āvāhayāmi sthāpayāmi**

Oṃ the Infinite Beyond Conception, the gross body, the subtle body and the causal body, we bow to the Shining Ones. We invoke you, invite you and establish your presence.

- 30 -

ॐ भूर्भुवः स्वः पृथिव्यै नमः पृथ्वीमावाहयामि स्थापयामि

**oṃ bhūrbhuvaḥ svaḥ pṛthivyai namaḥ pṛthvīmāvāhayāmi sthāpayāmi**

Oṃ the Infinite Beyond Conception, the gross body, the subtle body and the causal body, we bow to the Earth. We invoke you, invite you and establish your presence.

- 31 -

ॐ भूर्भुवः स्वः गङ्गादिनदीभ्यो नमः गङ्गादिनदीः आवाहयामि स्थापयामि

**oṃ bhūrbhuvaḥ svaḥ gaṅgādinadībhyo namaḥ gaṅgādinadīḥ āvāhayāmi sthāpayāmi**

Oṃ the Infinite Beyond Conception, the gross body, the subtle body and the causal body, we bow to the Ganges and other rivers. We invoke you, invite you and establish your presence.

- 32 -

ॐ भूर्भुवः स्वः सप्तसागरेभ्यो नमः सप्तसागरानावाहयामि स्थापयामि

**oṃ bhūrbhuvaḥ svaḥ saptasāgarebhyo namaḥ saptasāgarānāvāhayāmi sthāpayāmi**

Oṃ the Infinite Beyond Conception, the gross body, the subtle body and the causal body, we bow to the Seven Seas. We invoke you, invite you and establish your presence.

- 33 -

ॐ भूर्भुवः स्वः मेरवे नमः मेरुमावाहयामि स्थापयामि

**oṃ bhūrbhuvaḥ svaḥ merave namaḥ merumāvāhayāmi sthāpayāmi**

Oṃ the Infinite Beyond Conception, the gross body, the subtle body and the causal body, we bow to Mount Meru. We invoke you, invite you and establish your presence.

- 34 -

ॐ भूर्भुवः स्वः गदाय नमः गदामावाहयामि स्थापयामि

**oṃ bhūrbhuvaḥ svaḥ gadāya namaḥ gadāmāvāhayāmi sthāpayāmi**

Oṃ the Infinite Beyond Conception, the gross body, the subtle body and the causal body, we bow to the Club. We invoke you, invite you and establish your presence.

- 35 -

ॐ भूर्भुवः स्वः त्रिशूलाय नमः त्रिशूलमावाहयामि स्थापयामि

**oṃ bhūrbhuvaḥ svaḥ triśūlāya namaḥ triśūlamāvāhayāmi sthāpayāmi**

Oṃ the Infinite Beyond Conception, the gross body, the subtle body and the causal body, we bow to the Trident. We invoke you, invite you and establish your presence.

- 36 -

ॐ भूर्भुवः स्वः वज्राय नमः वज्रमावाहयामि स्थापयामि

**oṃ bhūrbhuvaḥ svaḥ vajrāya namaḥ vajramāvāhayāmi sthāpayāmi**

Oṃ the Infinite Beyond Conception, the gross body, the subtle body and the causal body, we bow to the Thunderbolt. We invoke you, invite you and establish your presence.

- 37 -

ॐ भूर्भुवः स्वः शक्तये नमः शक्तिमावाहयामि स्थापयामि

**oṃ bhūrbhuvaḥ svaḥ śaktaye namaḥ śaktimāvāhayāmi sthāpayāmi**

Oṃ the Infinite Beyond Conception, the gross body, the subtle body and the causal body, we bow to Energy. We invoke you, invite you and establish your presence.

- 38 -

ॐ भूर्भुवः स्वः दण्डाय नमः दण्डमावाहयामि स्थापयामि

**oṃ bhūrbhuvaḥ svaḥ daṇḍāya namaḥ daṇḍamāvāhayāmi sthāpayāmi**

Oṃ the Infinite Beyond Conception, the gross body, the subtle body and the causal body, we bow to the Staff. We invoke you, invite you and establish your presence.

- 39 -

ॐ भूर्भुवः स्वः खड्गाय नमः खड्गमावाहयामि स्थापयामि

**oṃ bhūrbhuvaḥ svaḥ khaḍgāya namaḥ khaḍgamāvāhayāmi sthāpayāmi**

Oṃ the Infinite Beyond Conception, the gross body, the subtle body and the causal body, we bow to the Sword. We invoke you, invite you and establish your presence.

- 40 -

ॐ भूर्भुवः स्वः पाशाय नमः पाशमावाहयामि स्थापयामि

**oṃ bhūrbhuvaḥ svaḥ pāśāya namaḥ pāśamāvāhayāmi sthāpayāmi**

Oṃ the Infinite Beyond Conception, the gross body, the subtle body and the causal body, we bow to the Net. We invoke you, invite you and establish your presence.

- 41 -

ॐ भूर्भुवः स्वः अङ्कुशाय नमः अङ्कुशमावाहयामि स्थापयामि

**oṃ bhūrbhuvaḥ svaḥ aṅkuśāya namaḥ aṅkuśamāvāhayāmi sthāpayāmi**

Oṃ the Infinite Beyond Conception, the gross body, the subtle body and the causal body, we bow to the Goad. We invoke you, invite you and establish your presence.

- 42 -

ॐ भूर्भुवः स्वः गौतमाय नमः गौतममावाहयामि स्थापयामि

**oṃ bhūrbhuvaḥ svaḥ gautamāya namaḥ gautamamāvāhayāmi sthāpayāmi**

Oṃ the Infinite Beyond Conception, the gross body, the subtle body and the causal body, we bow to Ṛṣi Gautam. We invoke you, invite you and establish your presence.

- 43 -

ॐ भूर्भुवः स्वः भरद्वाजाय नमः भरद्वाजमावाहयामि स्थापयामि

**oṃ bhūrbhuvaḥ svaḥ bharadvājāya namaḥ bharadvājamāvāhayāmi sthāpayāmi**

Oṃ the Infinite Beyond Conception, the gross body, the subtle body and the causal body, we bow to Ṛṣi Bharadvāj. We invoke you, invite you and establish your presence.

- 44 -

ॐ भूर्भुवः स्वः विश्वामित्राय नमः विश्वामित्रमावाहयामि स्थापयामि

**oṃ bhūrbhuvaḥ svaḥ viśvāmitrāya namaḥ viśvāmitramāvāhayāmi sthāpayāmi**

Oṃ the Infinite Beyond Conception, the gross body, the subtle body and the causal body, we bow to Ṛṣi Viśvāmitra we invoke you, invite you and establish your presence.

- 45 -

ॐ भूर्भुवः स्वः कश्यपाय नमः कश्यपमावाहयामि स्थापयामि

**oṃ bhūrbhuvaḥ svaḥ kaśyapāya namaḥ kaśyapamāvāhayāmi sthāpayāmi**

Oṃ the Infinite Beyond Conception, the gross body, the subtle body and the causal body, we bow to Ṛṣi Kaśyapa. We invoke you, invite you and establish your presence.

- 46 -

ॐ भूर्भुवः स्वः जमदग्नये नमः जमदग्निमावाहयामि स्थापयामि

**oṃ bhūrbhuvaḥ svaḥ jamadagnaye namaḥ jamadagnimāvāhayāmi sthāpayāmi**

Oṃ the Infinite Beyond Conception, the gross body, the subtle body and the causal body, we bow to Ṛṣi Jamadagni. We invoke you, invite you and establish your presence.

- 47 -

ॐ भूर्भुवः स्वः वसिष्ठाय नमः वसिष्ठमावाहयामि स्थापयामि

**oṃ bhūrbhuvaḥ svaḥ vasiṣṭhāya namaḥ vasiṣṭhamāvāhayāmi sthāpayāmi**

Oṃ the Infinite Beyond Conception, the gross body, the subtle body and the causal body, we bow to Ṛṣi Vaṣisṭha. We invoke you, invite you and establish your presence.

- 48 -

ॐ भूर्भुवः स्वः अत्रये नमः अत्रिमावाहयामि स्थापयामि

**oṃ bhūrbhuvaḥ svaḥ atraye namaḥ atrimāvāhayāmi sthāpayāmi**

Oṃ the Infinite Beyond Conception, the gross body, the subtle body and the causal body, we bow to Ṛṣi Atri. We invoke you, invite you and establish your presence.

- 49 -

ॐ भूर्भुवः स्वः अरुन्धत्यै नमः अरुन्धतीमावाहयामि स्थापयामि

**oṃ bhūrbhuvaḥ svaḥ arundhatyai namaḥ arundhatīmāvāhayāmi sthāpayāmi**

Oṃ the Infinite Beyond Conception, the gross body, the subtle body and the causal body, we bow to Devi Arundati, wife of Vaṣiṣṭha, example of purity. We invoke you, invite you and establish your presence.

- 50 -

ॐ भूर्भुवः स्वः ऐन्द्र्यै नमः ऐन्द्रीमावाहयामि स्थापयामि

**oṃ bhūrbhuvaḥ svaḥ aindryai namaḥ aindrīmāvāhayāmi sthāpayāmi**

Oṃ the Infinite Beyond Conception, the gross body, the subtle body and the causal body, we bow to Aindri, the energy of the Rule of the Pure. We invoke you, invite you and establish your presence.

- 51 -

ॐ भूर्भुवः स्वः कौमार्य्यै नमः कौमारीमावाहयामि स्थापयामि

**oṃ bhūrbhuvaḥ svaḥ kaumāryyai namaḥ kaumārīmāvāhayāmi sthāpayāmi**

Oṃ the Infinite Beyond Conception, the gross body, the subtle body and the causal body, we bow to Kumari, the energy of the ever pure one. We invoke you, invite you and establish your presence.

- 52 -

ॐ भूर्भुवः स्वः ब्राह्म्यै नमः ब्राह्मीमावाहयामि स्थापयामि

**oṃ bhūrbhuvaḥ svaḥ brāhmyai namaḥ brāhmīmāvāhayāmi sthāpayāmi**

Oṃ the Infinite Beyond Conception, the gross body, the subtle body and the causal body, we bow to Brāhmi, the energy of Creative Consciousness. We invoke you, invite you and establish your presence.

- 53 -

ॐ भूर्भुवः स्वः वाराह्यै नमः वाराहीमावाहयामि स्थापयामि

**oṃ bhūrbhuvaḥ svaḥ vārāhyai namaḥ vārāhīmāvāhayāmi sthāpayāmi**

Oṃ the Infinite Beyond Conception, the gross body, the subtle body and the causal body, we bow to Vārāhi, the energy of the Boar of Sacrifice. We invoke you, invite you and establish your presence.

- 54-

ॐ भूर्भुवः स्वः चामुण्डायै नमः चामुण्डामावाहयामि स्थापयामि

**oṃ bhūrbhuvaḥ svaḥ cāmuṇḍāyai namaḥ cāmuṇḍāmāvāhayāmi sthāpayāmi**

Oṃ the Infinite Beyond Conception, the gross body, the subtle body and the causal body, we bow to Camuṇḍa, the Conquerer of Passion and Meaness. We invoke you, invite you and establish your presence.

- 55 -

ॐ भूर्भुवः स्वः वैष्णव्यै नमः वैष्णवीमावाहयामि स्थापयामि

**oṃ bhūrbhuvaḥ svaḥ vaiṣṇavyai namaḥ vaiṣṇavīmāvāhayāmi sthāpayāmi**

Oṃ the Infinite Beyond Conception, the gross body, the subtle body and the causal body, we bow to Vaiṣṇāvi, the energy of All-Pervading Consciousness. We invoke you, invite you and establish your presence.

- 56 -

ॐ भूर्भुवः स्वः माहेश्वर्यै नमः माहेश्वरीमावाहयामि स्थापयामि

**oṃ bhūrbhuvaḥ svaḥ māheśvaryai namaḥ māheśvarīmāvāhayāmi sthāpayāmi**

Oṃ the Infinite Beyond Conception, the gross body, the subtle body and the causal body, we bow to Māheśvarī, the energy of the Supreme Sovereign. We invoke you, invite you and establish your presence.

- 57 -

ॐ भूर्भुवः स्वः वैनायक्यै नमः वैनायकीमावाहयामि स्थापयामि

**oṃ bhūrbhuvaḥ svaḥ vaināyakyai namaḥ vaināyakīmāvāhayāmi sthāpayāmi**

Oṃ the Infinite Beyond Conception, the gross body, the subtle body and the causal body, we bow to Vainākī, the energy of excellent conduct. We invoke you, invite you and establish your presence.

## aṣṭāśakti pūjā

worship of the eight forms of passion

ऊग्रचण्डा तु वरदा मध्याह्नार्कसमप्रभा ।
सा मे सदास्तु वरदा तस्मै नित्यं नमो नमः ॥

**ūgracaṇḍā tu varadā madhyāhnārkasamaprabhā**
**sā me sadāstu varadā tasmai nityaṃ namo namaḥ**

The Terrible Slayer of Passion, Giver of Boons, who shines within the middle of the Sun. May He always give to me boons. Therefore, I always bow and bow.

ॐ ह्रीं श्रीं ऊग्रचण्डायै नमः

**oṃ hrīṃ śrīṃ ūgracaṇḍāyai namaḥ**

Oṃ Māyā, Increase, I bow to the Terrible Slayer of Passion.

प्रचण्डे पुत्रदे नित्यं प्रचण्डगणसंस्थिते ।

सर्वानन्दकरे देवि तुभ्यं नित्यं नमो नमः ॥

**pracaṇḍe putrade nityaṃ pracaṇḍagaṇasaṃsthite**
**sarvānandakare devi tubhyaṃ nityaṃ namo namaḥ**

Whose Nature Removes Passion, always give children. Situated with the multitude of what preceds Passion, oh Goddess, cause all bliss. I always bow to you and bow to you.

ॐ ह्रीं श्रीं प्रचण्डायै नमः

**oṃ hrīṃ śrīṃ pracaṇḍāyai namaḥ**

Oṃ Māyā, Increase, I bow to She Whose Nature Removes Passion.

लक्ष्मीस्त्वं सर्वभूतानां सर्वभूताभयप्रदा ।

देवि त्वं सर्वकार्येषु वरदा भव सर्वदा ॥

**lakṣmīstvaṃ saravabhūtānāṃ sarvabhūtābhayapradā**
**devi tvaṃ sarvakāryeṣu varadā bhava sarvadā**

You are Lakṣmī, all existence; you grant freedom from fear to all existence. Oh Goddess, you reside within all effects. Always give boons.

ॐ ह्रीं श्रीं चण्डोग्रायै नमः

**oṃ hrīṃ śrīṃ caṇḍogrāyai namaḥ**

Oṃ Māyā, Increase, I bow to She Who Slays Passion.

या सिद्धिरिति नाम्ना च देवेशवरदायिनी ।

कलिकल्मषनाशाय नमामि चण्डनायिकाम् ॥

**yā siddhiriti nāmnā ca deveśavaradāyinī**
**kalikalmaṣanāśāya namāmi caṇḍanāyikām**

Her name brings perfection, and She is the Supreme among the Gods who grants boons. I bow down to She who destroys the iniquities of darkness, the Leader of Passion.

ॐ ह्रीं श्रीं चण्डनायिकायै नमः

**oṃ hrīṃ śrīṃ caṇḍanāyikāyai namaḥ**

Oṃ Māyā, Increase, I bow to the Leader of Passion.

देवि चण्डात्मिके चण्डि चण्डारिविजयप्रदे ।

धर्मार्थमोक्षदे दुर्गे नित्यं मे वरदा भव ॥

**devi caṇḍātmike caṇḍi caṇḍārivijayaprade**
**dharmārthamokṣade durge nityaṃ me varadā bhava**

Oh Goddess, to the soul of She Who Tears Apart Passion, She Who Tears Apart Thought, and She Who Conquers over Passion; hey Durgā, give me the boons of the Ideal of Perfection, the necessities for physical sustenance and Liberation.

ॐ ह्रीं श्रीं चण्डायै नमः

**oṃ hrīṃ śrīṃ caṇḍāyai namaḥ**

Oṃ Māyā, Increase, I bow to She who Conquers over Passion.

या सृष्टिस्थितिसंहारगुणत्रयसमन्विता ।

या परा परमा शक्तिश्चण्डवत्यै नमो नमः ॥

**yā sṛṣṭisthitisaṃhāraguṇatrayasamanvitā**
**yā parā paramā śaktiścaṇḍavatyai namo namaḥ**

Hers are creation, preservation and dissolution; the three qualities are equally present. To She who is Higher than the Highest Energy, to the Spirit of Passion I bow, I bow.

ॐ ह्रीं श्रीं चण्डवत्यै नमः

**oṃ hrīṃ śrīṃ caṇḍavatyai namaḥ**

Oṃ Māyā, Increase, I bow to the Spirit of Passion.

चण्डरूपात्मिका चण्डा चण्डनायकनायिका ।

सर्वसिद्धिप्रदा देवी तस्यै नित्यं नमो नमः ॥

**caṇḍarūpātmikā caṇḍā caṇḍanāyakanāyikā**
**sarvasiddhipradā devī tasyai nityaṃ namo namaḥ**

The form of the soul of Passion, She who Conquers over Passion, the Leader of the Leaders of Passion, oh Goddess, give all attainments of perfection. Therefore, always I bow, I bow.

ॐ ह्रीं श्रीं चण्डरूपायै नमः

**oṃ hrīṃ śrīṃ caṇḍarūpāyai namaḥ**

Oṃ Māyā, Increase, I bow to the Form of Passion.

बालार्करुणनयना सर्वदा भक्तवत्सला ।

चण्डासुरस्य मथनी वरदा त्वतिचण्डिका ॥

**bālārkaruṇanayanā sarvadā bhaktavatsalā**
**caṇḍāsurasya mathanī varadā tvaticaṇḍikā**

You have the Strength of the Sun and are always compassionate to devotees. The Warrior of Passion has a churning rod. Give boons, oh you who Tear Apart Extreme Passion.

ॐ ह्रीं श्रीं अतिचण्डिकायै नमः

**oṃ hrīṃ śrīṃ aticaṇḍikāyai namaḥ**

Oṃ Māyā, Increase, I bow to You who Tears Apart Extreme Passion.

ऊग्रचण्डा प्रचण्डा च चण्डोग्रा चण्डनायिका ।

चण्डा चण्डवती चैव चण्डरूपातिचण्डिका ॥

**ūgracaṇḍā pracaṇḍā ca caṇḍogrā caṇḍanāyikā**
**caṇḍā caṇḍavatī caiva caṇḍarūpāticaṇḍikā**

The Terrible Slayer of Passion, Whose Nature Removes Passion, She Who Slays Passion, the Leader of Passion, She Who Conquers Over Passion, the Spirit of Passion, the Form of Passion and She who Tears Apart Extreme Passion.

ॐ ह्रीं श्रीं अष्टाशक्तिभ्यो नमः

**oṃ hrīṃ śrīṃ aṣṭāśaktibhyo namaḥ**

Oṃ I bow to the eight forms of energy

## नव ग्रहण पूजा

**nava grahaṇa pūjā**

worship of the nine planets

ॐ जबाकुसुम सङ्काशं काश्यपयं महाद्युतिम् ।
तमोऽरिं सर्वपापघ्नं प्रनतोऽस्मि दिवाकरम् ॥
ॐ ह्रीं ह्रीं सूर्याय नमः

**oṃ jabākusuma saṅkāśaṃ**
**kāśyapayaṃ mahādyutim**
**tamo-riṃ sarvapāpaghnaṃ**
**pranato-smi divākaram**
**oṃ hrīṃ hrīṃ sūryāya namaḥ**

Oṃ Crimson red like a hybiscus flower, the Great Light shines onto the earth, removing all the darkness and eradicating sin. We bow down with devotion to that Shining Light. Oṃ we bow to the Sun, Light of Wisdom, Dispeller of Ignorance.

दधि सङ्ख तुषाराभं क्षीरोदार्णसम्भवम् ।
नमामि शशिनम् सोमम् शम्भोर्मुकुट भुषनम् ॥
ॐ ऐं क्लीं सोमाय नमः

**dadhi saṅkha tuṣārābhaṃ kṣīrodārṇasambhavam**
**namāmi śaśinam somam**
**śambhormukuṭa bhuṣanam**
**oṃ aiṃ klīṃ somāya namaḥ**

Creamy white like a container of curds and most pleasing, the Moon is born from the churning of the milk ocean. We bow down to the effulgent emblem of devotion, which is an ornament on the crown of Lord Śiva. Oṃ we bow to the Moon, emblem of devotion.

धरणीगर्भसम्भुतम् विद्युत्कान्ति समप्रभम् ।

कुमारं शक्तिहस्तं च तं मङ्गलम् प्रनमाम्यहम् ॥

ॐ हुं श्रीं मङ्गलाय नमः

**dharaṇīgarbhasambhutam**
**vidyutkānti samaprabham**
**kumāraṃ śaktihastaṃ ca**
**taṃ maṅgalam pranamāmyaham**
**oṃ huṃ śrīṃ maṅgalāya namaḥ**

Supporting the womb of all existence, Mars shines forth with the radiance of beauty enhanced by love, the son wielding energy in his hand. We bow down to Mars, Bearer of Welfare. Oṃ we bow down to Mars, Bearer of Welfare.

प्रियङ्गुकलिकश्यामम् रूपेणाऽप्रतिमं बुधम् ।

सौम्यं सौम्यगुणोपेतं तं बुधम् प्रनमाम्यहम् ॥

ॐ ऐं स्त्रीं श्रीं बुद्धाय नमः

**priyaṅgukalikaśyāmam**
**rūpeṇā-pratimaṃ budham**
**saumyaṃ saumyaguṇopetaṃ**
**taṃ budham pranamāmyaham**
**oṃ aiṃ strīṃ śrīṃ budhāya namaḥ**

Whose beloved body is dark like darkness, whose image is like the form of Intelligence, whose qualities are most beautiful, to that Mercury, emblem of Intelligence, we bow down in devotion. Oṃ we bow down to Mercury, the emblem of Intelligence.

देवानां च ऋषिनां च गुरुं काञ्चनसन्निभम् ।
बुद्धि भुतं त्रिलोकेशम् तं नमामि बृहास्पतिम् ॥
ॐ ऐं क्लीं हुं बृहस्पतये नमः

**devānāṃ ca ṛṣināṃ ca**
**guruṃ kāñcana sannibham**
**buddhi bhutaṃ trilokeśam**
**taṃ namāmi bṛhāspatim**
**oṃ aiṃ klīṃ huṃ bṛhaspataye namaḥ**

The Guru of the Gods and also the ṛṣis, who is like the highest wealth, who is the most intelligent of all beings, to that Jupiter, Guru of the Gods, we bow down in devotion. Oṃ we bow down to the Guru of the Gods.

हिम कुन्द मृणालाभं दैत्यानां परमं गुरुम् ।
सर्वशास्त्रप्रवक्तारं भार्गवम् प्रनमाम्यहम् ॥
ॐ ह्रीं श्रीं शुक्राय नमः

**hima kunda mṛṇālābhaṃ**
**daityānāṃ paramaṃ gurum**
**sarvaśāstrapravaktāraṃ**
**bhārgavam pranamāmyaham**
**oṃ hrīṃ śrīṃ śukrāya namaḥ**

Like sandal and jasmine that have been crushed, the foremost Guru of the forces of duality, who expounds all the scriptures; to that descendant of Bṛgu we bow down in devotion. Oṃ we bow down to Venus, the emblem of love and attachment.

नीलाम्बुजसमाभासं रविपुत्रं यमाग्रजम् ।

छायामार्तण्डसम्भूतं तं नमामि शनैश्चरम् ॥

ॐ ऐं ह्रीं श्रीं शनैश्चराय नमः

**nīlāmbujasamābhāsaṃ**
**raviputraṃ yamāgrajam**
**chāyāmārtaṇḍasambhūtaṃ**
**taṃ namāmi śanaiścaram**
**oṃ aiṃ hrīṃ śrīṃ śanaiścarāya namaḥ**

Looking like a blue cloud, the son of the Sun, he is foremost of those who control. He can even put his shadow over the glorious sun. To that Saturn, emblem of control, we bow down in devotion. Oṃ we bow down to Saturn, the emblem of control.

अर्द्धकायं महावीर्यं चन्द्रादित्यविमर्दनम् ।

सिंहिकागर्भ सम्भूतं तं राहु प्रनमाम्यहम् ॥

ॐ ऐं ह्रीं राहवे नमः

**arddhakāyaṃ mahāvīryaṃ candrādityavimardanam**
**siṃhikāgarbha sambhūtaṃ taṃ rāhu**
**pranamāmyaham**
**oṃ aiṃ hrīṃ rāhave namaḥ**

The great warrior divides even the sun and moon in half. He is born from the womb of Siṃhikā, and we bow down in devotion to the North Node, who commands direction. Oṃ we bow down to the North Node, who commands direction.

पालाशपुष्प सङ्काशं तारकाग्रहमस्तकम् ।

रौद्रं रौद्रात्मकं घोरं तं केतु प्रनमाम्यहम् ॥

ॐ ह्रीं ऐं केतवे नमः

**pālāśapuṣpa saṅkāśaṃ tārakāgrahamastakam**
**raudraṃ raudrātmakaṃ ghoraṃ**
**taṃ ketu pranamāmyaham**
**oṃ hrīṃ aiṃ ketave namaḥ**

Red like a pālāśa flower, who makes the starry-eyed constellation to set; he is terrible and awsome to see, and we bow down in devotion to the South Node, who presents obstacles. Oṃ we bow down to the South Node, who presents obstacles.

ब्रह्मा मुरारिस्त्रिपुरान्तकारी भानुः शशी भूमिसुतो बुधश्च ।
गुरुश्च शुक्रः शनि राहु केतवः सर्वे ग्रहा शान्तिकरा भवन्तु ॥

**brahmā murāristripurāntakārī**
**bhānuḥ śaśī bhūmisuto budhaśca**
**guruśca śukraḥ śani rāhu ketavaḥ**
**sarve grahā śāntikarā bhavantu**

Brahmā, Viṣṇu and Śiva always contemplate the Sun, Moon, Earth, Mercury, Jupiter, Venus, Saturn, the North and South Nodes. May all the constellations remain in Peace.

ॐ नव ग्रहेभ्योः नमः

**oṃ nava grahebhyoḥ namaḥ**

Oṃ we bow to the nine planets.

## yoginī pūjā

worship of the sixty-four yoginīs

1. ॐ ह्रीं श्रीं ब्रह्माण्यै नमः

**oṃ hrīṃ śrīṃ brahmāṇyai namaḥ**

Oṃ Māyā, Increase, I bow to Creative Energy.

2. ॐ ह्रीं श्रीं चण्डिकायै नमः

**oṃ hrīṃ śrīṃ caṇḍikāyai namaḥ**

Oṃ Māyā, Increase, I bow to She who Tears Apart Thoughts.

3. ॐ ह्रीं श्रीं रौद्र्यै नमः

**oṃ hrīṃ śrīṃ raudryai namaḥ**

Oṃ Māyā, Increase, I bow to Fearful One.

4. ॐ ह्रीं श्रीं गौर्य्यै नमः

**oṃ hrīṃ śrīṃ gauryyai namaḥ**

Oṃ Māyā, Increase, I bow to She who is Rays of Light.

5. ॐ ह्रीं श्रीं इन्द्राण्यै नमः

**oṃ hrīṃ śrīṃ indrāṇyai namaḥ**

Oṃ Māyā, Increase, I bow to the Energy of the Rule of the Pure.

6. ॐ ह्रीं श्रीं कौमार्य्यै नमः

**oṃ hrīṃ śrīṃ kaumāryyai namaḥ**

Oṃ Māyā, Increase, I bow to the Ever Pure One.

7. ॐ ह्रीं श्रीं भैरव्यै नमः

**oṃ hrīṃ śrīṃ bhairavyai namaḥ**

Oṃ Māyā, Increase, I bow to the Fearless One.

8. ॐ ह्रीं श्रीं दुर्गायै नमः

**oṃ hrīṃ śrīṃ durgāyai namaḥ**

Oṃ Māyā, Increase, I bow to the Reliever of Difficulties

9. ॐ ह्रीं श्रीं नरसिंह्यै नमः

**oṃ hrīṃ śrīṃ narasiṃhyai namaḥ**

Oṃ Māyā, Increase, I bow to the Man-Lion of Courage.

10. ॐ ह्रीं श्रीं कालिकायै नमः

**oṃ hrīṃ śrīṃ kālikāyai namaḥ**

Oṃ Māyā, Increase, I bow to She Who is Beyond Time.

11. ॐ ह्रीं श्रीं चामुण्डायै नमः

**oṃ hrīṃ śrīṃ cāmuṇḍāyai namaḥ**

Oṃ Māyā, Increase, I bow to She Who Conquers Over Passion and Meanness.

12. ॐ ह्रीं श्रीं शिवदूत्यै नमः

**oṃ hrīṃ śrīṃ śivadūtyai namaḥ**

Oṃ Māyā, Increase, I bow to She Who Sends Śiva as an ambassador.

13. ॐ ह्रीं श्रीं वाराह्यै नमः

**oṃ hrīṃ śrīṃ vārāhyai namaḥ**

Oṃ Māyā, Increase, I bow to the Boar of Sacrifice.

14. ॐ ह्रीं श्रीं कौशिक्यै नमः

**oṃ hrīṃ śrīṃ kauśikyai namaḥ**

Oṃ Māyā, Increase, I bow to She Who Manifests from Within.

15. ॐ ह्रीं श्रीं माहेश्वर्य्यै नमः

**oṃ hrīṃ śrīṃ māheśvaryyai namaḥ**

Oṃ Māyā, Increase, I bow to the Great Seer of All.

16. ॐ ह्रीं श्रीं शाङ्कर्य्यै नमः

**oṃ hrīṃ śrīṃ śāṅkaryyai namaḥ**

Oṃ Māyā, Increase, I bow to the Cause of Peace

17. ॐ ह्रीं श्रीं जयन्त्यै नमः

**oṃ hrīṃ śrīṃ jayantyai namaḥ**

Oṃ Māyā, Increase, I bow to Victory.

18. ॐ ह्रीं श्रीं सर्वमङ्गलायै नमः

**oṃ hrīṃ śrīṃ sarvamaṅgalāyai namaḥ**

Oṃ Māyā, Increase, I bow to She Who is All Welfare.

19. ॐ ह्रीं श्रीं काल्यै नमः

**oṃ hrīṃ śrīṃ kālyai namaḥ**

Oṃ Māyā, Increase, I bow to She Who is Beyond Time.

20. ॐ ह्रीं श्रीं करालिन्यै नमः

**oṃ hrīṃ śrīṃ karālinyai namaḥ**

Oṃ Māyā, Increase, I bow to She with the Gaping Mouth.

21. ॐ ह्रीं श्रीं मेधायै नमः

**oṃ hrīṃ śrīṃ medhāyai namaḥ**

Oṃ Māyā, Increase, I bow to the Intellect of Love.

22. ॐ ह्रीं श्रीं शिवायै नमः

**oṃ hrīṃ śrīṃ śivāyai namaḥ**
Oṃ Māyā, Increase, I bow to the Energy of Śiva.

23. ॐ ह्रीं श्रीं साकम्भर्य्यै नमः

**oṃ hrīṃ śrīṃ sākambharyyai namaḥ**
Oṃ Māyā, Increase, I bow to She Who Nourishes with Vegetables.

24. ॐ ह्रीं श्रीं भीमायै नमः

**oṃ hrīṃ śrīṃ bhīmāyai namaḥ**
Oṃ Māyā, Increase, I bow to She Who is Fearless.

25. ॐ ह्रीं श्रीं शान्तायै नमः

**oṃ hrīṃ śrīṃ śāntāyai namaḥ**
Oṃ Māyā, Increase, I bow to Peace.

26. ॐ ह्रीं श्रीं भ्रामर्य्यै नमः

**oṃ hrīṃ śrīṃ bhrāmaryyai namaḥ**
Oṃ Māyā, Increase, I bow to She Who is like a Bee.

27. ॐ ह्रीं श्रीं रुद्राण्यै नमः

**oṃ hrīṃ śrīṃ rudrāṇyai namaḥ**
Oṃ Māyā, Increase, I bow to She Who Relieves the Sufferings of all.

28. ॐ ह्रीं श्रीं अम्बिकायै नमः

**oṃ hrīṃ śrīṃ ambikāyai namaḥ**
Oṃ Māyā, Increase, I bow to the Divine Mother.

29. ॐ ह्रीं श्रीं क्षमायै नमः

**oṃ hrīṃ śrīṃ kṣamāyai namaḥ**

Oṃ Māyā, Increase, I bow to Patient Forgiveness.

30. ॐ ह्रीं श्रीं धात्र्यै नमः

**oṃ hrīṃ śrīṃ dhātryai namaḥ**

Oṃ Māyā, Increase, I bow to the Creatress.

31. ॐ ह्रीं श्रीं स्वाहायै नमः

**oṃ hrīṃ śrīṃ svāhāyai namaḥ**

Oṃ Māyā, Increase, I bow to the oblation 'I Am One with God!'

32. ॐ ह्रीं श्रीं स्वधायै नमः

**oṃ hrīṃ śrīṃ svadhāyai namaḥ**

Oṃ Māyā, Increase, I bow to the Oblations to the Ancestors.

33. ॐ ह्रीं श्रीं अपर्णायै नमः

**oṃ hrīṃ śrīṃ aparṇāyai namaḥ**

Oṃ Māyā, Increase, I bow to She Who is Indivisible.

34. ॐ ह्रीं श्रीं महोदर्य्यै नमः

**oṃ hrīṃ śrīṃ mahodaryyai namaḥ**

Oṃ Māyā, Increase, I bow to She with the Big Belly.

35. ॐ ह्रीं श्रीं घोररूपायै नमः

**oṃ hrīṃ śrīṃ ghorarūpāyai namaḥ**

Oṃ Māyā, Increase, I bow to the Form of Whiteness.

36. ॐ ह्रीं श्रीं महाकाल्यै नमः

**oṃ hrīṃ śrīṃ mahākālyai namaḥ**

Oṃ Māyā, Increase, I bow to the Great She Who is Beyond Time.

37. ॐ ह्रीं श्रीं भद्रकाल्यै नमः

**oṃ hrīṃ śrīṃ bhadrakālyai namaḥ**

Oṃ Māyā, Increase, I bow to the Excellent One Who is Beyond Time.

38. ॐ ह्रीं श्रीं कपालिन्यै नमः

**oṃ hrīṃ śrīṃ kapālinyai namaḥ**

Oṃ Māyā, Increase, I bow to She Who Wears Skulls.

39. ॐ ह्रीं श्रीं क्षेमङ्कर्य्यै नमः

**oṃ hrīṃ śrīṃ kṣemaṅkaryyai namaḥ**

Oṃ Māyā, Increase, I bow to She Who Destroys.

40. ॐ ह्रीं श्रीं ऊग्रचण्डायै नमः

**oṃ hrīṃ śrīṃ ūgracaṇḍāyai namaḥ**

Oṃ Māyā, Increase, I bow to the Terrible Slayer of Passion.

41. ॐ ह्रीं श्रीं चण्डोग्रायै नमः

**oṃ hrīṃ śrīṃ caṇḍogrāyai namaḥ**

Oṃ Māyā, Increase, I bow to She Who Slays Passion.

42. ॐ ह्रीं श्रीं चण्डनायिकायै नमः

**oṃ hrīṃ śrīṃ caṇḍanāyikāyai namaḥ**

Oṃ Māyā, Increase, I bow to the Leader of Passion.

43. ॐ ह्रीं श्रीं चण्डायै नमः

**oṃ hrīṃ śrīṃ caṇḍāyai namaḥ**

Oṃ Māyā, Increase, I bow to She Who Slays Passion.

44. ॐ ह्रीं श्रीं चण्डवत्यै नमः

**oṃ hrīṃ śrīṃ caṇḍavatyai namaḥ**

Oṃ Māyā, Increase, I bow to the Spirit of Passion.

45. ॐ ह्रीं श्रीं चण्ड्यै नमः

**oṃ hrīṃ śrīṃ caṇḍyai namaḥ**

Oṃ Māyā, Increase, I bow to She Who Tears Apart Extreme Passion.

46. ॐ ह्रीं श्रीं महामोहायै नमः

**oṃ hrīṃ śrīṃ mahāmohāyai namaḥ**

Oṃ Māyā, Increase, I bow to She Who Covers the World with Ignorance.

47. ॐ ह्रीं श्रीं महामायायै नमः

**oṃ hrīṃ śrīṃ mahāmāyāyai namaḥ**

Oṃ Māyā, Increase, I bow to She Who is the Great Māyā.

48. ॐ ह्रीं श्रीं प्रियङ्कर्य्यै नमः

**oṃ hrīṃ śrīṃ priyaṅkaryyai namaḥ**

Oṃ Māyā, Increase, I bow to She Who Causes Love.

49. ॐ ह्रीं श्रीं बलविकरण्यै नमः

**oṃ hrīṃ śrīṃ balavikaraṇyai namaḥ**
Oṃ Māyā, Increase, I bow to She Who is Extremely Powerful.

50. ॐ ह्रीं श्रीं बलप्रमथन्यै नमः

**oṃ hrīṃ śrīṃ balapramathanyai namaḥ**
Oṃ Māyā, Increase, I bow to She Who is the Strength of Disembodied Spirits.

51. ॐ ह्रीं श्रीं मदनोन्मथन्यै नमः

**oṃ hrīṃ śrīṃ madanonmathanyai namaḥ**
Oṃ Māyā, Increase, I bow to She Who Churns with Love.

52. ॐ ह्रीं श्रीं सर्वभूतदमन्यै नमः

**oṃ hrīṃ śrīṃ sarvabhūtadamanyai namaḥ**
Oṃ Māyā, Increase, I bow to She Who Controls All Existence.

53. ॐ ह्रीं श्रीं ऊमायै नमः

**oṃ hrīṃ śrīṃ ūmāyai namaḥ**
Oṃ Māyā, Increase, I bow to the Mother of Protection.

54. ॐ ह्रीं श्रीं तारायै नमः

**oṃ hrīṃ śrīṃ tārāyai namaḥ**
Oṃ Māyā, Increase, I bow to She Who Shines like a Star.

55. ॐ ह्रीं श्रीं महानिद्रायै नमः

**oṃ hrīṃ śrīṃ mahānidrāyai namaḥ**

Oṃ Māyā, Increase, I bow to She Who is the Great Sleep.

56. ॐ ह्रीं श्रीं विजायायै नमः

**oṃ hrīṃ śrīṃ vijāyāyai namaḥ**

Oṃ Māyā, Increase, I bow to Victory.

57. ॐ ह्रीं श्रीं जयायै नमः

**oṃ hrīṃ śrīṃ jayāyai namaḥ**

Oṃ Māyā, Increase, I bow to Conquest.

58. ॐ ह्रीं श्रीं शैलपुत्र्यै नमः

**oṃ hrīṃ śrīṃ śailaputryai namaḥ**

Oṃ Māyā, Increase, I bow to the Goddess of Inspiration.

59. ॐ ह्रीं श्रीं ब्रह्मचारिण्यै नमः

**oṃ hrīṃ śrīṃ brahmacāriṇyai namaḥ**

Oṃ Māyā, Increase, I bow to the Goddess of Learning.

60. ॐ ह्रीं श्रीं चण्डघण्टायै नमः

**oṃ hrīṃ śrīṃ caṇḍaghaṇṭāyai namaḥ**

Oṃ Māyā, Increase, I bow to the Goddess of Practice.

61. ॐ ह्रीं श्रीं कूष्माण्डायै नमः

**oṃ hrīṃ śrīṃ kūṣmāṇḍāyai namaḥ**

Oṃ Māyā, Increase, I bow to the Goddess of Refinement.

62. ॐ ह्रीं श्रीं स्कन्दमात्र्यै नमः

**oṃ hrīṃ śrīṃ skandamātryai namaḥ**

Oṃ Māyā, Increase, I bow to the Goddess Who Nurtures Divinity.

63. ॐ ह्रीं श्रीं कात्यायन्यै नमः

**oṃ hrīṃ śrīṃ kātyāyanyai namaḥ**

Oṃ Māyā, Increase, I bow to the Goddess Who is Ever Pure.

64. ॐ ह्रीं श्रीं कालरात्र्यै नमः

**oṃ hrīṃ śrīṃ kālarātryai namaḥ**

Oṃ Māyā, Increase, I bow to the Goddess of the Great Night of Surrendering the Ego.

ॐ ह्रीं श्रीं महागौर्य्यै नमः

**oṃ hrīṃ śrīṃ mahāgauryyai namaḥ**

Oṃ Māyā, Increase, I bow to the Goddess of the Great Radiant Light.

ॐ ह्रीं श्रीं कोटियोगिनीभ्यो नमः

**oṃ hrīṃ śrīṃ koṭiyoginībhyo namaḥ**

Oṃ Māyā, Increase, I bow to the tens of millions of Goddesses.

## astra pūja

worship of the weapons of war

ॐ सर्वायुधानां प्रथमो निमितस्त्वं पिनाकिना ।
शूलात् सारं समाकृष्य कृत्वा मुष्ठि ग्रहं शुभम् ॥

**oṃ sarvāyudhānāṃ prathamo nimitastvaṃ pinākinā**
**śūlāt sāraṃ samākṛṣya kṛtvā muṣṭi grahaṃ śubham**

Oṃ First among all the implements of war is the trident. From the trident the ocean of existence comes together. Make a fist and accept the radiance.

ॐ त्रिशूलाय नमः

**oṃ triśūlāya namaḥ**

Oṃ I bow to the trident.

असिर्विशसनः खङ्गस्तीक्ष्नधारो दुरासदः ।
श्रीगर्भो विजयश्चैव धर्मपाल नमोऽस्तु ते ॥

**asirviśasanaḥ khaṅgastīkṣnadhāro durāsadaḥ**
**śrīgarbho vijayaścaiva dharmapāla namo-stu te**

The sword that protects the universe, you hold aloft the sharp blade against iniquity. In the respected womb of Victory, only to protect dharma, I bow down to you.

ॐ खड्गाय नमः

**oṃ khaḍgāya namaḥ**

Oṃ I bow to the sword.

चक्र त्वं विष्णुरूपोऽसि विष्णुपानौ सदा स्थितः ।
देवीहस्तस्थितो नित्यं शुदर्शन नमोऽस्तु ते ॥

**cakra tvaṃ viṣṇurūpo-si viṣṇupānau sadā sthitaḥ**
**devīhastasthito nityaṃ śudarśana namo-stu te**

Oh Discus, you are of the form of Viṣṇu, and you always reside in Viṣṇu's hands. Always stay in the hands of the Goddess. Excellent Intuitive Vision, I bow to you.

ॐ चक्राय नमः

**oṃ cakrāya namaḥ**

Oṃ I bow to the discus.

सर्वायुधानां श्रेष्ठोऽसि दैत्यसेनानिसूदनः ।
भयेभ्यः सर्वतो रक्ष तीक्ष्नबाण नमोऽस्तु ते ॥

**sarvāyudhānāṃ śreṣṭo-si daityasenānisūdanaḥ**
**bhayebhyaḥ sarvato rakṣa tīkṣnabāṇa namo-stu te**

You are the ultimate of all implements of war, eradicating the armies of duality. Always protect from all fear. I bow to the arrows.

ॐ तीक्ष्नबाणाय नमः

**oṃ tīkṣnabāṇāya namaḥ**

Oṃ I bow to the sharp arrows.

शक्तिस्त्वं सर्वदेवानां गुहस्य च विशेषतः ।
शक्तिरूपेण सर्वत्र रक्षां कुरु नमोऽस्तु ते ॥

**śaktistvaṃ sarvadevānāṃ guhasya ca viśeṣataḥ**
**śaktirūpeṇa sarvatra rakṣāṃ kuru namo-stu te**

You are the energy of all the Gods, especially hidden. By means of this energy always protect me. I bow to you.

ॐ शक्तये नमः

**oṃ śaktaye namaḥ**
Oṃ I bow to Energy.

षष्ठिरूपेण खेट त्वं वैरिसंहारकारकः ।
देवीहस्तस्थितो नित्यं मम रक्षां कुरुष्व च ॥

**ṣaṣṭirūpeṇa kheṭa tvaṃ vairisaṃhārakārakaḥ**
**devīhastasthito nityaṃ mama rakṣāṃ kuruṣva ca**
With the form of six points you are the shield, the cause of dissolution of adversity. Always stay in the hand of the Goddess, and protect me.

ॐ खेटकाय नमः

**oṃ kheṭakāya namaḥ**
Oṃ I bow to the Shield.

सर्वायुध महामात्र सर्वदेवारिसुदन ।
चाप मां सर्वतो रक्ष साकं सायकसत्तमैः ॥

**sarvāyudha mahāmātra sarvadevārisudana**
**cāpa māṃ sarvato rakṣa sākaṃ sāyakasattamaiḥ**
The great measurement of all warriors makes all the Gods victorious. Always protect me with the bow, with arrows ready to be hurled.

ॐ पूर्णचापाय नमः

**oṃ pūrṇacāpāya namaḥ**
Oṃ I bow to the bow.

पाश त्वं नागरूपोऽसि विषपूर्णो विषोदरः ।
शत्रुणां दुःसहो नित्यं नागपाश नमोऽस्तु ते ॥

**pāśa tvaṃ nāgarūpo-si viṣapūrṇo viṣodaraḥ**
**śatruṇāṃ duḥsaho nityaṃ nāgapāśa namo-stu te**

You are the bond in the form of a snake full of venom ready to strike. You always cause pain to enemies. Snake-bond, I bow to you.

ॐ नागपाशाय नमः

**oṃ nāgapāśāya namaḥ**

Oṃ I bow to the Snake-bond.

अङ्कुशोऽसि नमस्तुभ्यं गजानां नियमः सदा ।
लोकानां सर्वरक्षार्थं विधृतः पार्वतीकरे ॥

**aṅkuśo-si namastubhyaṃ gajānāṃ niyamaḥ sadā**
**lokānāṃ sarvarakṣārthaṃ vidhṛtaḥ pārvatīkare**

Curved Sword or prod, we bow to you. Always you discipline elephants. In order to protect the worlds, remain in Pārvatī's hands.

ॐ अङ्कुशाय नमः

**oṃ aṅkuśāya namaḥ**

Oṃ I bow to the Curved Sword.

हिनस्ति दैत्यतेजांसि स्वनेनापूर्य या जगत् ।
सा घण्टा पातु नो देवि पापेभ्योऽनः सुतानिव ॥

**hinasti daitya tejāṃsi svanenāpūrya yā jagat**
**sā ghaṇṭā pātu no devi pāpebhyo-naḥ sutāniva**

Oh Goddess, may the sound of your bell, which fills the perceivable world, destroying the prowess of all thoughts, protect us from evil as a Mother protects Her children.

ॐ घण्टाय नमः

**oṃ ghaṇṭāya namaḥ**
Oṃ I bow to the Bell.

परशो त्वं महातीक्ष्न सर्वदेवारिसूदनः ।
देवीहास्तस्थितो नित्यं शत्रुक्षय नमोऽस्तु ते ॥

**paraśo tvaṃ mahātīkṣna sarvadevārisūdanaḥ**
**devīhāstasthito nityaṃ śatrukṣaya namo-stu te**
Oh Battle Axe, you are very sharp as you defend all the Gods. Always stay in the hands of the Goddess. Destroyer of enemies, we bow to you.

ॐ परशवे नमः

**oṃ paraśave namaḥ**
Oṃ I bow to the Battle Axe.

ॐ ह्रीं श्रीं सर्वायुधधारिण्यै दुर्गायै नमः

**oṃ hrīṃ śrīṃ sarvāyudhadhāriṇyai durgāyai namaḥ**
Oṃ Māyā, Increase, I bow to Durgā, who holds all the weapons of war.

सर्वायुधानां श्रेष्ठानि यानि यानि त्रिपिष्ठपे ।
तानि तानि दधत्यै ते चण्डिकायै नमो नमः ॥

**sarvāyudhānāṃ śreṣṭāni yāni yāni tripiṣṭape**
**tāni tāni dadhatyai te caṇḍikāyai namo namaḥ**

She is the most excellent of all warriors, wherever, wherever in the three worlds. Where there exist forces of duality, we bow to You, to She Who Tears Apart Thought, we bow.

ॐ ह्रीं श्रीं सर्वायुधधारिण्यै चण्डिकायै नमः

**oṃ hrīṃ śrīṃ sarvāyudhadhāriṇyai caṇḍikāyai namaḥ**

Oṃ Māyā, Increase, I bow to Caṇḍikā who holds all the weapons of war.

## bāhya mātrikā nyāsa

establishment of the letters in the external body

Every object in creation has a name to correspond to its form. There is a name that is agreed upon by the customs of language, what we may call an object; and there is a natural sound that is being emitted as a consequence of the vibrations that are taking place in the object itself, the movement of protons, nutrons, electrons, etc. Every manifested object of creation has a vibration, whether perceivable or not, and every vibration emits a sound, whether audible to the physical organ of hearing or not. Every sound is expressible by a letter that-symbolizes the sound that most closely approximates the vibration indicated, so that all the letters of the alphabets symbolize the total possibility of all vibrations that can be evolved or can be expressed - the totality of creation.

This natural name is called a *Bījā Mantra*, often translated as *Seed Mantra*. These Bījās are another name for the Mātṛkās, the letters of the Saṃskṛta alphabet. In Saṃskṛta Philosophy, the microcosm is an exact replica of the macrocosm. Hence every physical body contains all the vibrations possible in the cosmos.

Bāhya Mātṛkā Nyāsa means the establishment of the letters of the Saṃskṛta Alphabet within the "Outside" or the gross body of the worshipper. Bāhya Mātṛkā Nyāsa ascribes a position in each of the centers of activity for each of the letters, so that the worshipper can understand and experience the totality of creation as existing within the physical body. By using the different Mudrās described, the worshipper begins by placing the sixteen vowels in their respective positions.

Thumb 1 Pointer 2 Middle 3 Ring 4 Pinky 5
R. means right and L. means left

ॐ अं नमः

**oṃ aṃ namaḥ** R.1.4 base top of head

ॐ आं नमः

**oṃ āṃ namaḥ** R.1.4 base mouth

ॐ इं नमः

**oṃ iṃ namaḥ** R. 4 R. eye

ॐ ईं नमः

**oṃ īṃ namaḥ** L. 4 L. eye

ॐ उं नमः

**oṃ uṃ namaḥ** R. 1 R. ear

ॐ ऊं नमः

**oṃ ūṃ namaḥ** L. 1 L. ear

ॐ ऋं नमः

**oṃ ṛṃ namaḥ** R. 1.5 R. nostril

ॐ ॠं नमः

**oṃ ṝṃ namaḥ** L. 1.5 L. nostril

ॐ ऌं नमः

**oṃ ḷṃ namaḥ** R. 2.3.4 R. cheek

ॐ ॡं नमः

**oṃ ḹṃ namaḥ** L. 2.3.4 L. cheek

ॐ एं नमः

**oṃ eṃ namaḥ** R. 3 upper lip

ॐ ऐं नमः

**oṃ aiṃ namaḥ** R. 3 lower lip

ॐ ओं नमः

**oṃ oṃ namaḥ** R. 4 upper teeth

ॐ औं नमः

**oṃ auṃ namaḥ** R. 4 lower teeth

ॐ अं नमः

**oṃ aṃ namaḥ** R. 3.4 crown of head

ॐ अः नमः

**oṃ aḥ namaḥ** R. 3.4 mouth

ॐ कं नमः

**oṃ kaṃ namaḥ** L. 1.3.5 R. shoulder

ॐ खं नमः

**oṃ khaṃ namaḥ** L. 1.3.5 R. crook of elbow

ॐ गं नमः

**oṃ gaṃ namaḥ** L. 1.3.5 R. wrist

ॐ घं नमः

**oṃ ghaṃ namaḥ** L. 1.3.5 R. joint of hand

ॐ ङं नमः

**oṃ ṅaṃ namaḥ** L. 1.3.5 R. fingertips

ॐ चं नमः

**oṃ caṃ namaḥ** R. 1.3.5 L. shoulder

ॐ छं नमः

**oṃ chaṃ namaḥ** R. 1.3.5 L. crook of elbow

ॐ जं नमः

**oṃ jaṃ namaḥ** R. 1.3.5 L. wrist

ॐ झं नमः

**oṃ jhaṃ namaḥ** R. 1.3.5 L. joint of hand

ॐ ञं नमः

**oṃ ñaṃ namaḥ** R. 1.3.5 L. fingertips

ॐ टं नमः

**oṃ ṭaṃ namaḥ** L. 1.3.5 R. hip

ॐ ठं नमः

**oṃ ṭhaṃ namaḥ** L. 1.3.5 R. knees

ॐ डं नमः

**oṃ ḍaṃ namaḥ** L. 1.3.5 R. ankle

ॐ ढं नमः

**oṃ ḍhaṃ namaḥ** L. 1.3.5 R. joints of toes

ॐ णं नमः

**oṃ ṇaṃ namaḥ** L. 1.3.5 R. tips of toes

ॐ तं नमः

**oṃ taṃ namaḥ** R. 1.3.5 L. hip

ॐ थं नमः

**oṃ thaṃ namaḥ** R. 1.3.5 L. knees

ॐ दं नमः

**oṃ daṃ namaḥ** R. 1.3.5 L. ankle

ॐ धं नमः

**oṃ dhaṃ namaḥ** R. 1.3.5 L. joints of toes

ॐ नं नमः

**oṃ naṃ namaḥ** R. 1.3.5 L. tips of toes

ॐ पं नमः

**oṃ paṃ namaḥ** L. 1.4 base R. side

ॐ फं नमः

**oṃ phaṃ namaḥ** R. 1.4 base L. side

ॐ बं नमः

**oṃ baṃ namaḥ** R. 1.4 base belly

ॐ भं नमः

**oṃ bhaṃ namaḥ** L. 1.4 base back

ॐ मं नमः

**oṃ maṃ namaḥ** R. 1.2.3.4.5. flat navel

ॐ यं नमः

**oṃ yaṃ namaḥ** R. 1.4 base heart

ॐ रं नमः

**oṃ raṃ namaḥ** L. 1.4 base R. shoulder

ॐ लं नमः

**oṃ laṃ namaḥ** R. 1.4 base back of neck

ॐ वं नमः

**oṃ vaṃ namaḥ** R. 1.4 base L. shoulder

ॐ शं नमः

**oṃ śaṃ namaḥ** R. 1.4 L. shoulder to hand full length

ॐ षं नमः

**oṃ ṣaṃ namaḥ** L. 1.4 R. shoulder to hand full length

ॐ सं नमः

**oṃ saṃ namaḥ** L. 1.4 R. hip to leg full

ॐ हं नमः

**oṃ haṃ namaḥ** R. 1.4 L. hip to leg full

ॐ ळं नमः

**oṃ ḷaṃ namaḥ** L. 1.4 sternum to navel

ॐ क्षं नमः

**oṃ kṣaṃ namaḥ** R. 1.4 sternum to throat

ॐ ऐं ह्रीं क्लीं चामुण्डायै विच्चे

**oṃ aiṃ hrīṃ klīṃ cāmuṇḍāyai vicce**

Oṃ aiṃ hrīṃ klīṃ cāmuṇḍāyai vicce.

## mātṛkā nyāsa

establishment of the letters in the cakras

Following Pāṇiṇī's Grammar, which is the most authoritative on the subject, in the Bāhya Mātṛkā Nyāsa there are thirty-five consonants. Actually the number of letters varies according to different enumerations regarding differing functions, and in the Mātṛkā Nyāsa that follows, only fifty letters are to be placed.

Saṃskṛt is commonly taught with fifty letters: sixteen vowels and thirty-four consonants. Occasionally it is taught with fifty-two letters, with the addition of *oṃ* and *hrīṃ*. For the purpose of these Nyāsas, we follow both the formats because the authorities considered to be the most accurate agree in all the versions consulted. The question of why they differ in the number of letters they contain will not be addressed here.

Mātṛkā Nyāsa places the Bījās, or natural names, inside the cakras, which are the energy centers within the body. In this meditation we conceive that not only is all existence moving in my every movement, as in the former Nyāsa, but also that all the vibrations of the universe comprise the very essence of my being.

*Haṃ* stands for the Prāṇātman, the second *ḷaṃ* for the Jīvātman and *kṣaṃ* for Paramātman. In this way Jīva puts on, so to speak, or wears the universe as a gown. All the vibrations of existence make up the cloak that covers the ever more subtle essence of consciousness, which is the Silent Witness to the Dance of Creation.

**Viśuddha** (5th Cakra) 16 petals

ॐ अं नमः

**oṃ aṃ namaḥ**

ॐ आं नमः

**oṃ āṃ namaḥ**

ॐ इं नमः

**oṃ iṃ namaḥ**

ॐ ईं नमः

**oṃ īṃ namaḥ**

ॐ उं नमः

**oṃ uṃ namaḥ**

ॐ ऊं नमः

**oṃ ūṃ namaḥ**

ॐ ऋं नमः

**oṃ ṛṃ namaḥ**

ॐ ॠं नमः

**oṃ ṝṃ namaḥ**

ॐ ऌं नमः

**oṃ ḷṃ namaḥ**

ॐ ॡं नमः

**oṃ ḹṃ namaḥ**

ॐ एं नमः

**oṃ eṃ namaḥ**

ॐ ऐं नमः

**oṃ aiṃ namaḥ**

ॐ ओं नमः

**oṃ oṃ namaḥ**

ॐ औं नमः

**oṃ auṃ namaḥ**

ॐ अं नमः

**oṃ aṃ namaḥ**

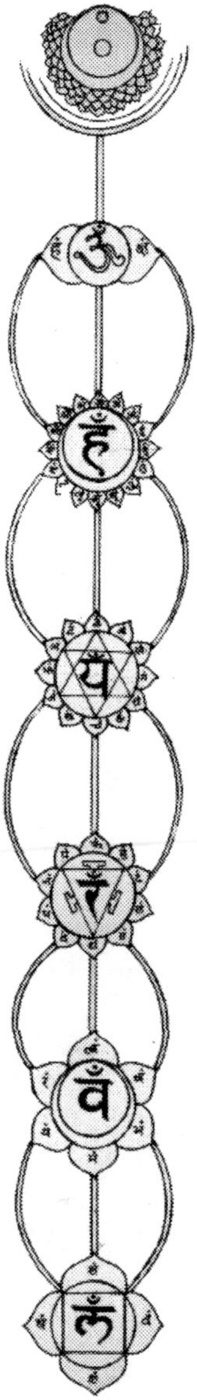

ॐ अः नमः

**oṃ aḥ namaḥ**

**Anahāta** (4th Cakra) 12 petals

ॐ कं नमः

**oṃ kaṃ namaḥ**

ॐ खं नमः

**oṃ khaṃ namaḥ**

ॐ गं नमः

**oṃ gaṃ namaḥ**

ॐ घं नमः

**oṃ ghaṃ namaḥ**

ॐ ङं नमः

**oṃ ṅaṃ namaḥ**

ॐ चं नमः

**oṃ caṃ namaḥ**

ॐ छं नमः

**oṃ chaṃ namaḥ**

ॐ जं नमः

**oṃ jaṃ namaḥ**

ॐ झं नमः

**oṃ jhaṃ namaḥ**

ॐ ञं नमः

**oṃ ñaṃ namaḥ**

ॐ टं नमः

**oṃ ṭaṃ namaḥ**

ॐ ठं नमः

**oṃ ṭhaṃ namaḥ**

**Maṇipura** (3rd Cakra) 10 petals

ॐ डं नमः

**oṃ ḍaṃ namaḥ**

ॐ ढं नमः

**oṃ ḍhaṃ namaḥ**

ॐ णं नमः

**oṃ ṇaṃ namaḥ**

ॐ तं नमः

**oṃ taṃ namaḥ**

ॐ थं नमः

**oṃ thaṃ namaḥ**

ॐ दं नमः

**oṃ daṃ namaḥ**

ॐ धं नमः

**oṃ dhaṃ namaḥ**

ॐ नं नमः

**oṃ naṃ namaḥ**

ॐ पं नमः

**oṃ paṃ namaḥ**

ॐ फं नमः

**oṃ phaṃ namaḥ**

**Swādiṣṭhana** (2nd Cakra) 6 petals

ॐ बं नमः

**oṃ baṃ namaḥ**

ॐ भं नमः

**oṃ bhaṃ namaḥ**

ॐ मं नमः

**oṃ maṃ namaḥ**

ॐ यं नमः

**oṃ yaṃ namaḥ**

ॐ रं नमः

**oṃ raṃ namaḥ**

ॐ लं नमः

**oṃ laṃ namaḥ**

**Mulādhāra** (1st Cakra) 4 petals

ॐ वं नमः

**oṃ vaṃ namaḥ**

ॐ शं नमः

**oṃ śaṃ namaḥ**

ॐ षं नमः

**oṃ ṣaṃ namaḥ**

ॐ सं नमः

**oṃ saṃ namaḥ**

## **Āgnyā** (6th Cakra) 2 petals

ॐ हं नमः

**oṃ haṃ namaḥ**

ॐ क्षं नमः

**oṃ kṣaṃ namaḥ**

ॐ ऐं ह्रीं क्लीं चामुण्डायै विच्चे

**oṃ aiṃ hrīṃ klīṃ cāmuṇḍāyai vicce**

Oṃ aiṃ hrīṃ klīṃ cāmuṇḍāyai vicce.

perform saṃhara mātṛkā nyāsa and bāhya mātṛkā nyāsa by repeating the above described processes in reverse order from the end to the beginning.

### **aṅga pūjā**

worship of the divine mother's body
using tattva mudrā on both hands touch:

ॐ दुर्गायै नमः पादौ पूजयामि

**oṃ durgāyai namaḥ pādau pūjayāmi** feet

I bow to the Reliever of Difficulties and worship Her feet.

ॐ गिरिजायै नमः गुल्फौ पूजयामि

**oṃ girijāyai namaḥ gulphau pūjayāmi** ankles

I bow to the Unconquerable One from the Mountains and worship Her ankles.

ॐ अपर्णायै नमः जानुनी पूजयामि

**oṃ aparṇāyai namaḥ jānunī pūjayāmi** knees

I bow to the Unseverable Energy and worship Her knees.

ॐ हरिप्रियायै नमः ऊरू पूजयामि

**oṃ haripriyāyai namaḥ ūrū pūjayāmi** thighs

I bow to the Beloved of Consciousness and worship Her thighs.

ॐ पार्वत्यै नमः कटिं पूजयामि

**oṃ pārvatyai namaḥ kaṭiṃ pūjayāmi** hips

I bow to the Daughter of the Mountains and worship Her hips.

ॐ आर्यायै नमः नाभिं पूजयामि

**oṃ āryāyai namaḥ nābhiṃ pūjayāmi** navel

I bow to the One Purified by Knowledge and worship Her navel.

ॐ जगन्मात्रे नमः उदरं पूजयामि

**oṃ jaganmātre namaḥ udaraṃ pūjayāmi** stomach

I bow to the Mother of the Perceivable Universe and worship Her stomach.

ॐ मंगलायै नमः कुक्षिं पूजयामि

**oṃ maṃgalāyai namaḥ kukṣiṃ pūjayāmi** sternum

I bow to the Energy of Welfare and worship Her sternum.

ॐ शिवायै नमः हृदयं पूजयामि

**oṃ śivāyai namaḥ hṛdayaṃ pūjayāmi** heart

I bow to the Energy of Infinite Goodness and worship Her heart.

ॐ महेश्वर्यै नमः कण्ठं पूजयामि

**oṃ maheśvaryai namaḥ kaṇṭhaṃ pūjayāmi** throat

I bow to the Energy of the Great Seer of All and worship Her throat.

ॐ विश्ववन्द्यायै नमः स्कन्धौ पूजयामि shoulders

**oṃ viśvavandyāyai namaḥ skandhau pūjayāmi**

I bow to She who is Praised by the Universe and worship Her shoulders.

ॐ काल्यै नमः बाहू पूजयामि

**oṃ kālyai namaḥ bāhū pūjayāmi** arms

I bow to She who Takes Away Darkness and worship Her arms.

ॐ आद्यायै नमः हस्तौ पूजयामि

**oṃ ādyāyai namaḥ hastau pūjayāmi** hands

I bow to She who is Sacred Study and worship Her hands.

ॐ वरदायै नमः मुखं पूजयामि

**oṃ varadāyai namaḥ mukhaṃ pūjayāmi** mouth

I bow to She who Grants Boons and worship Her mouth.

ॐ सुवाण्यै नमः नासिकां पूजयामि

**oṃ suvāṇyai namaḥ nāsikāṃ pūjayāmi** nose

I bow to She of Excellent Music and worship Her nose.

ॐ कमलाक्ष्म्यै नमः नेत्रे पूजयामि

**oṃ kamalākṣmyai namaḥ netre pūjayāmi** three eyes

I bow to the Lotus-eyed and worship Her eyes.

ॐ अम्बिकायै नमः शिरः पूजयामि

**oṃ ambikāyai namaḥ śiraḥ pūjayāmi** top of head

I bow to the Mother of All and worship Her head.

ॐ देव्यै नमः सर्वाङ्ग पूजयामि

**oṃ devyai namaḥ sarvāṅga pūjayāmi** entire body

I bow to the Goddess and worship Her entire body.

हं रं ईं ह्रीं

**haṃ raṃ īṃ hrīṃ**

ॐ हकारः स्थूलदेहः स्याद्रकार सूक्ष्मदेहकः ।
ईकारः कारणात्मासौ ह्रीङ्कारोऽहं तुरीयकम् ॥

**oṃ hakāraḥ sthūladehaḥ syād**
**rakāra sūkṣmadehakaḥ**
**īkāraḥ kāraṇātmāsau hrīṅkāro-haṃ turīyakam**

Oṃ The letter *Ha* indicates the Gross Body; the letter *Ra* is the Subtle Body. The letter *Ī* is the Causal Body; and as the entire letter *Hrīṃ*, I am beyond manifestation.

## **pīṭha nyāsa**

establishment of the place of internal worship

with tattva mudrā touch the places
indicating a yantra on your chest:

\- 1 -

ॐ आधारशक्तये नमः

**oṃ ādhāraśaktaye namaḥ**

Oṃ I bow to the primal energy that sustains existence.

\- 2 -

ॐ कुर्म्माय नमः

**oṃ kurmmāya namaḥ**

Oṃ I bow to the Tortoise that supports creation.

\- 3 -

ॐ अनन्ताय नमः

**oṃ anantāya namaḥ**

Oṃ I bow to Infinity (personified as a thousand hooded snake that holds aloft the worlds).

\- 4 -

ॐ पृथिव्यै नमः

**oṃ pṛthivyai namaḥ**

Oṃ I bow to the Earth.

\- 5 -

ॐ क्षीरसमूद्राय नमः

**oṃ kṣīrasamūdrāya namaḥ**

Oṃ I bow to the milk ocean, or ocean of nectar, the infinite expanse of existence from which all of creation manifested.

- 6 -

ॐ श्वेतद्वीपाय नमः

**oṃ śvetadvīpāya namaḥ**

Oṃ I bow to the Island of Purity, which is in the ocean.

- 7 -

ॐ मणिमन्दपाय नमः

**oṃ maṇimandapāya namaḥ**

Oṃ I bow to the Palace of Gems, which is on the island, the home of the Divine Mother.

- 8 -

ॐ कल्पवृक्षाय नमः

**oṃ kalpavṛkṣāya namaḥ**

Oṃ I bow to the Tree of Fulfillment, which satisfies all desires, growing in the palace courtyard.

- 9 -

ॐ मणिवेदिकायै नमः

**oṃ maṇivedikāyai namaḥ**

Oṃ I bow to the altar containing the gems of wisdom.

- 10 -

ॐ रत्नसिंहासनाय नमः

**oṃ ratnasiṃhāsanāya namaḥ**

Oṃ I bow to the throne of the jewel.

- 11 -

ॐ धर्म्माय नमः

**oṃ dharmmāya namaḥ**

Oṃ I bow to the Way of Truth and Harmony.

- 12 -

ॐ ज्ञानाय नमः

**oṃ jñānāya namaḥ**

Oṃ I bow to Wisdom.

- 13 -

ॐ वैराग्याय नमः

**oṃ vairāgyāya namaḥ**

Oṃ I bow to Detachment.

- 14 -

ॐ ईश्वर्ज्याय नमः

**oṃ īśvarjyāya namaḥ**

Oṃ I bow to the Imperishable Qualities.

- 15 -

ॐ अधर्म्माय नमः

**oṃ adharmmāya namaḥ**

Oṃ I bow to Disharmony.

- 16 -

ॐ अज्ञानाय नमः

**oṃ ajñānāya namaḥ**

Oṃ I bow to Ignorance.

- 17 -

ॐ अवैराग्याय नमः

**oṃ avairāgyāya namaḥ**

Oṃ I bow to Attachment.

- 18 -

ॐ अनीश्वर्ज्याय नमः

**oṃ anīśvarjyāya namaḥ**

Oṃ I bow to the Transient.

- 19 -

ॐ अनन्ताय नमः

**oṃ anantāya namaḥ**

Oṃ I bow to the Infinite.

- 20 -

ॐ पद्माय नमः

**oṃ padmāya namaḥ**

Oṃ I bow to the Lotus.

- 21 -

अं अर्कमण्डलाय द्वादशकलात्मने नमः

**aṃ arkamaṇḍalāya dvādaśakalātmane namaḥ**

"A" we bow to the twelve aspects of the realm of the sun. Tapinī, Tāpinī, Dhūmrā, Marīci, Jvālinī, Ruci, Sudhūmrā, Bhoga-dā, Viśvā, Bodhinī, Dhārinī, Kṣamā: Containing heat, Emanating Heat, Smoky, Ray-Producing, Burning, Lustrous, Purple or Smoky-Red, Granting Enjoyment, Universal, Which Makes Known, Productive of Consciousness, Which Supports, Which Forgives.

- 22 -

उं सोममण्डलाय षोडशकलात्मने नमः

**uṃ somamaṇḍalāya ṣoḍaśakalātmane namaḥ**

"U" we bow to the sixteen aspects of the realm of the moon: Amṛtā, Prāṇadā, Puṣā, Tuṣṭi, Puṣṭi, Rati, Dhṛti, Śaśinī, Candrikā, Kānti, Jyotsnā, Śrī, Prīti, Aṅgadā, Pūrṇā, Pūrṇāmṛtā; Nectar, Which Sustains life, Which Supports, Satisfying, Nourishing, Playful, Constant, Unfailing, Producer of Joy, Beauty Enhanced by Love, Light, Grantor of Prosperity, Affectionate, Purifying the Body, Complete, Full of Bliss.

- 23 -

मं वह्निमण्डलाय दशकलात्मने नमः

**maṃ vahnimaṇḍalāya daśakalātmane namaḥ**

"M" we bow to the ten aspects of the realm of fire: Dhūmrā, Arciḥ, Jvalinī, Śūkṣmā, Jvālinī, Visphuliṅginī, Suśrī, Surūpā, Kapilā, Havya-Kavya-Vahā: Smoky-Red, Flaming, Shining, Subtle, Burning, Sparkling, Beautiful, Well-Formed, Tawny, Messenger to the Gods and Ancestors.

- 24 -

ॐ सं सत्त्वाय नमः

**oṃ saṃ sattvāya namaḥ**

Oṃ I bow to activity, execution, light, knowledge, being.

- 25 -

ॐ रं रजसे नमः

**oṃ raṃ rajase namaḥ**

Oṃ I bow to desire, inspiration, becoming.

- 26 -

ॐ तं तमसे नमः

**oṃ taṃ tamase namaḥ**

Oṃ I bow to wisdom, to the darkness that exposes light, to rest.

- 27 -

ॐ आं आत्मने नमः

**oṃ āṃ ātmane namaḥ**

Oṃ I bow to the Soul.

- 28 -

ॐ अं अन्तरात्मने नमः

**oṃ aṃ antarātmane namaḥ**

Oṃ I bow to the Innermost Soul.

- 29 -

ॐ पं परमात्मने नमः

**oṃ paṃ paramātmane namaḥ**

Oṃ I bow to the Universal Soul, or the Consciousness thatexceeds manifestation.

- 30 -

ॐ ह्रीं ज्ञानात्मने नमः

**oṃ hrīṃ jñānātmane namaḥ**

Oṃ I bow to the Soul of Infinite Wisdom.

**āvāhaṇa**

invitation

अनेकरत्न संयुक्तं नानामणि गणान्वितम् ।

कार्तस्वरमयं दिव्यमासनं प्रतिगृह्यताम् ॥

ॐ ऐं ह्रीं क्लीं चामुण्डायै विच्चे आसनं समर्पयामि

**anekaratna saṃyuktaṃ nānāmaṇi gaṇānvitam**
**kārtasvaramayaṃ divyamāsanaṃ pratigṛhyatām**
**oṃ aiṃ hrīṃ klīṃ cāmuṇḍāyai vicce āsanaṃ samarpayāmi**

United with many gems and a multitude of various jewels, voluntarily accept my offering of a divine seat. With the offering of a seat, oṃ aiṃ hrīṃ klīṃ cāmuṇḍāyai vicce.

establishment within

**āvāhaṇi mudrā** (I invite you, please come.)

ॐ ऐं ह्रीं क्लीं चामुण्डायै विच्चे इहागच्छ

**oṃ aiṃ hrīṃ klīṃ cāmuṇḍāyai vicce ihāgaccha**

Oṃ aiṃ hrīṃ klīṃ cāmuṇḍāyai vicce, I invite you, please come.

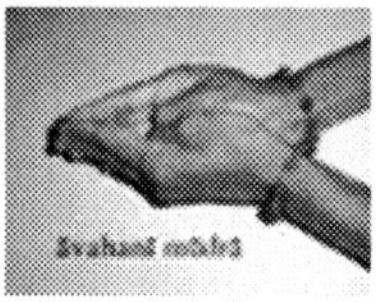

**sthāpanī mudrā** (I establish you within.)

इह तिष्ठ

**iha tiṣṭha**

I establish you within.

**sannidhāpanī mudrā** (I know you have many devotees who are requesting your attention, but I request that you pay special attention to me.)

इह सन्निरुध्यस्व

**iha sannirudhyasva**

I am binding you to remain here.

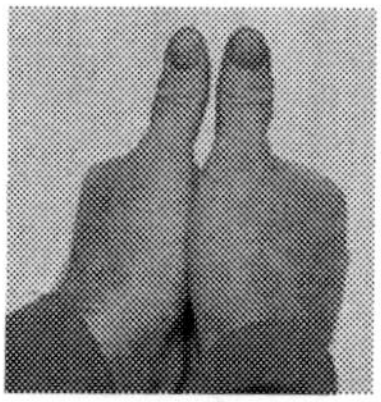

**saṃrodhanī mudrā** (I am sorry for any inconvenience caused.)

इह सनिहित भव

**iha sanihita bhava**

You bestow abundant wealth.

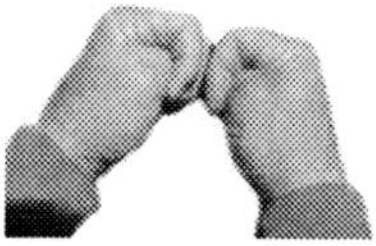

**atmā samarpaṇa mudrā** (I surrender my soul to you.)

अत्राधिष्ठानं कुरु

**atrādhiṣṭhānaṃ kuru**

I am depending on you to forgive me in this matter.

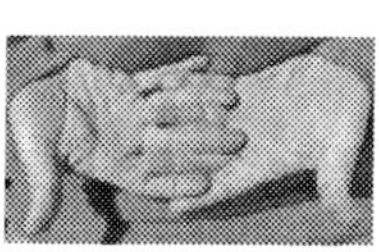

**prakṣan** (I bow to you with devotion.)

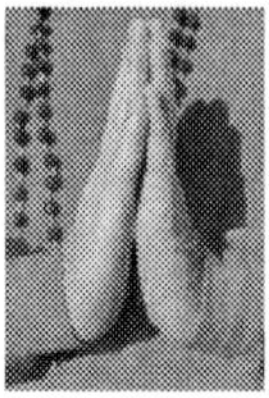

देवि मम पूजां गृहाण
देवि भक्तशूलवे परित्राण करायिते ।
जावोट् त्वं पूजैषामि तावोट् त्वं सुस्थिरा भव ॥

**devi mama pūjāṃ gṛhāṇa**
**devi bhaktaśūlave paritrāṇa karāyite**
**jāvoṭ tvaṃ pūjaiṣāmi tāvoṭ tvaṃ susthirā bhava**

Oh Goddess, please accept my worship. Oh God, remove all pain from your devotees. For so long as I worship you, please remain sitting still.

## prāṇa pratiṣṭhā

establishment of life

ॐ अं आं ह्रीं क्रों यं रं लं वं शं षं सं हों हं सः

**oṃ aṃ āṃ hrīṃ kroṃ yaṃ raṃ laṃ vaṃ śaṃ ṣaṃ saṃ hoṃ haṃ saḥ**

Oṃ The Infinite Beyond Conception, Creation (the first letter), Consciousness, Māyā, the cause of the movement of the subtle body to perfection and beyond; the path of fulfillment: control, subtle illumination, one with the earth, emancipation, the soul of peace, the soul of delight, the soul of unity (all this is I), perfection, Infinite Consciousness, I am this.

ॐ ऐं ह्रीं क्लीं चामुण्डायै विच्चे प्राणा इह प्राणाः

**oṃ aiṃ hrīṃ klīṃ cāmuṇḍāyai vicce prāṇā iha prāṇāḥ**

Oṃ aiṃ hrīṃ klīṃ cāmuṇḍāyai vicce. You are the life of this life!

ॐ अं आं ह्रीं क्रों यं रं लं वं शं षं सं हों हं सः

**oṃ aṃ āṃ hrīṃ kroṃ yaṃ raṃ laṃ vaṃ śaṃ ṣaṃ saṃ hoṃ haṃ saḥ**

Oṃ The Infinite Beyond Conception, Creation (the first letter), Consciousness, Māyā, the cause of the movement of the subtle body to perfection and beyond; the path of fulfillment: control, subtle illumination, one with the earth, emancipation, the soul of peace, the soul of delight, the soul of unity (all this is I), perfection, Infinite Consciousness, I am this.

ॐ ऐं ह्रीं क्लीं चामुण्डायै विच्चे जीव इह स्थितः

**oṃ aiṃ hrīṃ klīṃ cāmuṇḍāyai vicce jīva iha sthitaḥ**

Oṃ aiṃ hrīṃ klīṃ cāmuṇḍāyai vicce. You are situated in this life (or individual consciousness).

ॐ अं आं ह्रीं क्रों यं रं लं वं शं षं सं हों हं सः

**oṃ aṃ āṃ hrīṃ kroṃ yaṃ raṃ laṃ vaṃ śaṃ ṣaṃ saṃ hoṃ haṃ saḥ**

Oṃ The Infinite Beyond Conception, Creation (the first letter), Consciousness, Māyā, the cause of the movement of the subtle body to perfection and beyond; the path of fulfillment: control, subtle illumination, one with the earth, emancipation, the soul of peace, the soul of delight, the soul of unity (all this is I), perfection, Infinite Consciousness, I am this.

ॐ ऐं ह्रीं क्लीं चामुण्डायै विच्चे सर्वेन्द्रियाणि

**oṃ aiṃ hrīṃ klīṃ cāmuṇḍāyai vicce sarvendriyāṇi**

Oṃ aiṃ hrīṃ klīṃ cāmuṇḍāyai vicce. You are all these organs (of action and knowledge).

ॐ अं आं ह्रीं क्रों यं रं लं वं शं षं सं हों हं सः

**oṃ aṃ āṃ hrīṃ kroṃ yaṃ raṃ laṃ vaṃ śaṃ ṣaṃ saṃ hoṃ haṃ saḥ**

Oṃ The Infinite Beyond Conception, Creation (the first letter), Consciousness, Māyā, the cause of the movement of the subtle body to perfection and beyond; the path of fulfillment: control, subtle illumination, one with the earth, emancipation, the soul of peace, the soul of delight, the soul of unity (all this is I), perfection, Infinite Consciousness, I am this.

ॐ ऐं ह्रीं क्लीं चामुण्डायै विच्चे वाग् मनस्त्वक्चक्षुः-श्रोत्र-घ्राण-प्राणा इहागत्य सुखं चिरं तिष्ठन्तु स्वाहा

**oṃ aiṃ hrīṃ klīṃ cāmuṇḍāyai vicce vāg manastvakcakṣuḥ śrotra ghrāṇa prāṇā ihāgatya sukhaṃ ciraṃ tiṣṭhantu svāhā**

Oṃ aiṃ hrīṃ klīṃ cāmuṇḍāyai vicce. You are all these vibrations, mind, sound, eyes, ears, tongue, nose and life force. Bring forth infinite peace and establish it forever, I am One with God!

## kara nyāsa

establishment in the hands

ॐ ह्रां अंगुष्ठाभ्यां नमः

**oṃ hrāṃ aṇguṣṭhābhyāṃ namaḥ** *thumb forefinger*

Oṃ hrāṃ in the thumb, I bow.

ॐ ह्रीं तर्जनीभ्यां स्वाहा

**oṃ hrīṃ tarjanībhyāṃ svāhā** *thumb forefinger*

Oṃ hrīṃ in the forefinger, I am One with God!

ॐ ह्रूं मध्यमाभ्यां वषट्

**oṃ hrūṃ madhyamābhyāṃ vaṣaṭ** *thumb middle finger*
Oṃ hrūṃ in the middle finger, Purify!

ॐ ह्रैं अनामिकाभ्यां हुं

**oṃ hraiṃ anāmikābhyāṃ huṃ** *thumb ring finger*
Oṃ hraiṃ in the ring finger, Cut the Ego!

ॐ ह्रौं कनिष्ठिकाभ्यां वौषट्

**oṃ hrauṃ kaniṣṭhikābhyāṃ vauṣaṭ** *thumb little finger*
Oṃ hrauṃ in the little finger, Ultimate Purity!

Roll hand over hand forwards while reciting *karatal kar*,
and backwards while chanting *pṛṣṭhābhyāṃ*,
then clap hands when chanting *astrāya phaṭ.*

ॐ ह्रः करतल कर पृष्ठाभ्यां अस्त्राय फट् ॥

**oṃ hraḥ karatal kar pṛṣṭhābhyāṃ astrāya phaṭ**
Oṃ hraḥ I bow to the Goddesses with the weapon of Virtue.

ॐ ऐं ह्रीं क्लीं चामुण्डायै विच्चे

**oṃ aiṃ hrīṃ klīṃ cāmuṇḍāyai vicce**
Oṃ aiṃ hrīṃ klīṃ cāmuṇḍāyai vicce.

**aṅga nyāsa**

establishment in the body

*Holding tattva mudrā, touch heart.*

ॐ ह्रां हृदयाय नमः

**oṃ hrāṃ hṛdayāya namaḥ** *touch heart*
Oṃ hrāṃ in the heart, I bow.

*Holding tattva mudrā, touch top of head.*

ॐ ह्रीं शिरसे स्वाहा

**oṃ hrīṃ śirase svāhā** *top of head*

Oṃ hrīṃ on the top of the head, I am One with God!

*With thumb extended, touch back of head.*

ॐ ह्रूं शिखायै वषट्

**oṃ hrūṃ śikhāyai vaṣaṭ** *back of head*

Oṃ hrūṃ on the back of the head, Purify!

*Holding tattva mudrā, cross both arms.*

ॐ ह्रैं कवचाय हुं

**oṃ hraiṃ kavacāya huṃ** *cross both arms*

Oṃ hraiṃ crossing both arms, Cut the Ego!

*Holding tattva mudrā, touch two eyes and in between at once with three middle fingers.*

ॐ ह्रौं नेत्रत्रयाय वौषट्

**oṃ hrauṃ netratrayāya vauṣaṭ** *touch three eyes*

Oṃ hrauṃ in the three eyes, Ultimate Purity!

Roll hand over hand forwards while reciting *karatal kar*,
and backwards while chanting *pṛṣṭhābhyāṃ*,
then clap hands when chanting *astrāya phaṭ*.

ॐ ह्रः करतल कर पृष्ठाभ्यां अस्त्राय फट् ॥

**oṃ hraḥ karatal kar pṛṣṭhābhyāṃ astrāya phaṭ**

Oṃ hraḥ I bow to the Goddesses with the weapon of Virtue.

ॐ ऐं ह्रीं क्लीं चामुण्डायै विच्चे

**oṃ aiṃ hrīṃ klīṃ cāmuṇḍāyai vicce**

Oṃ aiṃ hrīṃ klīṃ cāmuṇḍāyai vicce.

*108 times japa*

**stapana**

establishment upon the yantra

ॐ अम्बे ऽअम्बिकेऽम्बालिके न मा नयति कश्चन ।
ससस्त्यश्वकः सुभद्रिकां कापीलोवासिनीम् ॥

**oṃ ambe -ambike-mbālike na mā nayati kaścana**
**sasastyaśvakaḥ subhadrikāṃ kāpīlovāsinīm**

Mother of the Perceivable Universe, Mother of the Conceivable Universe, Mother of the Universe of Intuitive Vision, lead me to that True Existence. As excellent crops (or grains) are harvested, so may I be taken to reside with the Infinite Consciousness.

ॐ जयन्ती मङ्गला काली भद्रकाली कपालिनी ।
दुर्गा क्षमा शिवा धात्री स्वाहा स्वधा नमोऽस्तु ते ॥

**oṃ jayantī maṅgalā kālī bhadra kālī kapālinī**
**durgā kṣamā śivā dhātrī svāhā svadhā namo-stu te**

Oṃ. She Who Conquers Over All, All-Auspicious, She Who is Beyond Time, the Excellent One Beyond Time, the Bearer of the Skulls of Impure Thought, the Reliever of Difficulties, Loving Forgiveness, Supporter of the Universe, Oblations of I am One with God, Oblations of Ancestral Praise, to You, we bow.

दुर्गां शिवां शान्तिकरीं ब्रह्माणीं ब्रह्मणः प्रियाम् ।
सर्वलोक प्रणेत्रीञ्च प्रणमामि सदा शिवाम् ॥

**durgāṃ śivāṃ śāntikarīṃ brahmāṇīṃ brahmaṇaḥ priyām**
**sarvaloka praṇetrīñca praṇamāmi sadā śivām**

The Reliever of Difficulties, Exposer of Goodness, Cause of Peace, Infinite Consciousness, Beloved by Knowers of Consciousness; all the inhabitants of all the worlds always bow to Her, and I am bowing to Goodness Herself.

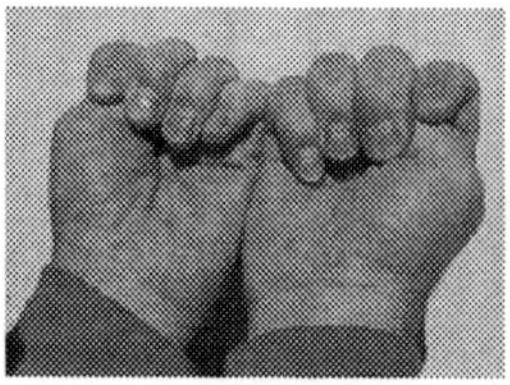

***āvāhaṇi mudrā***

*(I invite you, please come.)*

ॐ ह्रीं चण्डिके इहागच्छ

**oṃ hrīṃ caṇḍike ihāgaccha**

Oṃ Māyā, Energy which Tears Apart Thought, I invite you, please come.

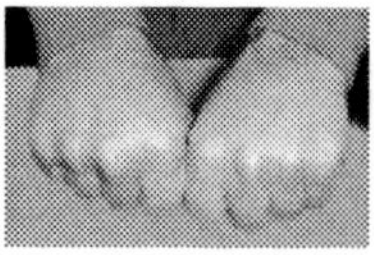

***sthāpanī mudrā***

*(I establish you within.)*

इह तिष्ठ

**iha tiṣṭha**

I establish you within.

***sannidhāpanī mudrā*** *(Mother, I know you have many devotees who are requesting your attention, but I request that you pay special attention to me.)*

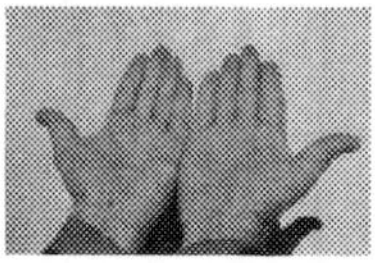

इह सनिहित भव

**iha sanihita bhava**

You bestow abundant wealth.

**saṃrodhanī mudrā**

*(I am sorry for any inconvenience.)*

अत्राधिष्ठानं कुरु

**atrādhiṣṭhānaṃ kuru**

I am depending upon you to forgive me in this matter.

**prakṣan**

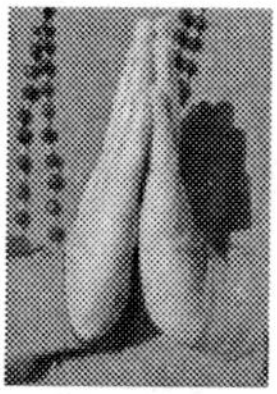

*(I bow to you with devotion.)*

देवि मम पूजां गृहाण

देवि भक्तशूलवे परित्राण करायिते ।

जावोट् त्वं पूजैषामि तावोट् त्वं सुस्थिरा भव ॥

**devi mama pūjāṃ gṛhāṇa**
**devi bhaktaśūlave paritrāṇa karāyite**
**jāvoṭ tvaṃ pūjaiṣāmi tāvoṭ tvaṃ susthirā bhava**

Oh Goddess, please accept my worship. Oh Goddess, remove all pain from your devotees. For so long as I worship you, please remain sitting still.

**pūjā naivedya**

offerings of worship

invitation

आगच्छेह महादेवि सर्वसम्पत्प्रदायिनि ।

यावद् व्रतं समाप्येत तावत्त्वं सन्निधौ भव ॥

ॐ ऐं ह्रीं क्लीं चामुण्डायै विच्चे आवाहनं समर्पयामि

**āgaccheha mahādevi sarvasampatpradāyini**
**yāvad vratam samāpyeta tāvattvam sannidhau bhava**
**om aim hrīm klīm cāmuṇḍāyai vicce āvāhanam samarpayāmi**

Please come here, oh Great Goddess, Giver of All Wealth! Please remain sitting still until this vow of worship is complete. With this offering of an invitation oṃ aiṃ hrīṃ klīṃ cāmuṇḍāyai vicce.

seat

अनेकरत्नसंयुक्तं नानामणिगणान्वितम् ।

कार्तस्वरमयं दिव्यमासनं प्रतिगृह्यताम् ॥

ॐ ऐं ह्रीं क्लीं चामुण्डायै विच्चे आसनं समर्पयामि

**anekaratna saṃyuktaṃ nānāmaṇi gaṇānvitam**
**kārtasvaramayaṃ divyamāsanaṃ pratigṛhyatām**
**oṃ aiṃ hrīṃ klīṃ cāmuṇḍāyai vicce āsanaṃ samarpayāmi**

United with many gems and a multitude of various jewels, voluntarily accept my offering of a divine seat. With this offering of a seat oṃ aiṃ hrīṃ klīṃ cāmuṇḍāyai vicce.

foot bath

ॐ गङ्गादिसर्वतीर्थेभ्यो मया प्रार्थनयाहृतम् ।

तोयमेतत् सुखस्पर्शं पाद्यार्थं प्रतिगृह्यताम् ॥

ॐ ऐं ह्रीं क्लीं चामुण्डायै विच्चे पाद्यं समर्पयामि

**oṃ gaṅgādi sarva tīrthebhyo mayā prārthanayāhṛtam**
**toyametat sukha sparśaṃ pādyārthaṃ pratigṛhyatām**
**oṃ aiṃ hrīṃ klīṃ cāmuṇḍāyai vicce pādyaṃ samarpayāmi**

Oṃ The Gaṅges and other waters from all the places of pilgrimage are mingled together in this our prayer. Please accept the comfortable touch of these waters offered to wash your lotus feet. With this offering of foot bath waters oṃ aiṃ hrīṃ klīṃ cāmuṇḍāyai vicce.

water for washing hands and mouth

कर्पूरेण सुगन्धेन सुरभिस्वादु शीतलम् ।

तोयमाचमनीयार्थं देवीदं प्रतिगृह्यताम् ॥

ॐ ऐं ह्रीं क्लीं चामुण्डायै विच्चे आचमनीयं समर्पयामि

**karpūreṇa sugandhena surabhisvādu śītalam**
**toyamācamanīyārthaṃ devīdaṃ pratigṛhyatām**
**oṃ aiṃ hrīṃ klīṃ cāmuṇḍāyai vicce ācamanīyaṃ samarpayāmi**

With camphor and excellent scent, cool with excellent taste, this water is being offered for washing. Oh Goddess, please accept it. With this offering of washing waters oṃ aiṃ hrīṃ klīṃ cāmuṇḍāyai vicce.

arghya

निधीनां सर्वदेवानां त्वमनर्घ्यगुणा ह्यसि ।

सिंहोपरिस्थिते देवि ! गृहाणार्घ्यं नमोऽस्तु ते ॥

ॐ ऐं ह्रीं क्लीं चामुण्डायै विच्चे अर्घ्यं समर्पयामि

**nidhīnāṃ sarvadevānāṃ tvamanarghyaguṇā hyasi**
**siṃhoparisthite devi gṛhāṇārghyaṃ namo-stu te**
**oṃ aiṃ hrīṃ klīṃ cāmuṇḍāyai vicce arghyaṃ samarpayāmi**

Presented to all the Gods, you, oh Arghya, bring an abundance of pleasure. Oh Goddess who is seated upon the lion, accept this arghya. I bow to you. With this offering of arghya oṃ aiṃ hrīṃ klīṃ cāmuṇḍāyai vicce.

madhuparka

दधिमधुघृतसमायुक्तं पात्रयुग्मं समन्वितम् ।

मधुपर्कं गृहाण त्वं शुभदा भव शोभने ॥

ॐ ऐं ह्रीं क्लीं चामुण्डायै विच्चे मधुपर्कं समर्पयामि

**dadhi madhu ghṛtasamāyuktaṃ**
**pātrayugmaṃ samanvitam**
**madhuparkaṃ gṛhāṇa tvaṃ śubhadā bhava śobhane**
**oṃ aiṃ hrīṃ klīṃ cāmuṇḍāyai vicce madhuparkaṃ samarpayāmi**

Yogurt, honey, ghee mixed together, and blended fine in a vessel; please accept this madhuparka, shining with radiant purity. With this offering of madhuparka oṃ aiṃ hrīṃ klīṃ cāmuṇḍāyai vicce.

milk bath

ॐ कामधेनुसमुद्भूतं सर्वेषां जीवनं परम् ।

पावनं यज्ञहेतुश्च स्नानार्थं प्रतिगृह्यताम् ॥

ॐ ऐं ह्रीं क्लीं चामुण्डायै विच्चे पयस्नानं समर्पयामि

**oṃ kāmadhenu samudbhūtaṃ**
**sarveṣāṃ jīvanaṃ param**
**pāvanaṃ yajña hetuśca snānārthaṃ pratigṛhyatām**
**oṃ aiṃ hrīṃ klīṃ cāmuṇḍāyai vicce paya snānaṃ samarpayāmi**

Oṃ Coming from the ocean of being, the Fulfiller of all Desires, Grantor of Supreme Bliss to all souls. For the motive of purifying or sanctifying this holy union, we request you to accept this bath. With this offering of milk for your bath oṃ aiṃ hrīṃ klīṃ cāmuṇḍāyai vicce.

yogurt bath

ॐ पयसस्तु समुद्भूतं मधुराम्लं शशिप्रभम् ।

दध्यानितं मया दत्तं स्नानार्थं प्रतिगृह्यताम् ॥

ॐ ऐं ह्रीं क्लीं चामुण्डायै विच्चे दधिस्नानं समर्पयामि

**oṃ payasastu samudbhūtaṃ**
**madhurāmlaṃ śaśiprabham**
**dadhyānitaṃ mayā dattaṃ**
**snānārthaṃ pratigṛhyatām**
**oṃ aiṃ hrīṃ klīṃ cāmuṇḍāyai vicce dadhi snānaṃ samarpayāmi**

Oṃ Derived from milk from the ocean of being, sweet and pleasing like the glow of the moon, let these curds eternally be our ambassador, as we request you to accept this bath. With this offering of yogurt for your bath oṃ aiṃ hrīṃ klīṃ cāmuṇḍāyai vicce.

ghee bath

ॐ नवनीतसमुत्पन्नं सर्वसन्तोषकारकम् ।

घृतं तुभ्यं प्रदास्यामि स्नानार्थं प्रतिगृह्यताम् ॥

ॐ ऐं ह्रीं क्लीं चामुण्डायै विच्चे घृतस्नानं समर्पयामि

**oṃ navanīta samutpannaṃ sarvasantoṣakārakam**
**ghṛtaṃ tubhyaṃ pradāsyāmi**
**snānārthaṃ pratigṛhyatām**
**oṃ aiṃ hrīṃ klīṃ cāmuṇḍāyai vicce ghṛta snānaṃ samarpayāmi**

Oṃ Freshly prepared from the ocean of being, causing all fulfillment, we offer this delightful ghee (clarified butter) and request you to accept this bath. With this offering of ghee for your bath oṃ aiṃ hrīṃ klīṃ cāmuṇḍāyai vicce.

honey bath

ॐ तरुपुष्पसमुद्भूतं सुस्वादु मधुरं मधु ।

तेजोपुष्टिकरं दिव्यं स्नानार्थं प्रतिगृह्यताम् ॥

ॐ ऐं ह्रीं क्लीं चामुण्डायै विच्चे मधुस्नानं समर्पयामि

**oṃ tarupuṣpa samudbhūtam**
**susvādu madhuraṃ madhu**
**tejo puṣṭikaraṃ divyaṃ snānārtham pratigṛhyatām**
**oṃ aiṃ hrīṃ klīṃ cāmuṇḍāyai vicce madhu snānaṃ samarpayāmi**

Oṃ Prepared from flowers of the ocean of being, enjoyable as the sweetest of the sweet, causing the fire of divine nourishment to burn swiftly, we request you to accept this bath. With this offering of honey for your bath oṃ aiṃ hrīṃ klīṃ cāmuṇḍāyai vicce.

sugar bath

ॐ इक्षुसारसमुद्भूता शर्करा पुष्टिकारिका ।
मलापहारिका दिव्या स्नानार्थं प्रतिगृह्यताम् ॥
ॐ ऐं ह्रीं क्लीं चामुण्डायै विच्चे शर्करास्नानं समर्पयामि

**oṃ ikṣusāra samudbhūtā śarkarā puṣṭikārikā**
**malāpahārikā divyā snānārthaṃ pratigṛhyatām**
**oṃ aiṃ hrīṃ klīṃ cāmuṇḍāyai vicce śarkarā snānaṃ samarpayāmi**

Oṃ From the lake of sugar-cane, from the ocean of being, which causes the nourishment of sugar to give divine protection from all impurity, we request you to accept this bath. With this offering of sugar for your bath oṃ aiṃ hrīṃ klīṃ cāmuṇḍāyai vicce.

five nectars bath

ॐ पयो दधि घृतं चैव मधु च शर्करायुतम् ।
पञ्चामृतं मयाऽऽनीतं स्नानार्थं प्रतिगृह्यताम् ॥
ॐ ऐं ह्रीं क्लीं चामुण्डायै विच्चे पञ्चामृतस्नानं समर्पयामि

**oṃ payo dadhi ghṛtaṃ caiva**
**madhu ca śarkarāyutam**
**pañcāmṛtaṃ mayā--nītaṃ**
**snānārthaṃ pratigṛhyatām**
**oṃ aiṃ hrīṃ klīṃ cāmuṇḍāyai vicce pañcāmṛta snānaṃ samarpayāmi**

Oṃ Milk, curd, ghee and then honey and sugar mixed together; these five nectars are our ambassador, as we request you to accept this bath. With this offering of five nectars for your bath oṃ aiṃ hrīṃ klīṃ cāmuṇḍāyai vicce.

scented oil

ॐ नानासुगन्धिद्रव्यं च चन्दनं रजनीयुतम् ।
उद्वर्तनं मया दत्तं स्नानार्थं प्रतिगृह्यताम् ॥
ॐ ऐं ह्रीं क्लीं चामुण्डायै विच्चे उद्वर्तनस्नानं समर्पयामि

**oṃ nānāsugandhidravyaṃ ca**
**candanaṃ rajanīyutam**
**udvartanaṃ mayā dattaṃ**
**snānārthaṃ pratigṛhyatām**
**oṃ aiṃ hrīṃ klīṃ cāmuṇḍāyai vicce udvartana snānaṃ samarpayāmi**

Oṃ With various beautifully smelling ingredients, as well as the scent of sandal, we offer you this scented oil, Oh Goddess. With this offering of scented oil oṃ aiṃ hrīṃ klīṃ cāmuṇḍāyai vicce.

scent bath

गन्धद्वरां दुराधर्षां नित्यपुष्टां करीषिणीम् ।
ईश्वरीं सर्वभूतानां तामिहोपह्वये श्रियम् ॥
ॐ ऐं ह्रीं क्लीं चामुण्डायै विच्चे गन्धस्नानं समर्पयामि

**gandhadvārāṃ durādharṣāṃ nityapuṣṭāṃ karīṣiṇīm**
**īśvarīṃ sarvabhūtānāṃ tāmihopahvaye śriyam**
**oṃ aiṃ hrīṃ klīṃ cāmuṇḍāyai vicce gandha snānaṃ samarpayāmi**

She is the cause of the scent which is the door to religious ecstasy, unconquerable (never-failing), continually nurturing for all time. May we never tire from calling that manifestation of the Highest Respect, the Supreme Goddess of all existence. With this offering of scented bath oṃ aiṃ hrīṃ klīṃ cāmuṇḍāyai vicce.

water bath

ॐ गङ्गे च जमुने चैव गोदावरि सरस्वति ।

नर्मदे सिन्धुकावेरि स्नानार्थं प्रतिगृह्यताम् ॥

ॐ ऐं ह्रीं क्लीं चामुण्डायै विच्चे गङ्गास्नानं समर्पयामि

**oṃ gaṅge ca jamune caiva godāvari sarasvati**
**narmade sindhu kāveri snānārthaṃ pratigṛhyatām**
**oṃ aiṃ hrīṃ klīṃ cāmuṇḍāyai vicce gaṅgā snānaṃ samarpayāmi**

Oṃ Please accept the waters from the Gaṅges, Jamunā, Godāvarī, Sarasvatī, Narmadā, Sindhu and Kāverī, which have been provided for your bath. With this offering of Ganges bath waters oṃ aiṃ hrīṃ klīṃ cāmuṇḍāyai vicce.

cloth

ॐ शीतवातोष्णसंत्राणं लज्जायै रक्षणं परं ।

देहालंकरणं वस्त्रं अथ शान्तिं प्रयच्छ मे ॥

ॐ ऐं ह्रीं क्लीं चामुण्डायै विच्चे वस्त्रं समर्पयामि

**oṃ śīta vātoṣṇa saṃ trāṇaṃ**
**lajjāyai rakṣaṇaṃ paraṃ**
**dehālaṅkaraṇaṃ vastraṃ**
**atha śāntiṃ prayaccha me**
**oṃ aiṃ hrīṃ klīṃ cāmuṇḍāyai vicce vastraṃ samarpayāmi**

To take away the cold and the wind and to fully protect your modesty, we adorn your body with this cloth, and thereby find the greatest Peace. With this offering of wearing apparel oṃ aiṃ hrīṃ klīṃ cāmuṇḍāyai vicce.

sacred thread

ॐ यज्ञोपवीतं परमं पवित्रं प्रजापतेर्यत् सहजं पुरस्तात् ।
आयुष्यमग्रं प्रतिमुञ्च शुभ्रं यज्ञोपवीतं बलमस्तु तेजः ॥

**oṃ yajñopavītaṃ paramaṃ pavitraṃ**
**prajāpateryat sahajaṃ purastāt**
**āyuṣyamagraṃ pratimuñca śubhraṃ**
**yajñopavītaṃ balamastu tejaḥ**

Oṃ the sacred thread of the highest purity is given by Prajāpati, the Lord of Creation, for the greatest facility. You bring life and illuminate the greatness of liberation. Oh sacred thread, let your strength be of radiant light.

शमो दमस्तपः शौचं क्षान्तिरार्जवमेव च ।
ज्ञानं विज्ञानमास्तिक्यं ब्रह्मकर्म स्वभावजम् ॥

**śamo damastapaḥ śaucaṃ kṣāntirārjavameva ca**
**jñānaṃ vijñānamāstikyaṃ**
**brahmakarma svabhāvajam**

Peacefulness, self-control, austerity, purity of mind and body, patience and forgiveness, sincerity and honesty, wisdom, knowledge, and self-realization, are the natural activities of a Brahmaṇa.

नवभिस्तन्तुभिर्युक्तं त्रिगुणं देवतामयं ।
उपवीतं मया दत्तं गृहाण त्वं सुरेश्वरि ॥

ॐ ऐं ह्रीं क्लीं चामुण्डायै विच्चे यज्ञोपवीतं समर्पयामि

**navamiṣṭantubhiryuktaṃ triguṇaṃ devatā mayaṃ**
**upavītaṃ mayā dattaṃ gṛhāṇa tvaṃ sureśvari**
**oṃ aiṃ hrīṃ klīṃ cāmuṇḍāyai vicce yajñopavītaṃ samarpayāmi**

With nine desirable threads all united together, exemplifying the three guṇas (or three qualities of harmony of our deity), this sacred thread will be our ambassador. Oh Ruler of the Gods, please accept. With this offering of a sacred thread oṃ aiṃ hrīṃ klīṃ cāmuṇḍāyai vicce.

rudrākṣa

त्र्यम्बकं यजामहे सुगन्धिं पुष्टिवर्द्धनम् ।

उर्व्वारुकमिव बन्धनान्मृत्योर्म्मुक्षीयमामृतात् ॥

ॐ ऐं ह्रीं क्लीं चामुण्डायै विच्चे रुद्राक्षं समर्पयामि

**tryambakaṃ yajāmahe**
**sugandhiṃ puṣṭivarddhanam**
**urvvārukamiva bandhanānmṛtyormmukṣīyamāmṛtāt**
**oṃ aiṃ hrīṃ klīṃ cāmuṇḍāyai vicce rudrākṣaṃ samarpayāmi**

We worship the Father of the three worlds, of excellent fame, Grantor of Increase. As a cucumber is released from its bondage to the stem, so may we be freed from Death to dwell in immortality. With this offering of rudrākṣa oṃ aiṃ hrīṃ klīṃ cāmuṇḍāyai vicce.

red powder

ॐ सिन्दूरमरुणाभासं जपाकुसुमसन्निभम् ।

पूजिताऽसि मया देवि प्रसीद परमेश्वरिः ॥

ॐ ऐं ह्रीं क्लीं चामुण्डायै विच्चे सिन्दूरं समर्पयामि

**oṃ sindūramaruṇābhāsaṃ japākusumasannibham**
**pūjitā-si mayā devi prasīda parameśvariḥ**
**oṃ aiṃ hrīṃ klīṃ cāmuṇḍāyai vicce sindūraṃ samarpayāmi**

Oṃ This red colored powder indicates Love, who drives the chariot of the Light of Wisdom, with which we are worshipping our Goddess. Please be pleased, Oh Great Seer of All. With this offering of red colored powder oṃ aiṃ hrīṃ klīṃ cāmuṇḍāyai vicce.

kuṅkum

ॐ कुङ्कुमं कान्तिदं दिव्यं कामिनी कामसम्भवम् ।

कुङ्कुमेनाऽर्चिते देवि प्रसीद परमेश्वरिः ॥

ॐ ऐं ह्रीं क्लीं चामुण्डायै विच्चे कुङ्कुमं समर्पयामि

**oṃ kuṅkumaṃ kāntidaṃ divyaṃ**
**kāminī kāmasambhavam**
**kuṅkumenā-rcite devi prasīda parameśvariḥ**
**oṃ aiṃ hrīṃ klīṃ cāmuṇḍāyai vicce kuṅkumaṃ samarpayāmi**

You are being adorned with this divine red powder, which is made more beautiful by the love we share with you, and is so pleasing. Oh Goddess, when we present this red powder be pleased, Oh Supreme Ruler of All. With this offering of red colored powder oṃ aiṃ hrīṃ klīṃ cāmuṇḍāyai vicce.

sandal paste

ॐ श्रीखण्डचन्दनं दिव्यं गन्धाढ्यं सुमनोहरम् ।

विलेपनं च देवेशि चन्दनं प्रतिगृह्यताम् ॥

ॐ ऐं ह्रीं क्लीं चामुण्डायै विच्चे चन्दनं समर्पयामि

**oṃ śrī khaṇḍacandanaṃ divyaṃ**
**gandhāḍyaṃ sumano haram**
**vilepanaṃ ca deveśi candanaṃ pratigṛhyatām**
**oṃ aiṃ hrīṃ klīṃ cāmuṇḍāyai vicce candanaṃ samarpayāmi**

You are being adorned with this beautiful divine piece of sandal wood, ground to a paste which is so pleasing. Please accept this offering of sandal paste, Oh Supreme Sovereign of all the Gods. With this offering of sandal paste oṃ aiṃ hrīṃ klīṃ cāmuṇḍāyai vicce.

tumeric

ॐ हरिद्रारञ्जिता देवि सुख-सौभाग्यदायिनि ।

तस्मात्त्वं पूजयाम्यत्र दुःख शान्तिं प्रयच्छमे ॥

ॐ ऐं ह्रीं क्लीं चामुण्डायै विच्चे हरिद्रां समर्पयामि

**oṃ haridrārañjitā devi sukha saubhāgyadāyini**
**tasmāttvaṃ pūjayāmyatra duḥkha śāntiṃ prayacchame ||**
**oṃ aiṃ hrīṃ klīṃ cāmuṇḍāyai vicce haridrāṃ samarpayāmi**

Oh Goddess, you are being gratified by this tumeric, the giver of comfort and beauty. When you are worshipped like this, then you must bestow upon us the greatest peace. With this offering of tumeric oṃ aiṃ hrīṃ klīṃ cāmuṇḍāyai vicce.

bracelets

ॐ माणिक्यमुक्ताखण्डयुक्ते सुवर्णकारेण च संस्कृते ये ।
ते किङ्किणीभिः स्वरिते सुवर्णे
मयाऽर्पिते देवि गृहाण कङ्कणे ॥
ॐ ऐं ह्रीं क्लीं चामुण्डायै विच्चे कङ्कणे समर्पयामि

**oṃ māṇikya muktā khaṇḍayukte**
**suvarṇakāreṇa ca saṃskṛte ye**
**te kiṅkiṇībhiḥ svarite suvarṇe**
**mayā-rpite devi gṛhāṇa kaṅkaṇe**
**oṃ aiṃ hrīṃ klīṃ cāmuṇḍāyai vicce kaṅkaṇe samarpayāmi**

Oṃ United with gems and pearls, excellent gold and the alphabets of Saṃskṛta, this bracelet is yours and radiance I am offering. Oh Goddess, accept this bracelet. With this offering of a bracelet oṃ aiṃ hrīṃ klīṃ cāmuṇḍāyai vicce.

conch ornaments

ॐ शङ्खञ्च विविधं चित्रं बाहूनाञ्च विभूषणम् ।
मया निवेदितं भक्त्या गृहाण परमेश्वरि ॥
ॐ ऐं ह्रीं क्लीं चामुण्डायै विच्चे शङ्खालङ्कारं समर्पयामि

**oṃ śaṅkhañca vividhaṃ citraṃ**
**bāhūnāñca vibhūṣaṇam**
**mayā niveditaṃ bhaktyā gṛhāṇa parameśvari**
**oṃ aiṃ hrīṃ klīṃ cāmuṇḍāyai vicce**
**śaṅkhālaṅkāraṃ samarpayāmi**

I am offering you with devotion ornaments worn upon the arms made of various qualities of conch shell. Please accept them, oh Supreme Divinity. With this offering of ornaments made of conch shell oṃ aiṃ hrīṃ klīṃ cāmuṇḍāyai vicce.

ornaments

ॐ दिव्यरत्नसमायुक्ता वह्निभानुसमप्रभाः ।

गात्राणि शोभयिष्यन्ति अलङ्काराः सुरेश्वरि ॥

ॐ ऐं ह्रीं क्लीं चामुण्डायै विच्चे अलङ्कारान् समर्पयामि

**oṃ divyaratnasamāyuktā vahnibhānusamaprabhāḥ**
**gātrāṇi śobhayiṣyanti alaṅkārāḥ sureśvari**
**oṃ aiṃ hrīṃ klīṃ cāmuṇḍāyai vicce alaṅkārān samarpayāmi**

Oṃ United with divine jewels that are radiant like fire, and stones which are shining, please accept these ornaments, oh Supreme among the Gods. With this offering of ornaments oṃ aiṃ hrīṃ klīṃ cāmuṇḍāyai vicce.

rice

अक्षतान् निर्मलान् शुद्धान् मुक्ताफलसमन्वितान् ।

गृहाणेमान् महादेवि देहि मे निर्मलां धियम् ॥

ॐ ऐं ह्रीं क्लीं चामुण्डायै विच्चे अक्षतान् समर्पयामि

**akṣatān nirmalān śuddhān muktāphalasamanvitān**
**gṛhāṇemān mahādevi dehi me nirmalāṃ dhiyam**
**oṃ aiṃ hrīṃ klīṃ cāmuṇḍāyai vicce akṣatān samarpayāmi**

Oh Great Goddess, please accept these grains of rice, spotlessly clean, bestowing the fruit of liberation, and give us a spotlessly clean mind. With this offering of grains of rice oṃ aiṃ hrīṃ klīṃ cāmuṇḍāyai vicce.

food offering

ॐ सत्पात्रं शुद्धसुहविर्व्विविधानेकभक्षणम् ।
निवेदयामि देवेशि सर्वतृप्तिकरं परम् ॥

**oṃ satpātraṃ śuddhasuhavirv vividhānekabhakṣaṇam**
**nivedayāmi deveśi sarvatṛptikaraṃ param**

Oṃ This ever-present platter containing varieties of the purest offerings of food we are presenting to the Lord of Gods to cause all satisfaction, most excellent and transcendental.

ॐ अन्नपूर्णे सदा पूर्णे शङ्करप्राणवल्लभे ।
ज्ञानवैराग्यसिद्ध्यर्थं भिक्षां देहि नमोऽस्तु ते ॥

**oṃ annapūrṇe sadā pūrṇe śaṅkara prāṇavallabhe**
**jñānavairāgyasiddhyarthaṃ**
**bhikṣāṃ dehi namo-stu te**

Oṃ Goddess who is full, complete and perfect with food and grains, always full, complete and perfect, the strength of the life force of Śiva, the Cause of Peace. For the attainment of perfection in wisdom and renunciation, please give us offerings. We bow down to you.

माता च पार्वती देवी पिता देवो महेश्वरः ।
बान्धवाः शिवभक्ताश्च स्वदेशो भुवनत्रयम् ॥

**mātā ca pārvatī devī pitā devo maheśvaraḥ**
**bāndhavāḥ śivabhaktāśca svadeśo bhuvanatrayam**

Our Mother is the Goddess, Pārvatī, and our Father is the Supreme Lord, Maheśvara. The Consciousness of Infinite Goodness, Śiva, Lord of the three worlds, is being extolled by his devotees.

ॐ ऐं ह्रीं क्लीं चामुण्डायै विच्चे भोगनैवेद्यम् समर्पयामि

**oṃ aiṃ hrīṃ klīṃ cāmuṇḍāyai vicce bhog-naivedyam samarpayāmi**

With this presentation of food oṃ aiṃ hrīṃ klīṃ cāmuṇḍāyai vicce.

drinking water

ॐ समस्तदेवदेवेशि सर्वतृप्तिकरं परम् ।

अखण्डानन्दसम्पूर्णं गृहाण जलमुत्तमम् ॥

ॐ ऐं ह्रीं क्लीं चामुण्डायै विच्चे पानार्थं जलम् समर्पयामि

**oṃ samasta devadeveśi sarvatṛptikaraṃ param**
**akhaṇḍānanda sampūrṇaṃ gṛhāṇa jalamuttamam**
**oṃ aiṃ hrīṃ klīṃ cāmuṇḍāyai vicce pānārthaṃ jalam samarpayāmi**

Oṃ Goddess of All the Gods and the fullness of Infinite Bliss, please accept this excellent drinking water. With this offering of drinking water oṃ aiṃ hrīṃ klīṃ cāmuṇḍāyai vicce.

betel nuts

पूगीफलं महद्दिव्यं नागवल्ली दलैर्युतम् ।

एलादिचूर्णसंयुक्तं ताम्बूलं प्रतिगृह्यताम् ॥

ॐ ऐं ह्रीं क्लीं चामुण्डायै विच्चे ताम्बूलं समर्पयामि

**pūgīphalaṃ mahaddivyaṃ nāgavallī dalairyutam**
**elādicūrṇasaṃyuktaṃ tāmbūlaṃ pratigṛhyatām**
**oṃ aiṃ hrīṃ klīṃ cāmuṇḍāyai vicce tāmbūlaṃ samarpayāmi**

These betel nuts, which are great and divine, come from vines that creep like a snake. United with cardamom ground to a powder, please accept this offering of mouth-freshening betel nuts. With this offering of mouth freshening betel nuts oṃ aiṃ hrīṃ klīṃ cāmuṇḍāyai vicce.

dakṣiṇā

ॐ पूजाफलसमृद्ध्यर्थं तवाग्रे स्वर्णमीश्वरि ।
स्थापितं तेन मे प्रीता पूर्णान् कुरु मनोरथान् ॥

**oṃ pūjāphalasmṛddhyarthaṃ tavāgre svarṇamīśvari sthāpitaṃ tena me prītā pūrṇān kuru manorathān**

Oṃ For the purpose of increasing the fruits of worship, Oh Supreme Goddess of all Wealth, we establish this offering of that which is dear to me. Bring to perfection the journey of my mind.

हिरण्यगर्भगर्भस्थं हेमबीजं विभावसोः ।
अनन्तपुण्यफलदमतः शान्तिं प्रयच्छ मे ॥

**hiraṅyagarbhagarbhasthaṃ hemabījaṃ vibhāvasoḥ anantapuṇyaphaladamataḥ śāntiṃ prayaccha me**

Oh Golden Womb, in whom all wombs are situated, shining brightly with the golden seed. Give infinite merits as fruits, we are wanting for peace.

ॐ ऐं ह्रीं क्लीं चामुण्डायै विच्चे दक्षिणां समर्पयामि

**oṃ aiṃ hrīṃ klīṃ cāmuṇḍāyai vicce dakṣiṇāṃ samarpayāmi**

Oṃ With this offering of wealth oṃ aiṃ hrīṃ klīṃ cāmuṇḍāyai vicce.

umbrella

छत्रं देवि जगद्धात्रि ! घर्मवातप्रणाशनम् ।

गृहाण हे महामाये ! सौभाग्यं सर्वदा कुरु ॥

ॐ ऐं ह्रीं क्लीं चामुण्डायै विच्चे छत्रं समर्पयामि

**chatraṃ devi jagaddhātri gharma vāta praṇāśanam**
**gṛhāṇa he mahāmāye saubhāgyaṃ sarvadā kuru**
**oṃ aiṃ hrīṃ klīṃ cāmuṇḍāyai vicce chatraṃ samarpayāmi**

Oh Goddess, Creator of the Universe! This umbrella will protect you from heat and wind. Please accept it, oh Great Māyā, and remain always beautiful. With this offering of an umbrella oṃ aiṃ hrīṃ klīṃ cāmuṇḍāyai vicce.

fly whisk

चामरं हे महादेवि चमरीपुच्छनिर्मितम् ।

गृहीत्वा पापराशीनां खण्डनं सर्वदा कुरु ॥

ॐ ऐं ह्रीं क्लीं चामुण्डायै विच्चे चामरं समर्पयामि

**cāmaraṃ he mahādevi camarīpucchanirmitam**
**gṛhītvā pāparāśīnāṃ khaṇḍanaṃ sarvadā kuru**
**oṃ aiṃ hrīṃ klīṃ cāmuṇḍāyai vicce cāmaraṃ samarpayāmi**

Oh Great Goddess, this fly whisk is made of yak's tail. Please accept it, and always whisk away all sin. With this offering of a fly whisk oṃ aiṃ hrīṃ klīṃ cāmuṇḍāyai vicce.

fan

बर्हिर्बर्हकृताकारं मध्यदण्डसमन्वितम् ।

गृह्यतां व्यजनं देवि देहस्वेदापनुत्तये ॥

ॐ ऐं ह्रीं क्लीं चामुण्डायै विच्चे तालवृन्तं समर्पयामि

**barhirbarhakṛtākāraṃ madhyadaṇḍa samanvitam**
**gṛhyatāṃ vyajanaṃ devi dehasvedāpanuttaye**
**oṃ aiṃ hrīṃ klīṃ cāmuṇḍāyai vicce tālavṛntaṃ samarpayāmi**

It moves back and forth with equanimity and has a stick in the middle. Please accept this fan, oh Goddess, to keep the perspiration from your body. With this offering of a fan oṃ aiṃ hrīṃ klīṃ cāmuṇḍāyai vicce.

mirror

दर्पणं विमलं रम्यं शुद्धबिम्बप्रदायकम् ।

आत्मबिम्बप्रदर्शनार्थर्पयामि महेश्वरि ! ॥

ॐ ऐं ह्रीं क्लीं चामुण्डायै विच्चे दर्पणं समर्पयामि

**darpaṇaṃ vimalaṃ ramyaṃ**
**śuddhabimbapradāyakam**
**ātmabimbapradarśanārtharpayāmi maheśvari**
**oṃ aiṃ hrīṃ klīṃ cāmuṇḍāyai vicce darpaṇaṃ samarpayāmi**

This beautiful mirror will give a pure reflection. In order to reflect my soul, I am offering it to you, oh Great Seer of all. With this offering of a mirror oṃ aiṃ hrīṃ klīṃ cāmuṇḍāyai vicce.

ārātrikam

ॐ चन्द्रादित्यौ च धरणी विद्युदग्निस्तथैव च ।

त्वमेव सर्वज्योतींषिं आरात्रिकं प्रतिगृह्यताम् ॥

ॐ ऐं ह्रीं क्लीं चामुण्डायै विच्चे आरात्रिकं समर्पयामि

**oṃ candrādityau ca dharaṇī vidyudagnistathaiva ca**
**tvameva sarvajyotīṣiṃ ārātrikaṃ pratigṛhyatām**
**oṃ aiṃ hrīṃ klīṃ cāmuṇḍāyai vicce ārātrikaṃ samarpayāmi**

Oṃ All knowing as the Moon, the Sun and the Divine Fire, you alone are all light, and this light we request you to accept. With this offering of light oṃ aiṃ hrīṃ klīṃ cāmuṇḍāyai vicce.

flower

मल्लिकादि सुगन्धीनि मालित्यादीनि वै प्रभो ।

मयाऽहृतानि पूजार्थं पुष्पाणि प्रतिगृह्यताम् ॥

ॐ ऐं ह्रीं क्लीं चामुण्डायै विच्चे पुष्पम् समर्पयामि

**mallikādi sugandhīni mālityādīni vai prabho**
**mayā-hṛtāni pūjārthaṃ puṣpāṇi pratigṛhyatām**
**oṃ aiṃ hrīṃ klīṃ cāmuṇḍāyai vicce puṣpam samarpayāmi**

Various flowers, such as mallikā and others of excellent scent, are being offered to you, Our Lord. All these flowers have come from the devotion of our hearts for your worship. Please accept them. With this offering of a flower oṃ aiṃ hrīṃ klīṃ cāmuṇḍāyai vicce.

यज्ञेन यज्ञमयजन्त देवास्तानि धर्म्माणि प्रथमान्यासन् ।

ते ह नाकं महिमानः सचन्त यत्र पूर्वे साध्याः सन्ति देवाः ॥

**yajñena yajñamayajanta devāstāni**
**dharmmāṇi prathamānyāsan**
**te ha nākaṃ mahimānaḥ sacanta yatra pūrve**
**sādhyāḥ santi devāḥ**

By sacrifice, the Gods gave birth to sacrifice, and the first principles of eternal Dharma were established. Those who live according to the glorious way, ultimately reach the highest abode where the Gods dwell in that ancient perfection.

ॐ राजाधिराजाय प्रसह्य साहिने नमो वयं वैश्रवणाय कुर्महे
स मे कामान् कामकामाय मह्यं कामेश्वरो वैश्रवणो ददातु ।
कुबेराय वैश्रवणाय महाराजाय नमः ॥

**oṃ rājādhirājāya prasahya sāhine namo vayaṃ vaiśravaṇāya kurmahe sa me kāmān kāmakāmāya mahyaṃ kāmeśvaro vaiśravaṇo dadātu kuberāya vaiśravaṇāya mahārājāya namaḥ**

Without any selfish interest we bow down to the universal being, the King of kings, the Lord of all desires, the Universal Being. May He grant to me the full and complete enjoyment of the desire of all desires: dharma (the ideal of perfection), artha (the material necessities of life), kāma (the perfection of desire) and mokṣa (self-realization).

ॐ स्वस्ति साम्राज्यं स्वाराज्यं वैराज्यं पारमेष्ठ्यं राज्यं
महाराज्यमाधिपत्यमयं समन्तपर्यायि स्यात् । सार्वभौमः
सार्वायुषां तदा परार्धात् पृथिव्यै समुद्रपर्यन्तायाऽएराडिति ।
तदप्येष श्लोकोऽभिगीतो मरुतः परिवेष्टारो मरुत्तस्या
ऽवसन् गृहे । आवीक्षितस्य कामप्रेर्विश्वेदेवाः सभासद इति ॥

**oṃ svasti sāmrājyaṃ svārājyaṃ vairājyaṃ pārameṣṭhyaṃ rājyaṃ mahārājyamādhipatyamayaṃ samantaparyāyai syāt sārvabhaumaḥ sārvāyuṣāṃ tadā parārdhāt pṛthivyai samudraparyantāyā-erāḍiti tadapyeṣa śloko-bhigīto marutaḥ pariveṣṭāro maruttasyā-vasan gṛhe āvīkṣitasya kāmaprerviśvedevāḥ sabhāsada iti**

Oṃ Let blessings flow to all of the kingdom, His own kingdom, the universal kingdom, the kingdom of the Supreme Divinity, the great kingdom of our Lord greater than the greatest, in the equilibrium of spiritual austerities. All that lives in the heavens or on the earth or in the seas is thus united. Those spiritual aspirants who sing these verses can aspire to dwell in the home of the purified. Having no unfulfilled desires, only desiring as the Universal Gods always.

ॐ विश्वतश्चक्षुरुत विश्वतो मुखो विश्वतो बाहुरुत
विश्वतस्पात् । सम्बाहुभ्यां धमति सम्पतत् त्रैर्द्यावा
भूमिं जनयन् देव एकः ॥

**oṃ viśvataścakṣuruta viśvato mukho viśvato bāhuruta viśvataspāt**
**sambāhubhyāṃ dhamati sampatat trairdyāvā bhūmiṃ janayan deva ekaḥ**

Oṃ He who sees the universe, the mouth of the universe, the arms of the universe, the feet of the universe. He is One God, whose two arms and two wings make possible all the activities of all that lives in the heavens and on earth.

## durgā pūjā

worship of durgā

### durgā gāyatrī

ॐ कात्यायनाय विद्महे कन्याकुमारी धीमहि ।

तन्नो दुर्गिः प्रचोदयात् ॐ ॥

**oṃ kātyāyanāya vidmahe kanyākumārī dhīmahi**
**tanno durgiḥ pracodayāt oṃ**

Oṃ We meditate on the Ever Pure One, we contemplate the Daughter Without Flaw or Imperfection. May that Goddess grant us increase.

एते गन्धपुष्पे ॐ ह्रीं श्रीं दुं दुर्गायै नमः

**ete gandhapuṣpe oṃ hrīṃ śrīṃ duṃ durgāyai namaḥ**

With these scented flowers oṃ I bow to the Goddess, Durgā, the Grantor of Increase, who Removes all Difficulties.

### dhyānam

meditation

ॐ जटाजूटसमायुक्तामर्द्धेन्दुकृतशेखराम् ।

लोचनत्रयसंयुक्तां पूर्णेन्दुसदृशाननाम् ॥

**oṃ jaṭājūṭasamāyuktāmarddhendukṛtaśekharām**
**locanatrayasaṃyuktāṃ pūrṇendusadṛśānanām**

Oṃ With loose-flowing tresses, poised with equanimity with the radiant half-moon upon her head, her three eyes are shining like the full moon.

तप्तकाञ्चनवर्णाभां सुप्रतिष्ठां सुलोचनाम् ।

नवयौवनसम्पन्नां सर्वाभरणभूषिताम् ॥

**taptakāñcanavarṇābhām supratiṣṭām sulocanām navayauvanasampannām sarvābharaṇabhūṣitām**

She is of the color of melted gold, of excellent birth and has beautiful eyes. She has nine manifestations, all resplendantly shining with ornaments.

सुचारुदशनां तद्वत् पीनोन्नतपयोधराम् ।
त्रिभङ्गस्थानसंस्थानां महिषासुरमर्दिनीम् ॥

**sucārudaśanām tadvat pīnonnatapayodharām tribhaṅgasthānasaṃsthānām mahiṣāsuramardinīm**

She holds aloft ten excellent weapons in her hands, and has three beautiful folds under her breasts - the Slayer of the Great Ego.

मृणालायतसंस्पर्श दशबाहु समन्विताम् ।
त्रिशूलं दक्षिणे ध्येयं खड्गं चक्रं क्रमादधः ॥

**mṛṇālāyatasaṃsparśa daśabāhu samanvitām triśūlaṃ dakṣiṇe dhyeyaṃ khaḍgaṃ cakraṃ kramādadhaḥ**

She bears the touch of death to the Ego in each of her ten arms. We meditate on the order of weapons, beginning at the upper right: trident, sword, discus,

तीक्ष्नवाणं तथा शक्तिं दक्षिणेषु विचिन्तयेत् ।
खेटकं पूर्णचापञ्च पाशमङ्कुशमेव च ॥

**tīkṣnavāṇaṃ tathā śaktiṃ dakṣiṇeṣu vicintayet kheṭakaṃ pūrṇacāpañca pāśamaṅkuśameva ca**

bow and arrow, and then energy we contemplate on her right side. The shield, club, noose, curved sword, and

घण्टां वा परशु वापि वामतः सन्निवेशयेत् ।

अधस्तान्महिषं तद्वद्विशिरस्कं प्रदर्शयेत् ॥

**ghaṇṭāṃ vā paraśu vāpi vāmataḥ sanniveśayet**
**adhastānmahiṣaṃ tadvadviśiraskaṃ pradarśayet**

the bell or battle axe we contemplate on her left side. Below lies the severed head of the Great Ego in the form of a buffalo.

शिरश्छेदोद्भवं तद्वद्दानवं खड्गपाणिनम् ।

हृदि शूलेन निर्भिन्नं निर्जदन्त्रविभूषितम् ॥

**śiraśchedodbhavaṃ tadvaddānavaṃ khaḍgapāṇinam**
**hṛdi śūlena nirbhinnaṃ nirjadantravibhūṣitam**

In place of the severed head, on his neck is the demonic image of the Great Ego with a sword in his hand. He is shown gritting his teeth from the spear that has pierced his heart.

रक्तारक्तीकृताङ्गञ्च रक्तविस्फूरितेक्षणम् ।

वेष्ठितं नागपाशेन भ्रूकुटीभीषणाननम् ॥

**raktāraktīkṛtāṅgañca raktavisphūritekṣaṇam**
**veṣṭhitaṃ nāgapāśena bhrūkuṭībhīṣaṇānanam**

Blood is flowing over his body and red is seen on all his limbs. The cobra snake in the form of a noose has wrapped itself around his brow and upper left arm.

सपाशवामहस्तेन धृतकेशन्तु दुर्गया ।

वमद्रुधिरवक्त्रञ्च देव्याः सिंहं प्रदर्शयेत् ॥

**sapāśavāmahastena dhṛtakeśantu durgayā**
**vamadrudhiravaktrañca devyāḥ siṃhaṃ pradarśayet**

On the side of the Goddess is shown the lion, Dharma, who is her conveyance and is facing the left.

देव्यास्तु दक्षिणं पादं समं सिंहोपरि स्थितम् ।
किञ्चिदूर्द्धं तथा वाममङ्गुष्ठं महिषोपरि ॥

**devyāstu dakṣiṇaṃ pādaṃ samaṃ siṃhopari sthitam**
**kiñcidūrddhaṃ tathā vāmamaṅguṣṭhaṃ mahiṣopari**

The Goddess's right foot is flatly positioned on top of the lion. Slightly elevated, only her left toe is on top of the Great Ego.

प्रसन्नवदनां देवीं सर्वकामफलप्रदां ।
स्तुयमानञ्च तद्रूपममरैः सन्निवेशयेत् ॥

**prasannavadanāṃ devīṃ sarvakāmaphalapradāṃ**
**stuyamānañca tadrūpamamaraiḥ sanniveśayet**

The Goddess is extremely pleased and grants the fruits of all desires to those who contemplate her excellent form and with one mind sing her praises:

ऊग्रचण्डा प्रचण्डा च चण्डोग्रा चण्डनायिका ।
चण्डा चण्डवती चैव चण्डरूपातिचण्डिका ॥

**ūgracaṇḍā pracaṇḍā ca caṇḍogrā caṇḍanāyikā**
**caṇḍā caṇḍavatī caiva caṇḍarūpāticaṇḍikā**

The Terrible Slayer of Passion, Whose Nature Removes Fear, She Who Slays Fear, She Who Sees Everywhere Freedom from Fear, She Who Tears Apart Fear, She Who Contains Fearlessness, The Form of the Erradicator of Fear and the Supreme She Who Tears Apart All Thoughts.

अष्टाभिः शक्तिभिस्ताभिः सततं परिवेष्ठिताम् ।

चिन्तयेज्ञगतां धात्रीं धर्म्मकामार्थमोक्षदाम् ॥

**aṣṭābhiḥ śaktibhistābhiḥ satatam pariveṣṭhitām**
**cintayejjagatām dhātrīm**
**dharmmakāmārthamokṣadām**

With these eight energies always surrounding her, we think of the Creator of the Perceivable Universe, who bestows the Way of Truth and Harmony, Satiation of Desires, Material Sustenance and Liberation, otherwise known as Self-Realization.

ॐ ह्रीं श्रीं दुं दुर्गायै नमः

**oṃ hrīṃ śrīṃ duṃ durgāyai namaḥ**

Oṃ I bow to the Goddess, Durgā, the Grantor of Increase, who Removes all Difficulties

### kara nyāsa

establishment in the hands

ॐ ह्रां अंगुष्ठाभ्यां नमः

**oṃ hrāṃ aṅguṣṭhābhyāṃ namaḥ** *thumb forefinger*

Oṃ hrāṃ in the thumb I bow.

ॐ ह्रीं तर्जनीभ्यां स्वाहा

**oṃ hrīṃ tarjanībhyāṃ svāhā** *thumb forefinger*

Oṃ hrīṃ in the forefinger, I am One with God!

ॐ ह्रूं मध्यमाभ्यां वषट्

**oṃ hrūṃ madhyamābhyāṃ vaṣaṭ** *thumb middlefinger*

Oṃ hrūṃ in the middle finger, Purify!

ॐ हैं अनामिकाभ्यां हुं

**oṃ hraiṃ anāmikābhyāṃ huṃ** *thumb ring finger*

Oṃ hraiṃ in the ring finger, Cut the Ego!

ॐ हौं कनिष्ठिकाभ्यां बौषट्

**oṃ hrauṃ kaniṣṭhikābhyāṃ vauṣaṭ** *thumb little finger*

Oṃ hrauṃ in the little finger, Ultimate Purity!

Roll hand over hand forwards while reciting *karatal kar*, and backwards while chanting *pṛṣṭhābhyāṃ*, then clap hands when chanting *astrāya phaṭ*.

ॐ हः करतल कर पृष्ठाभ्यां अस्त्राय फट् ॥

**oṃ hraḥ karatal kar pṛṣṭhābhyāṃ astrāya phaṭ**

Oṃ hraḥ I bow to the Goddess Durgā, with the weapon of Virtue.

ॐ ह्रीं श्रीं दुं दुर्गायै नमः

**oṃ hrīṃ śrīṃ duṃ durgāyai namaḥ**

Oṃ I bow to the Goddess, Durgā, the Grantor of Increase, who Removes all Difficulties

**aṅga nyāsa**

establishment in the body

*Holding tattva mudrā, touch heart.*

ॐ ह्रां हृदयाय नमः

**oṃ hrāṃ hṛdayāya namaḥ** *touch heart*

Oṃ hrāṃ in the heart, I bow.

*Holding tattva mudrā, touch top of head.*

ॐ ह्रीं शिरसे स्वाहा

**oṃ hrīṃ śirase svāhā** *top of head*

Oṃ hrīṃ on the top of the head, I am One with God!

*With thumb extended, touch back of head.*

ॐ ह्रूं शिखायै वषट्

**oṃ hrūṃ śikhāyai vaṣaṭ** *back of head*

Oṃ hrūṃ on the back of the head, Purify!

*Holding tattva mudrā, cross both arms.*

ॐ ह्रैं कवचाय हुं

**oṃ hraiṃ kavacāya huṃ** *cross both arms*

Oṃ hraiṃ crossing both arms, Cut the Ego!

*Holding tattva mudrā, touch two eyes and in between at once with three middle fingers.*

ॐ ह्रौं नेत्रत्रयाय वौषट्

**oṃ hrauṃ netratrayāya vauṣaṭ** *touch three eyes*

Oṃ hrauṃ in the three eyes, Ultimate Purity!

Roll hand over hand forwards while reciting *karatal kar*,
and backwards while chanting *pṛṣṭhābhyāṃ*,
then clap hands when chanting *astrāya phaṭ*.

ॐ ह्रः करतल कर पृष्ठाभ्यां अस्त्राय फट् ॥

**oṃ hraḥ karatal kar pṛṣṭhābhyāṃ astrāya phaṭ**

Oṃ hraḥ I bow to the Goddess Durgā, with the weapon of Virtue.

ॐ ह्रीं श्रीं दुं दुर्गायै नमः

**oṃ hrīṃ śrīṃ duṃ durgāyai namaḥ**

Oṃ I bow to the Goddess Durgā, the Grantor of Increase, who Removes all Difficulties

अथ दुर्गाद्वात्रिंशन्नाममाला

**atha durgā dvātriṃśannāma mālā**

The Rosary of thirty-two names of Durgā

दुर्गा दुर्गार्तिशमनी दुर्गापद्विनिवारिणी ।

दुर्गमच्छेदिनी दुर्गसाधिनी दुर्गनाशिनी ॥

**durgā durgārti śamanī durgā padvinivāriṇī**
**durgamacchedinī durga sādhinī durga nāśinī**

1. The Reliever of Difficulties
2. Who Puts Difficulties at Peace
3. The Dispeller of Difficult Adversities
4. Who Cuts Down Difficulties
5. The Performer of Discipline to Expel Difficulties
6. The Destroyer of Difficulties

दुर्गतोद्धारिणी दुर्गनिहन्त्री दुर्गमापहा ।

दुर्गमज्ञानदा दुर्गदैत्यलोकदवानला ॥

**durgatod dhāriṇī durga nihantrī durga māpahā**
**durgamajñānadā durga daityaloka davānalā**

7. Who Threatens Difficulties With Her Whip
8. Who Sends Difficulties to Ruin
9. Who Measures Difficulties
10. Who Makes Difficulties Unconscious
11. Who Destroys the World of Difficult Thoughts

दुर्गमा दुर्गमालोका दुर्गमात्मस्वरूपिणी ।
दुर्गमार्गप्रदा दुर्गमविद्या दुर्गमाश्रिता ॥

**durgamā durgamālokā durgamātmasvarūpiṇī**
**durgamārgapradā durgam avidyā durgamāśritā**

12. The Mother of Difficulties
13. Who is Beyond the World of Difficulties
14. The Intrinsic Nature of the Soul of Difficulties
15. Who Searches Through Difficulties
16. The Knowledge of Difficulties
17. The Extrication From Difficulties

दुर्गमज्ञानसंस्थाना दुर्गमध्यानभासिनी ।
दुर्गमोहा दुर्गमगा दुर्गमार्थस्वरूपिणी ॥

**durgam ajñāna saṃsthānā durgam adhyāna bhāsinī**
**durga mohā durgamagā durgamārtha svarūpiṇī**

18. The Continued Existence of Difficulties
19. Whose Meditation Remains Brilliant When in Difficulties
20. Who Deludes Difficulties
21. Who Resolves Difficulties
22. Who is the Intrinsic Nature of the Object of Difficulties

दुर्गमासुरसंहन्त्री दुर्गमायुधधारिणी ।
दुर्गमाङ्गी दुर्गमता दुर्गम्या दुर्गमेश्वरी ॥

**durgam āsura saṃhantrī durgam āyudha dhāriṇī**
**durgamāṅgī durgamatā durgamyā durgameśvarī**

23. The Annihilator of the Egotism of Difficulties
24. The Bearer of the Weapon Against Difficulties
25. The Refinery of Difficulties
26. Who is Beyond Difficulties
27. This Present Difficulty

28. The Empress of Difficulties

दुर्गभीमा दुर्गभामा दुर्गभा दुर्गदारिणी ।
नामावलिमिमां यस्तु दुर्गाया मम मानवः ।

**durgabhīmā durgabhāmā durgabhā durgadāriṇī**
**nāmāvalimimāṃ yastu durgāyā mama mānavaḥ**

29. Who is Terrible to Difficulties
30. The Lady of Difficulties
31. The Illuminator of Difficulties
32. Who Cuts Off Difficulties

Whoever will recite this garland of the names of Durgā,

पठेत् सर्वभयान्मुक्तो भविष्यति न संशयः ॥

**paṭhet sarva bhayān mukto bhaviṣyati na saṃśayaḥ**

the Reliever of Difficulties will be freed from every type of fear without a doubt.

श्रीदुर्गाष्टोत्तरशतनामस्तोत्रम्

**śrī durgāṣṭottara śatanāma stotram**

The Song containing one hundred eight names of the Respected Reliever of Difficulties

ईश्वर उवाच

**īśvara uvāca**

The Supreme Lord said:

शतनाम प्रवक्ष्यामि शृणुष्व कमलानने ।
यस्य प्रसादमात्रेण दुर्गा प्रीता भवेत् सती ॥

**śatanāma pravakṣyāmi śṛṇuṣva kamalānane**
**yasya prasādamātreṇa durgā prītā bhavet satī**

Oh Lotus Eyed, I elucidate the One-Hundred Eight Names by means of which the Reliever of Difficulties truly becomes extremely pleased:

ॐ सती साध्वी भवप्रीता भवानी भवमोचनी ।
आर्या दुर्गा जया चाद्या त्रिनेत्रा शूलधारिणी ॥

**oṃ satī sādhvī bhavaprītā bhavānī bhavamocanī**
**āryā durgā jayā cādyā trinetrā śūladhāriṇī**

1. Embodiment of Truth
2. Embodiment of Virtue
3. Lover of the Universe
4. Embodiment of the Universe
5. Who Releases the Bonds of the Universe
6. Purified by Knowledge
7. Reliever of Difficulties
8. Victory
9. Foremost
10. Having Three Eyes
11. Bearer of the Spear

पिनाकधारिणी चित्रा चण्डघण्टा महातपाः ।
मनो बुद्धिरहंकारा चित्तरूपा चिता चितिः ॥

**pināka dhāriṇī citrā caṇḍa ghaṇṭā mahātapāḥ**
**mano buddhir ahaṃkārā cittarūpā citā citiḥ**

12. Bearer of the Trident
13. Characterized by Diversity
14. Who Makes Beautiful Subtle Sounds
15. Who Performs the Great Discipline of Austerities
16. Mind
17. Intellect
18. Ego
19. The Form of Recollection
20. All Recollection
21. Consciousness

सर्वमन्त्रमयी सत्ता सत्यानन्द स्वरूपिणी ।

अनन्ता भाविनी भाव्या भव्याभव्या सदागतिः ॥

**sarva mantra mayī sattā satyānanda svarūpiṇī**
**anantā bhāvinī bhāvyā bhavyā bhavyā sadāgatiḥ**

22. The Essence of all Mantras
23. The Intrinsic Nature of Being
24. The Intrinsic Nature of the Bliss of Truth
25. Infinite
26. Who Brings Forth Creation
27. The Intensity of Reality
28. The Form of Welfare
29. Who Is Always the Same
30. Who Is Always in Motion

शाम्भवी देवमाता च चिन्ता रत्नप्रिया सदा ।

सर्वविद्या दक्षकन्या दक्षयज्ञविनाशिनी ॥

**śāmbhavī devamātā ca cintā ratnapriyā sadā**
**sarvavidyā dakṣakanyā dakṣayajña vināśinī**

31. Beloved by Consciousness
32. Mother of the Gods

33. Contemplation
34. Beloved Jewel
35. All Knowledge
36. Daughter of Ability
37. Destroyer of Dakṣa's Sacrifice

अपर्णानेकवर्णा च पाटला पाटलावती ।
पट्टाम्बर परीधाना कलमञ्जीररञ्जिनी ॥

**aparṇānekavarṇā ca pāṭalā pāṭalāvatī**
**paṭṭāmbara parīdhānā kalamañjīra rañjinī**

38. Without Limbs
39. Of Various Colors, Castes, Tribes
40. Of Red Hue
41. Adorned by Red Flowers
42. Adorned by Silk Garments
43. Whose Anklets Make a Beautiful Sound

अमेयविक्रमा क्रूरा सुन्दरी सुरसुन्दरी ।
वनदुर्गा च मातङ्गी मतङ्गमुनिपूजिता ॥

**ameya vikramā krūrā sundarī surasundarī**
**vanadurgā ca mātaṅgī mataṅga muni pūjitā**

44. Wielder of Infinite Strength
45. Who is Extremely Severe to Egos
46. Beautiful One
47. Beautiful One of the Gods
48. Reliever of Difficulties from the Forest
49. Embodiment of the Mother
50. Worshipped by the Greatest of Munis

ब्राह्मी माहेश्वरी चैन्द्री कौमारी वैष्णवी तथा ।
चामुण्डा चैव वाराही लक्ष्मीश्च पुरुषाकृतिः ॥

**brāhmī māheśvarī caindrī kaumārī vaiṣṇavī tathā**
**cāmuṇḍā caiva vārāhī lakṣmīśca puruṣākṛtiḥ**

51. Creative Energy
52. Energy of the Great Seer of All
53. Energy of the Rule of the Pure
54. Ever Pure One
55. Energy That Pervades All
56. Slayer of Passion and Anger
57. Most Excellent Desire of Union
58. Goddess of Wealth
59. Maker of Men

विमलोत्कर्षिणी ज्ञाना क्रिया नित्या च बुद्धिदा ।
बहुला बहुलप्रेमा सर्ववाहन वाहना ॥

**vimalot karṣiṇī jñānā kriyā nityā ca buddhidā**
**bahulā bahulapremā sarvavāhana vāhanā**

60. Spotlessly Pure
61. Eminent One
62. Embodiment of Wisdom
63. Embodiment of Action
64. Eternal
65. Bestower of Wisdom
66. Extensive
67. Extensive Love
68. Carrier of all Carriers

निशुम्भशुम्भहननी महिषासुरमर्दिनी ।
मधुकैटभहन्त्री च चण्डमुण्डविनाशिनी ॥

**niśumbha śumbha hananī mahiṣāsura mardinī**
**madhu kaiṭabha hantrī ca caṇḍa muṇḍa vināśinī**

69. Slayer of Self-Deprecation and Self-Conceit
70. Slayer of the Great Ego
71. Annihilator of Too Much and Too Little
72. Destroyer of Passion and Anger

सर्वासुरविनाशा च सर्वदानवघातिनी ।
सर्वशास्त्रमयी सत्या सर्वास्त्रधारिणी तथा ॥

**sarvāsuravināśā ca sarvadānava ghātinī**
**sarva śāstramayī satyā sarvāstra dhāriṇī tathā**

73. Destroyer of All Egotistical Thought
74. Slayer of All Duality
75. Essence of All Scriptures
76. Truth
77. Bearer of All Weapons

अनेकशस्त्रहस्ता च अनेकास्त्रस्य धारिणी ।
कुमारी चैककन्या च कैशोरी युवती यतिः ॥

**aneka śastra hastā ca anekāstrasya dhāriṇī**
**kumārī caika kanyā ca kaiśorī yuvatī yatiḥ**

78. With Numerous Weapons in Her Hands
79. Bearer of Numerous Weapons
80. Ever Pure One
81. Sole Daughter
82. Incomparable Beauty
83. Eternal Youth
84. Ascetic

अप्रौढा चैव प्रौढा च वृद्धमाता बलप्रदा ।

महोदरी मुक्तकेशी घोररूपा महाबला ॥

**aprauḍhā caiva prauḍhā ca vṛddhamātā balapradā**
**mahodarī muktakeśī ghorarūpā mahābalā**

85. Never Aging
86. Advanced in Age
87. Mother of Old Age
88. Giver of Strength
89. Great Eminence
90. With Loose Hair
91. Of Formidable Appearance
92. One Of Great Strength

अग्निज्वाला रौद्रमुखी कालरात्रिस्तपस्विनी ।

नारायणी भद्रकाली विष्णुमाया जलोदरी ॥

**agnijvālā raudramukhī kālarātristapasvinī**
**nārāyaṇī bhadrakālī viṣṇu māyā jalodarī**

93. Shining like Fire
94. Of Fearful Face
95. The Dark Night of Overcoming Egotism
96. Performer of Severe Spiritual Discipline
97. Exposer of Consciousness
98. Excellent One Beyond Time
99. Measurement of the All-Pervading Consciousness
100. Who Came from the Waters

शिवदूती कराली च अनन्ता परमेश्वरी ।

कात्यायनी च सावित्री प्रत्यक्षा ब्रह्मवादिनी ॥

**śivadūtī karālī ca anantā parameśvarī**
**kātyāyanī ca sāvitrī pratyakṣā brahma vādinī**

101. Ambassador of Consciousness
102. Formidable One
103. Infinite
104. Supreme Sovereign
105. Ever Pure One
106. Bearer of Light
107. Perception of the Gross World
108. Who Speaks of Infinite Consciousness

य इदं प्रपठेन्नित्यं दुर्गानामशताष्टकम् ।
नासाध्यं विद्यते देवि त्रिषु लोकेषु पार्वति ॥

**ya idaṃ prapaṭhen nityaṃ durgā nāmaśatāṣṭakam**
**nāsādhyaṃ vidyate devi triṣu lokeṣu pārvati**

Oh Goddess, Pārvatī, He who recites these one hundred eight names of the Reliever of Difficulties every day will find no difficulties in the three worlds.

धनं धान्यं सुतं जायां हयं हस्तिनमेव च ।
चतुर्वर्गं तथा चान्ते लभेन्मुक्तिं च शाश्वतीम् ॥

**dhanaṃ dhānyaṃ sutaṃ jāyāṃ**
**hayaṃ hastinameva ca**
**caturvargaṃ tathā cānte labhenmuktiṃ ca śāśvatīm**

He will find wealth, food, sons, a loving wife, horses, elephants, and the four objectives of human life will be satisfied. At the end of his earthly existence he will attain eternal liberation.

कुमारीं पूजयित्वा तु ध्यात्वा देवीं सुरेश्वरीम् ।
पूजयेत् परया भक्त्या पठेन्नामशताष्टकम् ॥

**kumārīṃ pūjayitvā tu dhyātvā devīṃ sureśvarīm**
**pūjayet parayā bhaktyā paṭhen nāmaśatāṣṭakam**

One should worship the Ever Pure One and meditate upon the female Ruler of Gods with the highest selfless devotion. Then the recitation of these one hundred eight names should be commenced.

तस्य सिद्धिर्भवेद् देवि सर्वैः सुरवरैरपि ।
राजानो दासतां यान्ति राज्यश्रियमवाप्नुयात् ॥

**tasya siddhir bhaved devi sarvaiḥ suravarairapi**
**rājāno dāsatāṃ yānti rājya śriyamavāpnuyāt**

Oh Goddess, whoever performs in this way attains the highest perfection of the Gods. Kings become his servants and he commands the wealth of kingdoms.

गोरोचनालक्तककुङ्कुमेन सिन्धुरकर्पूरमधुत्रयेण ।
विलिख्य यन्त्रं विधिना विधिज्ञो भवेत् सदा धारयतेपुरारिः ॥

**gorocanā laktaka kuṅkumena**
**sindhura karpūra madhutrayeṇa**
**vilikhya yantraṃ vidhinā vidhijño**
**bhavet sadā dhārayate purāriḥ**

With fragrant gum, lac, red powders, camphor, ghee, sugar and honey, one should draw the graphic representation of this truth according to the rules laid down in the scriptures. The knowledgeable one who will wear such an inscription becomes one with the Consciousness of Infinite Goodness.

भौमावास्यानिशामग्रे चन्द्रे शतभिषां गते ।
विलिख्य प्रपठेत् स्तोत्रं स भवेत् संपदां पदम् ॥

**bhaumāvāsyāniśāmagre candre śata bhiṣāṃ gate**
**vilikhya prapaṭhet stotraṃ**
**sa bhavet saṃpadāṃ padam**

On the evening before the New Moon Day, known as Bhaumavatī, when the celestial configuration is in the asterism known as Śatabhiśā, if one recites these mantras, he becomes the Lord of Wealth.

ॐ ह्रीं श्रीं दुं दुर्गायै नमः

**oṃ hrīṃ śrīṃ duṃ durgāyai namaḥ**

Oṃ I bow to the Goddess, Durgā, the Grantor of Increase, who Removes all Difficulties

## kālī pūjā

worship of kālī

### kālī gāyatrī

ॐ महाकाल्यै च विद्महे श्मशानवासिन्यै च धीमहि ।
तन्नो काली प्रचोदयात् ॥

**oṃ mahākālyai ca vidmahe śmaśāna vāsinyai ca dhīmahi tanno kālī pracodayāt**

Oṃ We meditate on the Great Goddess Who Takes Away Darkness, we contemplate She Who Resides in the Cremation Grounds (the ultimate form into which creation dissolves). May that Goddess grant us increase.

ध्यानम्

**dhyānam**

meditation

करालवदनां घोरां मुक्तकेशीं चतुर्भुजां ।
कालिकां दक्षिणां दिव्यां मुण्डमालाविभूषिताम् ॥

**karālavadanāṃ ghorāṃ muktakeśīṃ caturbhujām**
**kālikāṃ dakṣiṇāṃ divyāṃ muṇḍamālā vibhūṣitām**

The sound of her voice makes one dreadfully fearful. She has loose hair and four arms, She Who Takes Away the Darkness, of Divine Ability (or bearing the divine gift), and displays the garland of heads of impure thoughts.

सद्यश्छिन्नशिरःखड्गवामाधोर्द्ध्वकराम्भुजां ।
अभयां वरदाञ्चैव दक्षिणोर्द्धाधःपाणिकाम् ॥

**sadyaśchinnaśiraḥkhaṅga**
**vāmādhorddhva karāmbhujāṃ**
**abhayāṃ varadañcaiva dakṣiṇorddhādhaḥpāṇikām**

In her lower left hand is the recently severed head (of the Ego), in her upper left hand, which is raised, is the sword. With her lower right hand She grants fearlessness and with her upper right hand She gives blessings.

महामेघप्रभां श्यामां तथा चैव दिगम्बरीं ।
कण्ठावसक्तमुण्डालीगलद्रुधिरचर्च्चितां ॥

**mahāmegha prabhāṃ śyāmāṃ**
**tathā caiva digambarīṃ**
**kaṇṭhāvasaktamuṇḍālīgaladrudhiracarccitāṃ**

She shines like a big dark cloud and is clothed in space (naked, without any covering). From her neck dangles the garland of heads, dripping the blood of attachment from their severed necks.

कर्णावतंसतानीतशव युग्मभयानकां ।
घोरदंष्ट्रां करालास्यां पीनोन्नतपयोधराम् ॥

**karṇāvataṃsatānītaśava yugmabhayānakāṃ**
**ghoradaṃṣṭrāṃ karālāsyāṃ pīnonnatapayodharām**

Her two ears are adorned with ring-shaped ornaments, her body is withered like a corpse. Her large protruding teeth are extremely terrifying to the ego, and her large upraised breasts overflowing.

शवानां करसङ्घातैःकृतकाञ्चीं हसन्मुखीं ।
सृक्कद्वयगलद्रक्तधाराविस्फुरिताननां ॥

**śavānāṃ karasaṅghātaiḥkṛtakāñcīṃ hasanmukhīṃ**
**sṛkkadvayagaladraktadhārāvisphuritānanāṃ**

She wears a girdle made from the severed arms of the corpses of impurity that She has slain. Her face is filled with laughter. Pouring forth from the throats She has cut comes a torrent of blood, the life of all passion, in a glistening river.

घोररावां महारौद्रीं श्मशानालयवासिनीम् ।
बालार्कमण्डलाकारलोचनत्रितयान्वितां ॥

**ghorarāvāṃ mahāraudrīṃ śmaśānālayavāsinīm**
**bālārkamaṇḍalākāralocanatritayānvitāṃ**

Extremely frightful and greatly terrifying is this resident of the cremation grounds, this young woman with a figure like an asetic's begging bowl, with three eyes.

दन्तुरां दक्षिणव्यापि मुक्तालन्विकचोच्चयां ।
शवरूप महादेवहृदयोपरिसंस्थितां ॥

**danturāṃ dakṣiṇavyāpi muktālanvikacoccayāṃ**
**śavarūpa mahādevahṛdayoparisaṃsthitāṃ**

Pervading the South and filling up everywhere, unattached, She is resting with ease on the corpse like form of Mahādeva, the Great Lord of All, standing upon his heart.

शिवाभिर्घोररवाभिश्चतुर्द्दिक्षु समन्विता ।
महाकालेन च समं विपरीतरतातुरां ॥

**śivābhirghoraravābhiścaturddikṣu samanvitāṃ**
**mahākālena ca samaṃ viparītaratāturāṃ**

Śivā, the Energy of Infinite Goodness (Kālī) emits a dreadful roar that pervades the four directions, and Mahākāla, the Great Time (Śiva), equally reverses, or sends it back, with the greatest of delight.

सुखप्रसन्नवदनां स्मेराननसरोरुहां ।
एवं संचिन्तयेत् कालीं सर्वकामसमृद्धिदाम् ॥

**sukhaprasannavadanāṃ smerānana saroruhāṃ**
**evaṃ saṃcintayet kālīṃ sarvakāmasamṛddhidām**

If one contemplates Kālī, the Remover of Darkness, in this way, with her face of radiant beauty that gives pleasure, and its wide expansive smile, one will become prosperous and fulfill all desires.

ॐ क्रीं क्रीं क्रीं हुं हुं ह्रीं ह्रीं दक्षिणे कालिके क्रीं क्रीं क्रीं हुं हुं ह्रीं ह्रीं स्वाहा

**oṃ krīṃ krīṃ krīṃ huṃ huṃ hrīṃ hrīṃ dakṣiṇe kālike krīṃ krīṃ krīṃ huṃ huṃ hrīṃ hrīṃ svāhā**

The Cause that Moves the Subtle Body to the Infinite Perfection and Beyond, cut the ego! Cut the ego! Māyā! Māyā! Oh Goddess Who Removes All Darkness, the Cause Which Moves the Subtle Body to the Infinite Perfection and Beyond, cut the ego! Cut the ego! Māyā! Māyā! I am ONE with God!

ॐ क्रां अंगुष्ठाभ्यां नमः

**oṃ krāṃ aṅguṣṭhābhyāṃ namaḥ** *thumb forefinger*

Oṃ krāṃ in the thumb I bow.

ॐ क्रीं तर्जनीभ्यां स्वाहा

**oṃ krīṃ tarjanībhyāṃ svāhā** *thumb forefinger*

Oṃ krīṃ in the forefinger, I am One with God!

ॐ क्रूं मध्यमाभ्यां वषट्

**oṃ krūṃ madhyamābhyāṃ vaṣaṭ** *thumb middlefinger*

Oṃ krūṃ in the middle finger, Purify!

ॐ क्रैं अनामिकाभ्यां हुं

**oṃ kraiṃ anāmikābhyāṃ huṃ** *thumb ringfinger*

Oṃ kraiṃ in the ring finger, Cut the Ego!

ॐ क्रौं कनिष्ठिकाभ्यां वौषट्

**oṃ krauṃ kaniṣṭhikābhyāṃ vauṣaṭ** *thumb littlefinger*

Oṃ krauṃ in the little finger, Ultimate Purity!

Roll hand over hand forwards while reciting *karatal kar*,
and backwards while chanting *pṛṣṭhābhyāṃ*,
then clap hands when chanting *astrāya phaṭ*.

ॐ क्रः करतलकरपृष्ठाभ्यां अस्त्राय फट्

**oṃ kraḥ karatal kar pṛṣṭhābhyāṃ astrāya phaṭ**

Oṃ I bow to the Goddess Kālī with the weapon of Virtue.

ॐ क्रीं काल्यै नमः

**oṃ krīṃ kālyai namaḥ**

I bow to the Goddess Kālī Who Takes Away Darkness.

Holding tattva mudrā, touch heart.

ॐ क्रां हृदयाय नमः

**oṃ krāṃ hṛdayāya namaḥ** *touch heart*

Oṃ krāṃ in the heart, I bow.

Holding tattva mudrā, touch top of head.

ॐ क्रीं शिरसे स्वाहा

**oṃ krīṃ śirase svāhā** *top of head*

Oṃ krīṃ on the top of the head, I am One with God!

Make a fist with thumb extended, touch back of head.

ॐ क्रूं शिखायै वषट्

**oṃ krūṃ śikhāyai vaṣaṭ** *back of head*

Oṃ krūṃ on the back of the head, Purify!

Holding tattva mudrā, cross both arms.

ॐ क्रैं कवचाय हुं

**oṃ kraiṃ kavacāya huṃ** *cross both arms*

Oṃ kraiṃ crossing both arms, Cut the Ego!

Holding tattva mudrā, touch two eyes and in between
at once with three middle fingers.

ॐ क्रौं नेत्रत्रयाय वौषट्

**oṃ kraum̐ netratrayāya vauṣaṭ** *touch three eyes*

Oṃ krauṃ in the three eyes, Ultimate Purity!

Roll hand over hand forwards while reciting *karatal kar*,
and backwards while chanting *pṛṣṭhābhyāṃ*,
then clap hands when chanting *astrāya phaṭ*.

ॐ क्रः करतलकरपृष्ठाभ्यां अस्त्राय फट्

**oṃ kraḥ karatal kar pṛṣṭhābhyāṃ astrāya phaṭ**

Oṃ I bow to the Goddess Kālī with the weapon of Virtue.

ॐ क्रीं काल्यै नमः

**oṃ krīṃ kālyai namaḥ**

I bow to the Goddess Kālī Who Takes Away Darkness.

## आद्यास्तोत्रम्

## ādyā stotram

The Song of the Foremost
(Kālī as the Supreme Divinity)

शृणु वत्स प्रवक्ष्यामि आद्यास्तोत्रम् महाफलं ।

यः पठेत् सततं भक्त्या स एव विष्णुवल्लभः ॥

**śṛṇu vatsa pravakṣyāmi ādyā stotram mahāphalaṃ**
**yaḥ paṭhet satataṃ bhaktyā sa eva viṣṇu vallabhaḥ**

Listen, my child, while I elucidate the Song of the Foremost, which grants the great fruit. Whoever always recites this with devotion will have strength comparable with that of Viṣṇu.

मृत्युव्याधिभयं तस्य नास्ति किञ्चित् कलौ युगे ।
अपुत्रो लभते पुत्रं त्रिपक्षं श्रवणं यदि ॥

**mṛtyuvyādhibhayaṃ tasya nāsti kiñcit kalau yuge**
**aputro labhate putraṃ tripakṣaṃ śravaṇaṃ yadi**

Neither death nor illness will bring fear, nor anything else of the Kali Yuga. Those without children will attain children, if they listen (to this) three times (a day).

द्वौ मासौ बन्धनान् मुक्तिर्विप्रवक्त्रा श्रुतं यदि ।
मृतवत्सा जीववत्सा षण्मासान् श्रवणं यदि ॥

**dvau māsau bandhanān muktir**
**vipravaktrā śrutaṃ yadi**
**mṛtavatsā jīvavatsā ṣaṇmāsān śravaṇaṃ yadi**

If this is heard from the mouth of a twice-born for two months, one will be liberated from bondage. If one listens thus for six months, he will be liberated from the cycles of birth and death.

नौकायां सङ्कटे युद्धे पठनाज्जयमाप्नुयात् ।
लिखित्वा स्थापनाद् गेहे नाग्निचौरभयं क्वचित् ॥

**naukāyāṃ saṅkaṭe yuddhe paṭhanājjayamāpnuyāt**
**likhitvā sthāpanād gehe nāgnicaurabhayaṃ kvacit**

It is a boat to cross the difficulties of war; no one will be able to defeat the person who recites it. And if it is duly written and established in one's house, no fear will come from fire, thieves nor from other causes.

राजस्थाने जयी नित्यं प्रसन्नाः सर्वदेवताः ।
पापानि विलयं यान्ति मृतौ मुक्तिमवाप्नुयात् ॥

**rājasthāne jayī nityaṃ prasannāḥ sarvadevatāḥ**
**pāpāni vilayaṃ yānti mṛtau mukti mavāpnuyāt**

In the house of kings one will be eternally invincible and pleasing to all the Gods. Cleaving asunder the sins of all life, one will be liberated even from death.

ॐ ह्रीं ब्रह्माणी ब्रह्मलोके च वैकुण्ठे सर्वमङ्गला ।

इन्द्राणी अमरावत्याममम्बिका वरुणालये ॥

**oṃ hrīṃ brahmāṇī brahmaloke ca**
**vaikuṇṭhe sarvamaṅgalā**
**indrāṇī amarāvatyāmambikā varuṇālaye**

Oṃ Hrīṃ (the totality of Māyā that can be perceived, conceived or intuited) in the Brahma Loka, in the reality of Creative Consciousness, is Brahmāṇī, the Energy of Creative Consciousness. In Vaikuṇṭha, the home of Viṣṇu, is All Welfare. In the Land of the Immortals (the heaven of Indra), is Indrānī, the Energy of the Rule of the Pure, and Ambikā, the Divine Mother, in the home of Varuṇa, the Lord of Equilibrium.

यमालये कालरूपा कुबेरभवने शुभा ।

महानन्दाग्निकोणे च वायव्यां मृग वाहिनी ॥

**yamālaye kālarūpā kuberabhavane śubhā**
**mahānandāgni koṇe ca vāyavyāṃ mṛga vāhinī**

In the house of Death is the Dark Form and with the Lord of Wealth is the Radiant Luster. In the Southeast, the home of Agni, the Divine Fire, or Purifying Light of Meditation, is Great Delight, and in the Northwest, the home of Vāyu, is She Who rides on the deer.

नैर्ऋत्यां रक्तदन्ता च ऐशान्यां शूलधारिणी ।

पाताले वैष्णवीरूपा सिंहले देवमोहिनी ॥

**nairṛtyāṃ raktadantā ca aiśānyāṃ śūladhāriṇī**
**pātāle vaiṣṇavī rūpā siṃhale devamohinī**

In the Southwest is She with Red Teeth, and in the Northeast, She Who Holds the Spear. In the regions of hell is the form of Vaiṣṇavī, She Who Pervades All, and in Laṅkā is She Who mesmerizes the Gods.

सुरसा च मणिद्वीपे लङ्कायां भद्रकालिका ।

रामेश्वरी सेतुबन्धे विमला पुरुषोत्तमे ॥

**surasā ca manidvīpe laṅkāyāṃ bhadrakālikā**
**rāmeśvarī setubandhe vimalā puruṣottame**

In the Island of Jewels is the Mother of the Gods, and in the Island of Laṅkā, Bhadrakālikā, the Excellent One Beyond Time. The Supreme Lord of Rāma is at the bridge, and in the Excellent Fullness (or excellent individual) is Vimalā, Pure and Stainless.

विरजा औड्रदेशे च कामाख्या नीलपर्वते ।

कालिका बङ्गदेशे च अयोध्यायां महेश्वरी ॥

**virajā auḍradeśe ca kāmākhyā nīlaparvate**
**kālikā baṅgadeśe ca ayodhyāyāṃ maheśvarī**

The Great Warrior is in the country of Audra, and Kāmākhyā is in the Blue Mountains. In the country of Bengal is Kālikā, She Who Takes Away the Darkness, and in Ayodhyā, Maheśvarī, the Great Seer of All.

वाराणस्यामन्नपूर्णा गयाक्षेत्रे गयेश्वरी ।

कुरुक्षेत्रे भद्रकाली व्रजे कात्यायनी परा ॥

**vārāṇasyāmannapūrṇā gayākṣetre gayeśvarī**
**kurukṣetre bhadrakālī vraje kātyāyanī parā**

Annapūrnā, She Who Is Full of Food, is at Vārāṇasi, and in the fields of Gayā, Gayeśvarī, the Supreme Lord of the Abode. In Kurukṣetra, the Field of the Family, is Bhadrakālī, the Excellent One Beyond Time, and in the thunderbolt, the Excellence of Illumination, is the Supreme Ever Pure One.

द्वारकायां महामाया मथुरायां माहेश्वरी ।

क्षुधा त्वं सर्वभूतानां वेला त्वं सागरस्य च ॥

**dvārakāyāṃ mahāmāyā mathurāyāṃ māheśvarī**
**kṣudhā tvaṃ sarvabhūtānāṃ velā tvaṃ sāgarasya ca**

In Dvārakā is Mahāmāyā, the Great Limitation of Consciousness, and in Mathurā, the Energy of the Great Seer of All. You are Hunger to all Beings, and you are the flow of the tides to the sea.

नवमी कृष्णपक्षस्य शुक्लस्यैकादशी परा ।

दक्षस्य दुहिता देवी दक्षयज्ञविनाशिनी ॥

**navamī kṛṣṇa pakṣasya śuklasyaikādaśī parā**
**dakṣasya duhitā devī dakṣayajña vināśinī**

On the ninth day of the dark fortnight, and on the eleventh day of the bright fortnight, remember the Goddess who is Dakṣa's daughter, the Destroyer of Dakṣa's sacrifice.

रामस्य जानकी त्वं हि रावणध्वंसकारिणी ।

चण्डमुण्डवधे देवी रक्तबीजविनाशिनी ॥

**rāmasya jānakī tvaṃ hi rāvaṇadhvaṃsa kāriṇī**
**caṇḍamuṇḍavadhe devī raktabīja vināśinī**

Also you are Rāma's Jānakī (Sītā), the cause of Rāvaṇa's destruction, as well as the Goddess who slays Passion and Meanness, destroyer of the Seed of Desire.

निशुम्भशुम्भमथनी मधुकैटभघातिनी ।
विष्णुभक्तिप्रदा दुर्गा सुखदा मोक्षदा सदा ॥

**niśumbha śumbha mathanī madhu kaiṭabha ghātinī**
**viṣṇu bhakti pradā durgā sukhadā mokṣadā sadā**

You are the killer of Self-Conceit and Self-Deprecation, and destroyer of Two Much and Two Little. Oh Durgā, Reliever of all Difficulties, bestow eternal devotion upon this Consciousness; always give comfort and liberation.

इमं आद्या स्तवं पुण्यं यः पठेत् सततं नरः ।
सर्वज्वरभयं न स्यात् सर्वव्याधिविनाशनम् ॥

**imaṃ ādyā stavaṃ puṇyaṃ**
**yaḥ paṭhet satataṃ naraḥ**
**sarvajvarabhayaṃ na syāt sarvavyādhi vināśanam**

Whoever will constantly recite this meritorious Song of the Foremost will destroy all affliction, fear and disease.

कोटितीर्थफलञ्चासौ लभते नात्र संशयः ।
जया मे चाग्रतः पातु विजया पातु पृष्ठतः ॥

**koṭi tīrtha phalañcāsau labhate nātra saṃśayaḥ**
**jayā me cāgrataḥ pātu vijayā pātu pṛṣṭhataḥ**

The fruits of visiting millions of pilgrimage sites will be attained without a doubt. May Victory protect me in my front and Conquest protect my rear.

नारायणी शीर्षदेशे सर्वाङ्गे सिंहवाहिनी ।
शिवदूती उग्रचण्डा प्रत्यङ्गे परमेश्वरी ॥

**nārāyaṇī śīrṣadeśe sarvāṅge siṃhavāhinī**
**śivadūtī ugracaṇḍā pratyaṅge parameśvarī**

May the Great Exposer of Consciousness protect the area of the head, and may all the limbs be protected by She Who Rides on the Lion, also known as She for Whom Consciousness Is Ambassador, She Who is Terrible to Passion, the Supreme Empress of All and everybody;

विशालाक्षी महामाया कौमारी शङ्खिनी शिवा ।
चक्रिणी जयदात्री च रणमत्ता रणप्रिया ॥

**viśālākṣī mahāmāya kaumārī śaṅkhinī śivā**
**cakriṇī jayadātrī ca raṇamattā raṇapriyā**

The Goal of the Infinite, the Great Limitation of Consciousness, the Ever-Pure One, She Who Holds the Conch, the Energy of Infinite Goodness; She Who Holds the Discus, the Grantor of Victory, and She Who is Intoxicated with Delight, She Who is the Lover of Delight;

दुर्गा जयन्ती काली च भद्रकाली महोदरी ।
नारसिंही च वाराही सिद्धिदात्री सुखप्रदा ॥

**durgā jayantī kālī ca bhadrakālī mahodarī**
**nārasiṃhī ca vārāhī siddhidātrī sukhapradā**

The Reliever of Difficulties, She Who Is Always Victorious, She Who Takes Away Darkness, and the Excellent One

Beyond Time, the Wielder of Ignorance; She Who Is Half-Human and Half-Lion, and the Boar of Sacrifice, the Grantor of Perfection, Giver of Comfort;

भयङ्करी महारौद्री महाभयविनाशिनी ॥

**bhayaṅkarī mahāraudrī mahābhaya vināśinī**

Who Destroys all fear, the Great Terrifying One Who Destroys all Fear.

इति आद्यास्तोत्रम् समाप्तम् ॥

**iti ādyā stotram samāptam**

And that is the completion of the Song of the Foremost.

ॐ क्रीं क्रीं क्रीं हुं हुं ह्रीं ह्रीं दक्षिणे कालिके क्रीं क्रीं क्रीं हुं हुं ह्रीं ह्रीं स्वाहा ॥

**oṃ krīṃ krīṃ krīṃ huṃ huṃ hrīṃ hrīṃ dakṣiṇe kālike krīṃ krīṃ krīṃ huṃ huṃ hrīṃ hrīṃ svāhā**

Oṃ The Cause that Moves the Subtle Body to the Infinite Perfection and Beyond, Cut the Ego! Cut the Ego! Māyā! Māyā! Oh Goddess Who Removes All Darkness, the Cause that Moves the Subtle Body to the Infinite Perfection and Beyond, Cut the Ego! Cut the Ego! Māyā! Māyā! I am ONE with God!

ॐ कालि कालि महाकालि कालिके पापहारिणी ।
धर्मार्थमोक्षदे देवि नारायणि नमोऽस्तुते ॥

**oṃ kāli kāli mahākāli kālike pāpahāriṇī**
**dharmārthamokṣade devi nārāyaṇi namo-stute**

Oṃ Goddess Who Takes Away Darkness, Goddess Who Takes Away Darkness, Great Goddess Who Takes Away Darkness,

Beloved Goddess Who Takes Away Darkness, Who Takes Away All Sin. Give the way of peace and harmony, the necessities for physical sustenance, and liberation or self-realization. Oh Goddess, Exposer of Consciousness, we bow to you.

ॐ क्रीं काल्यै नमः

**oṃ krīṃ kālyai namaḥ**

Oṃ I bow to the Goddess Who Takes Away Darkness.

### lakṣmī pūjā

worship of lakṣmī

### lakṣmī gāyatrī

ॐ महालक्ष्म्यै च विद्महे सर्वशक्त्यै च धीमहे ।

तन्नो देवी प्रचोदयात् ॥

**oṃ mahālakṣmyai ca vidmahe**
**sarvaśaktyai ca dhīmahe**
**tanno devī pracodayāt**

Oṃ We meditate upon the Great Goddess of True Wealth, we contemplate She Who Embodies all Energy. May that Goddess grant us increase.

### dhyānam

meditation

ॐ पाशाक्षमालिकाम्बोज-सृणिभर्याम्यसौम्ययोः ।

पद्मासनस्तां ध्यायेच्च श्रियः त्रैलोक्यमातरम् ॥

**oṃ pāśākṣamālikāmboja-sṛṇibharyāmyasaumyayoḥ**
**padmāsanastāṃ dhyāyecca śriyaḥ trailokyamātaram**

Oṃ The bond, mālā of alphabets, a gourd, Her lovely hand gives freedom from fear of creation. We meditate upon the Goddess of the Highest Respect seated in the lotus posture, the Mother of the three worlds.

गौरवर्णां सुरूपाञ्च सर्वालङ्कार-भूषिताम् ।
रौक्मपद्मव्यग्रकरां वरदां दक्षिणेन तु ॥

**gauravarṇāṃ surūpāñca sarvālaṅkāra-bhūṣitām**
**raukmapadmavyagrakarāṃ varadāṃ dakṣiṇena tu**

She has a light color, with excellent form, all Her ornaments are shining. She holds a red lotus in Her hand, and Her right hand grants boons.

लक्ष्मिस्त्वं सर्वभूतानां नमस्ते विश्वभाविणी ।
देहि पुत्रं धानं देहि पाहि नित्यं नमोऽस्तु ते ॥

**lakṣmistvaṃ sarvabhūtānāṃ namaste viśvabhāviṇī**
**dehi putraṃ dhānaṃ dehi pāhi nityaṃ namo-stu te**

You are Lakṣmi and all existence bows to you, the Mother of the Universe. Give me children and give me wealth. Protect me eternally, I bow to you.

त्रैलोक्यपूजिते देवि कमले विष्णु बल्लभे ।
यथात्वं सुस्थिरा कृष्णे तथा भव मयि स्थिरा ॥

**trailokyapūjite devi kamale viṣṇu ballabhe**
**yathātvaṃ susthirā kṛṣṇe tathā bhava mayi sthirā**

The Goddess is worshipped in the three worlds as the Lotus One, the strength of Viṣṇu. Hey Energy of Kṛṣṇa, for as long as you sit still, let me be still as well.

ईश्वरी कमला लक्ष्मीश्चला भूतिर्हरिप्रिया ।

पद्मा पद्मालया सम्पद् हृष्टिः श्रीः पद्मधारिणी ॥

**īśvarī kamalā lakṣmīścalā bhūtirharipriyā**
**padmā padmālayā sampada**
**hṛṣṭhiḥ śrīḥ padmadhāriṇī**

You are Īśvarī, Kamalā, Lakṣmī, She Who Moves All, All Existence, Beloved of Viṣṇu, Lotus, Who Resides in Lotuses, All Support, Joy, Respect, Who Holds a Lotus.

द्वादशैतानि नामानि लक्ष्मीं संपूज्य यः पठेत् ।

स्थिरा लक्ष्मीर्भवेत्तस्य पुत्रजायादिभिः सह ॥

**dvādaśaitāni nāmāni lakṣmīṃ sampūjya yaḥ paṭhet**
**sthirā lakṣmīrbhavettasya putrajāyādibhiḥ saha**

These are the twelve names of Lakṣmī. If one reads them in worship, Lakṣmī becomes fixed in your being and your children will always be victorious.

## kara nyāsa

establishment in the hands

ॐ श्रां अंगुष्ठाभ्यां नमः

**oṃ śrāṃ aṅguṣṭhābhyāṃ namaḥ** *thumb forefinger*

Oṃ śrāṃ in the thumb I bow.

ॐ श्रीं तर्जनीभ्यां स्वाहा

**oṃ śrīṃ tarjanībhyāṃ svāhā** *thumb forefinger*

Oṃ śrīṃ in the forefinger, I am One with God!

ॐ श्रूं मध्यमाभ्यां वषट्

**oṃ śrūṃ madhyamābhyāṃ vaṣaṭ** *thumb middlefinger*
Oṃ śrūṃ in the middle finger, Purify!

ॐ श्रैं अनामिकाभ्यां हुं

**oṃ śraiṃ anāmikābhyāṃ huṃ** *thumb ring finger*
Oṃ śraiṃ in the ring finger, Cut the Ego!

ॐ श्रौं कनिष्ठिकाभ्यां वौषट्

**oṃ śrauṃ kaniṣṭhikābhyāṃ vauṣaṭ** *thumb little finger*
Oṃ śrauṃ in the little finger, Ultimate Purity!

Roll hand over hand forwards while reciting *karatal kar*,
and backwards while chanting *pṛṣṭhābhyāṃ*,
then clap hands when chanting *astrāya phaṭ.*

ॐ श्रः करतल कर पृष्ठाभ्यां अस्त्राय फट् ॥

**oṃ śraḥ karatal kar pṛṣṭhābhyāṃ astrāya phaṭ**
Oṃ śraḥ I bow to the Goddess Lakṣmī, with the weapon of Virtue.

ॐ श्रीं लक्ष्म्यै नमः

**oṃ śrīṃ lakṣmyai namaḥ**
Oṃ I bow to the Goddess Lakṣmī

## aṅga nyāsa

establishment in the body

*Holding tattva mudrā, touch heart.*

ॐ श्रां हृदयाय नमः

**oṃ śrāṃ hṛdayāya namaḥ** *touch heart*
Oṃ śrāṃ in the heart, I bow.

*Holding tattva mudrā, touch top of head.*

ॐ श्रीं शिरसे स्वाहा

**oṃ śrīṃ śirase svāhā** *top of head*

Oṃ śrīṃ on the top of the head, I am One with God!

*With thumb extended, touch back of head.*

ॐ श्रूं शिखायै वषट्

**oṃ śrūṃ śikhāyai vaṣaṭ** *back of head*

Oṃ śrūṃ on the back of the head, Purify!

*Holding tattva mudrā, cross both arms.*

ॐ श्रैं कवचाय हुं

**oṃ śraiṃ kavacāya huṃ** *cross both arms*

Oṃ śraiṃ crossing both arms, Cut the Ego!

*Holding tattva mudrā, touch two eyes and in between at once with three middle fingers.*

ॐ श्रौं नेत्रत्रयाय वौषट्

**oṃ śrauṃ netratrayāya vauṣaṭ** *touch three eyes*

Oṃ śrauṃ in the three eyes, Ultimate Purity!

Roll hand over hand forwards while reciting *karatal kar*, and backwards while chanting *pṛṣṭhābhyāṃ*, then clap hands when chanting *astrāya phaṭ*.

ॐ श्रः करतल कर पृष्ठाभ्यां अस्त्राय फट् ॥

**oṃ śraḥ karatal kar pṛṣṭhābhyāṃ astrāya phaṭ**

Oṃ śraḥ I bow to the Goddess Lakṣmī with the weapon of Virtue.

ॐ श्रीं लक्ष्म्यै नमः

**oṃ śrīṃ lakṣmyai namaḥ**
Oṃ I bow to the Goddess Lakṣmī.

**mahālakṣmī aṣṭakaṃ**

eight verses in praise of mahālakṣmī

नमस्तेऽस्तु महामाये श्रीपीठे सुरपूजिते ।

सङ्खचक्रगदाहस्ते महालक्ष्मि नमोऽस्तु ते ॥

**namaste-stu mahāmāye śrīpīṭhe surapūjite**
**saṅkhacakragadāhaste mahālakṣmi namo-stu te**
The dwelling place of the highest respected wealth, worshipped by all divine beings, Oh Infinite Container of Consciousness, we bow to you. To you who holds the conch shell, discus and club (or mace) in your hands, to the Great Goddess of True Wealth, we bow.

नमस्ते गरुडारूढे कोलासुरभयंकरि ।

सर्वपापहरे देवि महालक्ष्मि नमोऽस्तु ते ॥

**namaste garuḍārūḍhe kolāsurabhayaṃkari**
**sarvapāpahare devi mahālakṣmi namo-stu te**
She who rides upon the eagle Garuḍa, filling the demon Kola (the Perverter of the Family or Destroyer of Excellence) with fear, the Goddess Who Eradicates Sin, to the Great Goddess of True Wealth we bow.

सर्वज्ञे सर्ववरदेसर्वदुष्टभयङ्करि ।

सर्वदुःखहरे देवि महालक्ष्मि नमोऽस्तु ते ॥

**sarvajñe sarvavaradesarvaduṣṭabhayaṅkari**
**sarvaduḥkhahare devi mahālakṣmi namo-stu te**

Knower of all, Grantor of all wishes, instilling the fear of all evil, the Goddess Who Takes Away All Pain, to the Great Goddess of True Wealth we bow.

सिद्धिबुद्धिप्रदे देवि भुक्तिमुक्तिप्रदायिनि ।
मन्त्रपूते सदा देवि महालक्ष्मि नमोऽस्तु ते ॥

**siddhibuddhiprade devi bhuktimuktipradāyini**
**mantrapūte sadā devi mahālakṣmi namo-stu te**

Grantor of perfection and intelligence, Giver of enjoyment and liberation, wearing mantra as your form, to the Great Goddess of True Wealth we bow.

आध्यन्तरहिते देवि आध्यशक्तिमहेश्वरि ।
योगजे योगसम्भूते महालक्ष्मि नमोऽस्तु ते ॥

**ādhyantarahite devi ādhyaśaktimaheśvari**
**yogaje yogasambhūte mahālakṣmi namo-stu te**

Without beginning or end, Oh Goddess, the primordial energy, the Great Seer of All (or Great Ruler of All), who dwells always in union, who is born of union, to the Great Goddess of True Wealth we bow.

स्थूलसूक्ष्ममहारौद्रे महाशक्तिमहोदरे ।
महापापहरे देवि महालक्ष्मि नमोऽस्तु ते ॥

**sthūlasūkṣmamahāraudre mahāśaktimahodare**
**mahāpāpahare devi mahālakṣmi namo-stu te**

Wearing the gross body, wearing the subtle body, as the Great Reliever of Suffering, the Great Energy, the Cosmic Source of All, the Goddess Who Takes Away Great Sin, to the Great Goddess of True Wealth we bow.

पद्मासनस्थिते देवि परब्रह्मस्वरूपिणि ।
परमेशि जगन्मातर्महालक्ष्मि नमोऽस्तु ते ॥

**padmāsanasthite devi parabrahmasvarūpiṇi**
**parameśi jaganmātarmahālakṣmi namo-stu te**

Situated upon a lotus seat, Oh Goddess, the Intrinsic Nature of the Universal Consciousness, the Supreme Ruler, Mother of the Universe, to the Great Goddess of True Wealth we bow.

श्वेताम्बरधरे देवि नानालङ्कारभूषिते ।
जगत्स्थिते जगन्मातर्महालक्ष्मि नमोऽस्तु ते ॥

**svetāmbaradhare devi nānālaṅkārabhūṣite**
**jagatsthite jaganmātarmahālakṣmi namo-stu te**

Wearing a white cloth, Oh Goddess, with various ornaments shining, the Residence of the Worlds, the Mother of the Worlds, to the Great Goddess of True Wealth we bow.

महालक्ष्म्यष्टकं स्तोत्रं यः पठेद्भक्तिमानरः ।
सर्वसिद्धिमवाप्नोति राज्यं प्राप्नोति सर्वदा ॥

**mahālakṣmyaṣṭakaṃ stotraṃ yaḥ**
**paṭhedbhaktimānaraḥ**
**sarvasiddhimavāpnoti rājyaṃ prāpnoti sarvadā**

Whoever will recite these eight verses in praise of the Great Goddess of True Wealth with full devotion and attention, will attain to perfection for himself as well as for those who are under his influence.

एककाले पठेन्नित्यं महापापविनाशनम् ।
द्विकालं यः पठेन्नित्यं धनधान्यसमन्वितः ॥

**ekakāle paṭhennityaṃ mahāpāpavināśanam**
**dvikālaṃ yaḥ paṭhennityaṃ**
**dhanadhānyasamanvitaḥ**

Whoever regularly recites this one time, will be freed even from great sins. Who regularly recites twice will have abundance of wealth and grains.

त्रिकालं यः पठेन्नित्यं महाशत्रुविनाशनम् ।
महालक्ष्मीर्भवेन्नित्यं प्रसन्ना वरदा शुभा ॥

**trikālaṃ yaḥ paṭhennityaṃ mahāśatruvināśanam**
**mahālakṣmīrbhavennityaṃ prasannā varadā śubhā**

Whoever regularly recites three times will witness the destruction of the Great Enemy (Ego), and the Great Goddess of True Wealth, the Grantor of Welfare, the Giver of Boons, will always be pleased.

ॐ विश्वरूपस्य भार्ज्यासि पद्मे पद्मालये शुभे ।
सर्वतः पाहि मां देवी महालक्ष्मि नमोऽस्तु ते ॥

**oṃ viśvarūpasya bhārjyāsi padme padmālaye śubhe**
**sarvataḥ pāhi māṃ devī mahālakṣmi namo-stu te**

Oṃ the form of the universe, you are the wife of the universe, Lotus One, Who Resides in Lotuses, Pure One; always protect me, oh Goddess. Oh Great Goddess of True Wealth, I bow to you.

## sarasvatī pūjā

worship of sarasvatī

### sarasvatī gāyatrī

ॐ वाग् देव्यै च विद्महे कामराजाय धीमहे ।

तन्नो देवि प्रचोदयात् ॥

**oṃ vāg devyai ca vidmahe kāmarājāya dhīmahe**
**tanno devi pracodayāt**

Oṃ We meditate on the Goddess who encompasses all vibrations, we contemplate the queen of all desires. May that Goddess grant us increase.

### dhyānam

meditation

ॐ तरुणशकलमिन्दोविभ्रती शुभ्र कान्तिः

कुचभरनमिताङ्गी सन्निषण्णा सिताब्जे ।

निजकरकमलोद्यल्लेखनीपुस्तकश्रीः

सकलविभर्वसिद्ध्यै पातु वागदेवता नमः ॥

**oṃ taruṇaśakalamindovibhratī śubhra kāntiḥ**
**kūcabharanamitāṅgī sanniṣaṇṇā sitābje**
**nijakarakamalodyallekhanīpustakaśrīḥ**
**sakalavibharvasiddhyai pātu vāgdevatā namaḥ**

Her body is very young, shining with the radiance of Her beauty. Her jet black hair contrasts with the pure white of her body. With her lotus-like hands She writes in a book. To She Who Contains All Vibrations, to the Grantor of Perfection, to the Protector of All, we bow.

ॐ श्वेतपद्मासनादेवी श्वेतपुष्पोपशोभिता ।
श्वेताम्बरधरा नित्या श्वेतगन्धानुलेपना ॥

**oṃ śvetapadmāsanādevī śvetapuṣpopaśobhitā**
**śvetāmbaradharā nityā śvetagandhānulepanā**

The Goddess is seated upon a white lotus, displaying white flowers. She always wears a white cloth, and emits a pure and clean fragrance.

श्वेताक्षी शुभ्रहस्ता च श्वेतचन्दनचर्च्चिता ।
श्वेतवीणाधरा शुभ्रा श्वेतालङ्कारभूषिता ॥

**śvetākṣī śubhrahastā ca śvetacandanacarccitā**
**śvetavīṇādharā śubhrā śvetālaṅkārabhūṣitā**

Her clear white eyes are shining, her limbs are beautiful and She wears the markings of white sandle paste. She holds a white-colored musical instrument called the vīnā, and her pure white ornaments are shining.

वन्दिता सिद्धगन्धर्वैरर्चिता सुरदानवैः ।
पूजिता मुनिभिः सर्वैर्ऋषिभिः स्तुयते सदा ॥

**vanditā siddhagandharvairarcitā suradānavaiḥ**
**pūjitā munibhiḥ sarvairṛṣibhiḥ stuyate sadā**

All beings of perfection praise Her, as do the celestial singers of divine wisdom. Both the forces of cohesion and those of separation act through Her. She is worshipped by men of wisdom, and all Seers of Eternal Harmony constantly sing Her praise.

स्तोत्रेनानेन तां देवीं जगद्धात्रीं सरस्वतीं ।
ये स्मरन्ति त्रिसन्ध्यञ्च सर्वां विद्यां लभन्ति ते ॥

**stotreṇānena tāṃ devīṃ jagaddhātrīṃ sarasvatīṃ**
**ye smaranti trisandhyañca**
**sarvāṃ vidyāṃ labhanti te**

Whoever will remember this hymn of Sarasvatī, the Goddess of Wisdom, Creator of the Perceivable Universe, at the three times of prayer by means of this hymn, will attain all Knowledge.

**kara nyāsa**

establishment in the hands

ॐ सां अंगुष्ठाभ्यां नमः

**oṃ sāṃ aṅguṣṭhābhyāṃ namaḥ** *thumb forefinger*

Oṃ sāṃ in the thumb I bow.

ॐ सीं तर्जनीभ्यां स्वाहा

**oṃ sīṃ tarjanībhyāṃ svāhā** *thumb forefinger*

Oṃ sīṃ in the forefinger, I am One with God!

ॐ सूं मध्यमाभ्यां वषट्

**oṃ sūṃ madhyamābhyāṃ vaṣaṭ** *thumb middlefinger*

Oṃ sūṃ in the middle finger, Purify!

ॐ सैं अनामिकाभ्यां हुं

**oṃ saiṃ anāmikābhyāṃ huṃ** *thumb ring finger*

Oṃ saiṃ in the ring finger, Cut the Ego!

ॐ सौं कनिष्ठिकाभ्यां बौषट्

**oṃ sauṃ kaniṣṭhikābhyāṃ vauṣaṭ** *thumb little finger*

Oṃ sauṃ in the little finger, Ultimate Purity!

Roll hand over hand forwards while reciting *karatal kar*,
and backwards while chanting *pṛṣṭhābhyāṃ*,
then clap hands when chanting *astrāya phaṭ.*

ॐ सः करतल कर पृष्ठाभ्यां अस्त्राय फट् ॥

**oṃ saḥ karatal kar pṛṣṭhābhyāṃ astrāya phaṭ**

Oṃ saḥ I bow to the Goddess Sarasvatī with the weapon of Virtue.

ॐ सं सरस्वत्यै नमः

**oṃ saṃ sarasvatyai namaḥ**

Oṃ I bow to the Goddess Sarasvatī.

## aṅga nyāsa

establishment in the body

*Holding tattva mudrā, touch heart.*

ॐ सां हृदयाय नमः

**oṃ sāṃ hṛdayāya namaḥ** *touch heart*

Oṃ sāṃ in the heart, I bow.

*Holding tattva mudrā, touch top of head.*

ॐ सीं शिरसे स्वाहा

**oṃ sīṃ śirase svāhā** *top of head*

Oṃ sīṃ on the top of the head, I am One with God!

*With thumb extended, touch back of head.*

ॐ सूं शिखायै वषट्

**oṃ sūṃ śikhāyai vaṣaṭ** *back of head*

Oṃ sūṃ on the back of the head, Purify!

*Holding tattva mudrā, cross both arms.*

ॐ सैं कवचाय हुं

**oṃ saiṃ kavacāya huṃ** *cross both arms*

Oṃ saiṃ crossing both arms, Cut the Ego!

*Holding tattva mudrā, touch two eyes and in between at once with three middle fingers.*

ॐ सौं नेत्रत्रयाय वौषट्

**oṃ sauṃ netratrayāya vauṣaṭ** *touch three eyes*

Oṃ sauṃ in the three eyes, Ultimate Purity!

Roll hand over hand forwards while reciting *karatal kar*, and backwards while chanting *pṛṣṭhābhyāṃ*, then clap hands when chanting *astrāya phaṭ.*

ॐ सः करतल कर पृष्ठाभ्यां अस्त्राय फट् ॥

**oṃ saḥ karatal kar pṛṣṭhābhyāṃ astrāya phaṭ**

Oṃ saḥ I bow to the Goddess Sarasvatī with the weapon of Virtue.

ॐ सं सरस्वत्यै नमः

**oṃ saṃ sarasvatyai namaḥ**

Oṃ I bow to the Goddess Sarasvatī.

या कुन्देन्दु-तुषार-हार-धवला या सुभ्र-वस्त्रावृता ।
या वीणा-वर-दण्ड-मण्डितकरा या श्वेत-पद्मासना ॥

**yā kundendu-tuṣāra-hāra-dhavalā**
**yā subhra-vastrāvṛtā**
**yā vīṇā-vara-daṇḍa-maṇḍitakarā**
**yā śveta-padmāsanā**

She wears a beautiful garland made from the Queen of Jasmine Flowers covered with dew. She wears a white garment. Her hands are ornamented with a vīṇā, a blessing and a staff, and She is situated on a white lotus.

या ब्रह्माच्युत-शंकर-प्रभृतिभिर्देवैः सदा वन्दिता ।

सा मां पातु सरस्वती भगवती निःशेष-जाड्यापहा ॥

**yā brahmācyuta-śaṃkara-prabhṛtibhir**
**devaiḥ sadā vanditā**
**sā māṃ pātu sarasvatī bhagavatī niḥśeṣ-jāḍyāpahā**

She is worshipped by Brahmā, Viṣṇu and Śiva, along with all the other Gods. May that Sarasvatī, the Supreme Divinity, protect me unceasingly from the absence of intelligence.

ॐ भद्रकाल्यै नमो नित्यं सरस्वत्यै नमो नमः ।

वेदवेदाङ्गवेदान्त विद्यास्थानेभ्य एव च ॥

**oṃ bhadrakālyai namo nityaṃ**
**sarasvatyai namo namaḥ**
**vedavedaṅgavedānta vidyāsthānebhya eva ca**

Oṃ I always bow to the Excellent Remover of Darkness. Again and again I bow down to the Goddess Sarasvati. She is all Wisdom, including all apendages to wisdom, the highest Wisdom, and the repository of all knowledge.

ॐ सरस्वति महाभागे विद्ये कमलालोचने ।

विश्वरुपे विशालाक्षि विद्यां देहि नमोऽस्तु ते ॥

**oṃ sarasvati mahābhāge vidye kamalālocane**
**viśvarupe viśālākṣi vidyāṃ dehi namo-stu te**

Oṃ Goddess Sarasvati, of great parts, all Knowledge, with lotus eyes: You are the form of the universe, Seer of All, please give us knowledge, we bow down to you.

**brahmā pūjā**

worship of brahmā

**brahmā gāyatrī**

ॐ तत् पुरुषाय विद्महे परातत्त्वाय धीमहे ।

तन्नो ब्रह्माः प्रचोदयात् ॥

**oṃ tat puruṣāya vidmahe parātattvāya dhīmahe**
**tanno brahmāḥ pracodayāt**

Oṃ We meditate on that full and complete Consciousness, we contemplate the highest Principle. May that Creative Capacity give us increase.

**dhyānam**

meditation

ॐ ब्रह्मा कमण्डलुधरश्चतुर्वक्त्रश्चतुभूजः ।

कदाचिद्रक्तकमले हंसारूढः कदाचन ॥

**oṃ brahmā kamaṇḍaludharaścaturvaktraścatubhūjaḥ**
**kadācidraktakamale haṃsārūḍhaḥ kadācana**

Oṃ Brahmā holds the water pot of renunciation. He has four faces and four arms. He is colored as a red lotus. He rides upon a swan at all times.

वर्णेन रक्तगौराङ्गः प्रांशुस्तुंगाङ्ग ऊन्नतः ।

कमण्डलुर्वामिकरे श्रुवो हस्ते तु दक्षिणे ॥

**varṇena raktagaurāṅgaḥ prāṃśustuṃgāṅga ūnnataḥ**
**kamaṇḍalurvāmakare śruvo haste tu dakṣiṇe**

His color is red, His body is white; by His strength Gaṅgā rose. He keeps the water pot in His left hand, and the spoon for pouring oblations of ghee in His right.

दक्षिणाधवस्तथा माला वामाधश्च तथा श्रुवः ।
आज्यस्थाली वामपार्श्वे वेदाः सर्वेऽग्रतः स्थिताः ॥

**dakṣiṇādhavastathā mālā vāmādhaśca tathā śruvaḥ**
**ājyasthālī vāmapārśve vedāḥ sarve-grataḥ sthitāḥ**

In His lower right hand there is a mālā, and in His lower left hand is a spoon for pouring oblations. On His left side is the vessel containing ghee for oblations, and the four Vedas are situated around Him.

सावित्री वामपार्श्वस्था दक्षिणस्था सरस्वती ।
सर्वे चर्षयो ह्यग्रे कुर्ज्यादेभिश्च चिन्तनम् ॥

**sāvitrī vāmapārśvesthā dakṣiṇasthā sarasvatī**
**sarve carṣayo hyagre kurjyādebhiśca cintanam**

Sāvitrī is at His left side, and Sarasvatī is at His right. All the ṛṣis are gathered around. We think of the Progenitor of all beings born on earth.

ॐ बौं ब्रह्मणे नमः

**oṃ bauṃ brahmaṇe namaḥ**

Oṃ bauṃ we bow to Brahmā.

**kara nyāsa**

establishment in the hands

ॐ बां अंगुष्ठाभ्यां नमः

**oṃ bāṃ aṅguṣṭhābhyāṃ namaḥ** *thumb forefinger*

Oṃ bāṃ in the thumb I bow.

ॐ बीं तर्जनीभ्यां स्वाहा

**oṃ bīṃ tarjanībhyāṃ svāhā** *thumb forefinger*

Oṃ bīṃ in the forefinger, I am One with God!

ॐ बूं मध्यमाभ्यां वषट्

**oṃ būṃ madhyamābhyāṃ vaṣaṭ** *thumbmiddlefinger*

Oṃ būṃ in the middle finger, Purify!

ॐ बैं अनामिकाभ्यां हुं

**oṃ baiṃ anāmikābhyāṃ huṃ** *thumb ring finger*

Oṃ baiṃ in the ring finger, Cut the Ego!

ॐ बौं कनिष्ठिकाभ्यां बौषट्

**oṃ bauṃ kaniṣṭhikābhyāṃ vauṣaṭ** *thumb little finger*

Oṃ bauṃ in the little finger, Ultimate Purity!

Roll hand over hand forwards while reciting *karatal kar*, and backwards while chanting *pṛṣṭhābhyāṃ*, then clap hands when chanting *astrāya phaṭ*.

ॐ बः करतल कर पृष्ठाभ्यां अस्त्राय फट् ॥

**oṃ baḥ karatal kar pṛṣṭhābhyāṃ astrāya phaṭ**

Oṃ baḥ I bow to Brahmā, with the weapon of Virtue.

ॐ बौं ब्रह्मणे नमः

**oṃ bauṃ brahmaṇe namaḥ**

Oṃ bauṃ we bow to Brahmā.

**aṅga nyāsa**

establishment in the body

*Holding tattva mudrā, touch heart.*

ॐ बां हृदयाय नमः

**oṃ bāṃ hṛdayāya namaḥ** *touch heart*

Oṃ bāṃ in the heart, I bow.

*Holding tattva mudrā, touch top of head.*

ॐ बीं शिरसे स्वाहा

**oṃ bīṃ śirase svāhā** *top of head*

Oṃ bīṃ on the top of the head, I am One with God!

*With thumb extended, touch back of head.*

ॐ बूं शिखायै वषट्

**oṃ būṃ śikhāyai vaṣaṭ** *back of head*

Oṃ būṃ on the back of the head, Purify!

*Holding tattva mudrā, cross both arms.*

ॐ बैं कवचाय हुं

**oṃ baiṃ kavacāya huṃ** *cross both arms*

Oṃ baiṃ crossing both arms, Cut the Ego!

*Holding tattva mudrā, touch two eyes and in between at once with three middle fingers.*

ॐ बौं नेत्रत्रयाय वौषट्

**oṃ bauṃ netratrayāya vauṣaṭ** *touch three eyes*

Oṃ bauṃ in the three eyes, Ultimate Purity!

Roll hand over hand forwards while reciting *karatal kar*,
and backwards while chanting *pṛṣṭhābhyāṃ*,
then clap hands when chanting *astrāya phaṭ*.

ॐ बः करतल कर पृष्ठाभ्यां अस्त्राय फट् ॥

**oṃ baḥ karatal kar pṛṣṭhābhyāṃ astrāya phaṭ**

Oṃ baḥ I bow to Brahmā, with the weapon of Virtue.

ॐ बौं ब्रह्मणे नमः

**oṃ bauṃ brahmaṇe namaḥ**

Oṃ bauṃ we bow to Brahmā.

## viṣṇu pūjā

worship of viṣṇu

### viṣṇu gāyatrī

ॐ नारायणाय विद्महे वासुदेवाय धीमहे ।

तन्नो विष्णुः प्रचोदयात् ॥

**oṃ nārāyaṇāya vidmahe vaśudevāya dhīmahe**
**tanno viṣṇu pracodayāt**

Oṃ We meditate on the manifestation of Consciousness, we contemplate the Lord of the Earth. May that Viṣṇu grant us increase.

### dhyānam

meditation

शान्ताकारं भुजग-शयनं पद्मनाभं सुरेशम् ।

विश्वाधारं गगन-सदृशं मेघवर्णं शुभाङ्गम् ॥

**śāntākāraṃ bhujaga-śayanaṃ**
**padmanābhaṃ sureśam**
**viśvādhāraṃ gagana-sadṛśaṃ**
**meghavarṇaṃ śubhāṅgam**

The Cause of Peace is lying on a snake, from whose navel sprang the lotus. He is the Lord of Gods, who supports the universe, appearing as the sky, and is dark as a cloud, with a beautiful body.

लक्ष्मीकान्तं कमलनयनं योगिभिर्ध्यान-गम्यम् ।
वन्दे विष्णुं भव-भय-हरं सर्वलोकैकनाथम् ॥

**lakṣmīkāntaṃ kamalanayanaṃ**
**yogibhirdhyāna-gamyam**
**vande viṣṇuṃ bhava-bhaya-haraṃ**
**sarvalokaikanātham**

The Lord of Lakṣmī, with lotus eyes, is realized by Yogis in meditation. We worship Viṣṇu, who removes the fear of existence and who is Master of the all of the worlds.

यदा यदा हि धर्मस्य ग्लानिर्भवति भारत ।
अभ्युत्थानमधर्मस्य तादात्मानं सृजाम्यहम् ॥

**yadā yadā hi dharmasya glānirbhavati bhārata**
**abhyutthānamadharmasya tādātmānaṃ sṛjāmyaham**

Whenever the forces of dharma become weak, oh Bhārat, you who manifest light, in order to put down the forces of unrighteousness, my soul takes birth in creation.

परित्राणाय साधूनां विनाशाय च दुष्कृताम् ।
धर्मसंस्थापनार्थाय संभवामि युगे युगे ॥

**paritrāṇāya sādhūnāṃ vināśāya ca duṣkṛtām**
**dharmasaṃsthāpanārthāya saṃbhavāmi yuge yuge**

To protect those who strive for spiritual life, to destroy the performance of evil, in order to establish the principles of dharma, from time to time I make My presence manifest.

नैनं छिन्दन्ति शस्त्राणि नैनं दहति पावकः ।
न चैनं क्लेदयन्त्यापो न शोषयति मारुतः ॥

**nainaṃ chindanti śastrāṇi nainaṃ dahati pāvakaḥ**
**na cainaṃ kledayantyāpo na śoṣayati mārutaḥ**

No weapons can pierce it, nor can fire burn it; water cannot make it wet, nor can the wind blow it.

नमो ब्रह्मण्य देवाय गोब्रह्मणहिताय च ।
जगद्धिताय कृष्णाय गोविन्दाय नमो नमः ॥

**namo brahmaṇya devāya gobrahmaṇahitāya ca**
**jagaddhitāya kṛṣṇāya govindāya namo namaḥ**

I bow to the Lord of Creation, and to the examples of radiant light, to the Creator of the world, to Kṛṣṇa, to Govinda, I bow, I bow.

नमस्ते त्रिषु लोकेषु नमस्ते परतस्त्रिषु ।
नमस्ते दिक्षु सर्वासु त्वं हि सर्वमयो निधिः ॥

**namaste triṣu lokeṣu namaste paratastriṣu**
**namaste dikṣu sarvāsu tvaṃ hi sarvamayo nidhiḥ**

I bow to He who is manifest in the three worlds. I bow to He who is beyond the three worlds. I bow to He who is in every direction, may my thoughts remain fixed on Him.

नमस्ते भगवन् विष्णो लोकानां प्रभवाप्याय ।
त्वं हि कर्त्ता हृषीकेश संहर्ता चापराजितः ॥

**namaste bhagavan viṣṇo lokānāṃ prabhavāpyāya**
**tvaṃ hi karttā hṛṣīkeśa saṃhartā cāparājitaḥ**

I bow to the Supreme Lord Viṣṇu, who is the essence of all the worlds. He is the Doer of all, Controller of the senses, Dissolver and is undefeatable.

यथा विष्णुमयं सत्यं यथा विष्णुमयं जगत् ।
यथा विष्णुमयं सर्वं पाप्मा मे नश्यतां तथा ॥

**yathā viṣṇumayaṃ satyaṃ yathā viṣṇumayaṃ jagat**
**yathā viṣṇumayaṃ sarvaṃ**
**pāpmā me naśyatāṃ tathā**

It is this Viṣṇu that is my truth, and it is this Viṣṇu that is my world. It is this Viṣṇu that is my all. Please destroy all sin.

नारायणः परं ब्रह्म नारायणपरं तपः ।
नारायणपरो देवः सर्वं नारायणः सदा ॥

**nārāyaṇaḥ paraṃ brahma nārāyaṇaparaṃ tapaḥ**
**nārāyaṇaparo devaḥ sarvaṃ nārāyaṇaḥ sadā**

The manifestation of Consciousness is the Supreme Divinity, the manifestation of Consciousness is the highest austerity. The manifestation of Consciousness is the Supreme God. Everything is the manifestation of Consciousness.

**kara nyāsa**

establishment in the hands

ॐ क्लां अंगुष्ठाभ्यां नमः

**oṃ klāṃ aṅguṣṭhābhyāṃ namaḥ** *thumb forefinger*

Oṃ klāṃ in the thumb I bow.

ॐ क्लीं तर्जनीभ्यां स्वाहा

**oṃ klīṃ tarjanībhyāṃ svāhā** *thumb forefinger*

Oṃ klīṃ in the forefinger, I am One with God!

ॐ क्लूं मध्यमाभ्यां वषट्

**oṃ klūṃ madhyamābhyāṃ vaṣaṭ** *thumb middlefinger*

Oṃ klūṃ in the middle finger, Purify!

ॐ क्लैं अनामिकाभ्यां हुं

**oṃ klaiṃ anāmikābhyāṃ huṃ** *thumb ring finger*

Oṃ klaiṃ in the ring finger, Cut the Ego!

ॐ क्लौं कनिष्ठिकाभ्यां वौषट्

**oṃ klauṃ kaniṣṭhikābhyāṃ vauṣaṭ** *thumb little finger*

Oṃ klauṃ in the little finger, Ultimate Purity!

Roll hand over hand forwards while reciting *karatal kar*,
and backwards while chanting *pṛṣṭhābhyāṃ*,
then clap hands when chanting *astrāya phaṭ*.

ॐ क्लः करतल कर पृष्ठाभ्यां अस्त्राय फट् ॥

**oṃ klaḥ karatal kar pṛṣṭhābhyāṃ astrāya phaṭ**

Oṃ klaḥ I bow to Viṣṇu, with the weapon of Virtue.

ॐ क्लीं विष्णवे नमः

**oṃ klīṃ viṣṇave namaḥ**

Oṃ klīṃ I bow to Viṣṇu

## aṅga nyāsa

establishment in the body

*Holding tattva mudrā, touch heart.*

ॐ क्लां हृदयाय नमः

**oṃ klāṃ hṛdayāya namaḥ** *touch heart*

Oṃ klāṃ in the heart, I bow.

*Holding tattva mudrā, touch top of head.*

ॐ क्लीं शिरसे स्वाहा

**oṃ klīṃ śirase svāhā** *top of head*

Oṃ klīṃ on the top of the head, I am One with God!

*With thumb extended, touch back of head.*

ॐ क्लूं शिखायै वषट्

**oṃ klūṃ śikhāyai vaṣaṭ** *back of head*

Oṃ klūṃ on the back of the head, Purify!

*Holding tattva mudrā, cross both arms.*

ॐ क्लैं कवचाय हुं

**oṃ klaiṃ kavacāya huṃ** *cross both arms*

Oṃ klaiṃ crossing both arms, Cut the Ego!

*Holding tattva mudrā, touch two eyes and in between at once with three middle fingers.*

ॐ क्लौं नेत्रत्रयाय वौषट्

**oṃ baum netratrayāya vauṣaṭ** *touch three eyes*

Oṃ klauṃ in the three eyes, Ultimate Purity!

Roll hand over hand forwards while reciting *karatal kar*, and backwards while chanting *pṛṣṭhābhyāṃ*, then clap hands when chanting *astrāya phaṭ.*

ॐ क्लः करतल कर पृष्ठाभ्यां अस्त्राय फट् ॥

**oṃ klaḥ karatal kar pṛṣṭhābhyāṃ astrāya phaṭ**

Oṃ klaḥ I bow to Viṣṇu, with the weapon of Virtue.

ॐ क्लीं विष्णवे नमः

**oṃ klīṃ viṣṇave namaḥ**

Oṃ klīṃ I bow to Viṣṇu

## śiva pūjā

worship of śiva

ॐ सदा शिवाय विद्महे सहश्राक्षाय धीमहे ।

तन्नो शम्भो प्रचोदयात् ॥

**oṃ sadā śivāya vidmahe sahaśrākṣāya dhīmahe tanno śambho pracodayāt**

Oṃ We meditate upon the Perfect, Full, Complete, Always Continuing, Consciousness of Infinite Goodness, we contemplate He Whose Thousand Eyes see everywhere. May that Giver of Bliss grant us increase.

ॐ सद्योजातं प्रपद्यामि सद्योजातायवै नमो नमः ।

भवे भवे नाति भवे भवस्वमांभवोद्भवाय नमः ॥

**oṃ sadyojātaṃ prapadyāmi**
**sadyojātāyavai namo namaḥ**
**bhave bhave nāti bhave**
**bhavasvamāṃ bhavodbhavāya namaḥ**

Oṃ I extol the Birth of Truth as Pure Existence. Again and again I bow down to the Birth of Truth as Pure Existence. In being after being, beyond all being, who Himself is all Being, from whom came all being, to That Existence I bow.

वामदेवाय नमो ज्येष्ठाय नमः श्रेष्ठाय नमो रुद्राय नमः ।

कालाय नमः कलविकरणाय नमो बलविकरणाय नमो

बलाय नमो बलप्रमत्तनाय नमः ।

सर्वभूतदमनाय नमोमनोन्मनाय नमः ॥

**vāmadevāya namo jyeṣṭhāya namaḥ śreṣṭhāya**
**namo rudrāya namaḥ**
**kālāya namaḥ kalavikaraṇāya namo**
**balavikaraṇāya namo balāya namo**
**balapramattanāya namaḥ**
**sarvabhūtadamanāya namomanonmanāya namaḥ**

I bow to the Beautiful God Who Is Beloved. I bow to the Pleasant One, to the Ultimate One. I bow to the Reliever of Sufferings, I bow to Time, I bow to the Cause of the Illumination of Darkness, I bow to the Source of Strength, I bow to the Progenitor of Strength. I bow to the Fashioner of All the Elements, I bow to the Mind of All Minds.

अघोरेभ्योत्तघोरेभ्योघोरघेरतरेभ्यः ।

सर्वेभ्यःसर्वशर्वेभ्यो नमस्तेऽस्तुरुद्ररूपेभ्यः ॥

**aghorebhyottaghorebhyoghoragheratarebhyaḥ sarvebhyaḥsarvaśarvebhyo namaste-sturudrarūpebhyaḥ**

I bow to He Who Is Free From Fear, Who Instills the Fear of Evil, Who Saves the Righteous from Fear; Who Is Within All, the All of Everything, we give our respect to He Who Is the Form of the Reliever of Sufferings.

ॐ तत् पुरुषाय विद्महे महादेवाय धीमहि ।

तन्नो रुद्रः प्रचोदयात् ॥

**oṃ tat puruṣāya vidmahe mahādevāya dhīmahi tanno rudraḥ pracodayāt**

Oṃ We meditate on That Universal Consciousness, we contemplate the Great God. May that Reliever of Sufferings grant us increase.

ईशानः सर्वविद्यानमीश्वरः सर्वभूतानाम् ।

ब्रह्माधिपतिर्ब्रह्मणोधिपतिर्ब्रह्माशिवोमेऽस्तुसदाशिवोम् ॥

**īśānaḥ sarvavidyānamīśvaraḥ sarvabhūtānām brahmādhipatirbrahmaṇodhipatirbrahmāśivome-stusadāśivom**

The Seer of All, who is all Knowledge, the Lord of the Universe, who is all existence; before the Creative Consciousness, before the knowers of Consciousness, existing in eternal delight as the Consciousness of Infinite Goodness.

एते गन्धपुष्पे ॐ हराय नमः

**ete gandhapuṣpe oṃ harāya namaḥ**

With these scented flowers oṃ we bow to He who Takes Away.

एते गन्धपुष्पे ॐ महेश्वराय नमः

**ete gandhapuṣpe oṃ maheśvarāya namaḥ**

With these scented flowers oṃ we bow to to the Supreme Lord of All.

ॐ ध्यायेन्नित्यं महेशं रजतगिरिनिभं चारुचन्द्रावतंसं
रत्ना कल्पोज्वलांगं परशु मृगवयाभीति हस्तं प्रसन्नं ।
पद्मासीनं समन्तात् स्तुतऽममरगणैर्व्याघ्रकृत्तिं वसानं
विश्वाद्यं विश्वबीजं निखलभयहरं पञ्चवक्त्रं त्रिनेत्रं ॥

**oṃ dhyāyen nityaṃ maheśaṃ**
**rajata girinibhaṃ cāru candrā vataṃsaṃ**
**ratnā kalpo jvalāṃgaṃ**
**paraśu mṛga vayābhīti hastaṃ prasannaṃ**
**padmāsīnaṃ samantāt**
**stuta-mama ragaṇair vyāghra kṛtiṃ vasānaṃ**
**viśvādyaṃ viśva bījaṃ**
**nikhala bhayaharaṃ pañca vaktraṃ trinetraṃ**

We always meditate on He who shines like the white mountains, ornamented by a digit of the moon on His head. His body shines like jewels. In His left hands He displays an axe and the Mṛga Mudrā (Kalpataru Mudrā, with the thumb, middle and ring fingers joined with the pointer and pinky extended up) and in His two right hands He shows mudrās granting blessings and fearlessness. He is of beautiful appearance seated in the full lotus asana. On His four sides the Gods are present singing hymns of praise. His wearing apparel is a tiger's skin. He is before the universe and the cause of the universe. He removes all fear, has five faces and three eyes.

### kara nyāsa

establishment in the hands

ॐ नं अंगुष्ठाभ्यां नमः

**oṃ naṃ aṅguṣṭhābhyāṃ namaḥ** *thumb forefinger*

Oṃ naṃ in the thumb I bow.

ॐ मः तर्जनीभ्यां स्वाहा

**oṃ maḥ tarjanībhyāṃ svāhā** *thumb forefinger*

Oṃ maḥ in the forefinger, I am One with God!

ॐ शिं मध्यमाभ्यां वषट्

**oṃ śiṃ madhyamābhyāṃ vaṣaṭ** *thumb middlefinger*

Oṃ śiṃ in the middle finger, Purify!

ॐ वां अनामिकाभ्यां हुं

**oṃ vāṃ anāmikābhyāṃ huṃ** *thumb ringfinger*

Oṃ vāṃ in the ring finger, Cut the Ego!

ॐ यः कनिष्ठिकाभ्यां वौषट्

**oṃ yaḥ kaniṣṭhikābhyāṃ vauṣaṭ** *thumb little finger*

Oṃ yaḥ in the little finger, Ultimate Purity!

Roll hand over hand forwards while reciting *karatal kar*,
and backwards while chanting *pṛṣṭhābhyāṃ*,
then clap hands when chanting *astrāya phaṭ*.

ॐ नमः शिवाय करतल कर पृष्ठाभ्यां अस्त्राय फट् ॥

**oṃ namaḥ śivāya karatal kar pṛṣṭhābhyāṃ astrāya phaṭ**

Oṃ I bow to the Consciousness of Infinite Goodness with the weapon of Virtue.

ॐ नमः शिवाय

**oṃ namaḥ śivāya**

I bow to the Consciousness of Infinite Goodness.

**aṅga nyāsa**

establishment in the body

*Holding tattva mudrā, touch heart.*

ॐ नं हृदयाय नमः

**oṃ naṃ hṛdayāya namaḥ** *touch heart*

Oṃ naṃ in the heart, I bow.

*Holding tattva mudrā, touch top of head.*

ॐ मः शिरसे स्वाहा

**oṃ maḥ śirase svāhā** *top of head*

Oṃ maḥ on the top of the head, I am One with God!

*With thumb extended, touch back of head.*

ॐ शिं शिखायै वषट्

**oṃ śiṃ śikhāyai vaṣaṭ** *back of head*

Oṃ śiṃ on the back of the head, Purify!

*Holding tattva mudrā, cross both arms.*

ॐ वां कवचाय हुं

**oṃ vāṃ kavacāya huṃ** *cross both arms*

Oṃ vāṃ crossing both arms, Cut the Ego!

*Holding tattva mudrā, touch two eyes and in between at once with three middle fingers.*

ॐ यः नेत्रत्रयाय वौषट्

**oṃ yaḥ netratrayāya vauṣaṭ** *touch three eyes*

Oṃ yaḥ in the three eyes, Ultimate Purity!

Roll hand over hand forwards while reciting *karatal kar*, and backwards while chanting *pṛṣṭhābhyāṃ*, then clap hands when chanting *astrāya phaṭ*.

ॐ नमः शिवाय करतल कर पृष्ठाभ्यां अस्त्राय फट् ॥

**oṃ namaḥ śivāya karatal kar pṛṣṭhābhyāṃ astrāya phaṭ**

Oṃ I bow to the Consciousness of Infinite Goodness with the weapon of Virtue.

ॐ नमः शिवाय

**oṃ namaḥ śivāya**

I bow to the Consciousness of Infinite Goodness.

ॐ नं उदीच्यै नमः

**oṃ naṃ udīcyai namaḥ**

Oṃ I bow to naṃ in the north.

ॐ मः प्राच्यै नमः

**oṃ maḥ prācyai namaḥ**

Oṃ I bow to maḥ in the east.

ॐ शिं दक्षिणायै नमः

**oṃ śiṃ dakṣiṇāyai namaḥ**

Oṃ I bow to śiṃ in the south.

ॐ वां प्रतीच्यै नमः

**oṃ vāṃ pratīcyai namaḥ**

Oṃ I bow to vāṃ in the west.

ॐ यः वायव्यै नमः

**oṃ yaḥ vāyavyai namaḥ**

Oṃ I bow to yaḥ in the northwest.

ॐ नं ऐशान्यै नमः

**oṃ naṃ aiśānyai namaḥ**

Oṃ I bow to naṃ in the northeast.

ॐ मः आग्नेय्यै नमः

**oṃ maḥ āgneyyai namaḥ**

Oṃ I bow to maḥ in the southeast.

ॐ शिं नैर्ऋत्यै नमः

**oṃ śiṃ nairṛtyai namaḥ**

Oṃ I bow to śiṃ in the southwest.

ॐ वां ऊर्ध्वायै नमः

**oṃ vāṃ ūrdhvāyai namaḥ**
Oṃ I bow to vāṃ looking up.

ॐ यः भूम्यै नमः

**oṃ yaḥ bhūmyai namaḥ**
Oṃ I bow to yaḥ looking down.

ॐ नमः शिवाय

**oṃ namaḥ śivāya** *ten directions*
Oṃ I bow to the Consciousness of Infinite Goodness

एते गन्धपुष्पे ॐ सर्वाय क्षितिमूर्त्तये नमः

**ete gandhapuṣpe oṃ sarvāya kṣiti mūrttaye namaḥ**
With these scented flowers oṃ I bow to the Image of all Earth in the east.

एते गन्धपुष्पे ॐ भराय जलमूर्त्तये नमः

**ete gandhapuṣpe oṃ bharāya jala mūrttaye namaḥ**
With these scented flowers oṃ I bow to the Image who is full of water in the northeast.

एते गन्धपुष्पे ॐ रुद्राय अग्निमूर्त्तये नमः

**ete gandhapuṣpe oṃ rudrāya agni mūrttaye namaḥ**
With these scented flowers oṃ I bow to the Image of the Divine Fire, the Light of Meditation, who takes away the sufferings of all, in the north.

एते गन्धपुष्पे ॐ ऊग्राय वायुमूर्त्तये नमः

**ete gandhapuṣpe oṃ ūgrāya vāyu mūrttaye namaḥ**

With these scented flowers oṃ I bow to the Image of Wind who is fierce and blows as he pleases, in the northwest.

एते गन्धपुष्पे ॐ भीमाय आकाषमूर्त्तये नमः

**ete gandhapuṣpe oṃ bhīmāya ākāṣa mūrttaye namaḥ**

With these scented flowers oṃ I bow to the Image of Ether who is fearless, in the west.

एते गन्धपुष्पे ॐ पशुपतये यजमानमूर्त्तये नमः

**ete gandhapuṣpe oṃ paśupataye yajamāna mūrttaye namaḥ**

With these scented flowers oṃ I bow to the Sacrificer, the Lord of all animal life, in the southwest.

एते गन्धपुष्पे ॐ महादेवाय सोममूर्त्तये नमः

**ete gandhapuṣpe oṃ mahādevāya soma mūrttaye namaḥ**

With these scented flowers oṃ I bow to the Image of the Moon of Devotion, to the Great God, in the south.

एते गन्धपुष्पे ॐ ईशानाय सूर्यमूर्त्तये नमः

**ete gandhapuṣpe oṃ īśānāya sūrya mūrttaye namaḥ**

With these scented flowers oṃ I bow to the Image of the Sun or the Light of Wisdom, to the Lord of All, in the southeast.

ॐ नमोऽस्तु स्थाणुभूताय ज्योतिर्लिङ्गात्मने नमः ।
चतुर्मूर्त्तिवपुष्छाया भासिताङ्गाया शम्भवे ॥

**oṃ namo-stu stāṇubhūtāya jyotir liṅgātmane namaḥ**
**catur mūrttivapuṣchāyā bhāsitāṅgāyā śambhave**

Oṃ I bow to the Residence of All Existence, to the subtlest Consciousness of Light, I bow. The four images are His reflections, the body of the universe, Giver of Bliss.

ॐ नमः शिवाय

**oṃ namaḥ śivāya**

Oṃ I bow to the Consciousness of Infinite Goodness.

वन्दे देवमुमापतिं सुरगुरुं वन्दे जगत्कारणं
वन्दे पन्नगभूषणं मृगधरं वन्दे पशूनां पतिम् ।
वन्दे सूर्यशशाङ्कवह्निनयनं वन्दे मुकुन्दप्रियं
वन्दे भक्तजनाश्रयं च वरदं वन्दे शिवं शङ्करम् ॥

**vande devamumāpatiṃ suragurum**
**vande jagatkāraṇaṃ**
**vande pannagabhūṣaṇaṃ mṛgadharaṃ**
**vande paśūnāṃ patim**
**vande sūryaśaśāṅkavahninayanaṃ**
**vande mukundapriyaṃ**
**vande bhaktajanāśrayaṃ ca varadaṃ**
**vande śivaṃ śaṅkaram**

We extol the God who is the Lord of Umā, the Guru of the Gods. We extol the Cause of the perceivable universe. We extol He who has the radiance of emeralds, who shows the (mudrā) of the deer (also known as the wish-fulfilling tree). We extol He who is the Lord of all who are bound. We extol He whose three eyes are the Sun, the Moon and Fire. We extol the beloved of Viṣṇu. We extol the refuge of all devotees and the Giver of Boons. We extol the Consciousness of Infinite Goodness, the Cause of Bliss.

हे जिह्वे भज विश्वनाथ बद्रीकेदार भस्मम्बराः
भीमाशङ्करबैजनाथह्यवढे नागेशरामेश्वराः ।
ॐकारेममलेश्वरं स्मरहरं महङ्कालं मल्लिकाऽर्जुनम्
ध्यायेत् त्र्यंबकसोमनाथमनिशं एकादशे ॐ नमः ॥

**he jihve bhaja viśvanātha**
**badrīkedāra bhasmambarāḥ**
**bhīmāśaṅkarabaijanātha**
**hyavaḍhe nāgeśarāmeśvarāḥ**
**oṃkāremamaleśvaraṃ smaraharaṃ**
**mahaṅkālaṃ mallikā-rjunam**
**dhyāyet tryaṃbakasomanātha**
**maniśaṃ ekādaśe oṃ namaḥ**

Oh Tongue, sing the praises of the Lord of the Universe who dwells at Badrī-Kedārnāth and wears ashes. He stays at Bhīmāśaṅkara, Baijanātha, Nāgeśvara, Rāmeśvarā; Oṃkāreśvarā, Mamaleśvaraṃ, Mahaṅkālaṃ, Mallikārjunam, Tryaṃbaka, Somanātha. Oṃ we bow and meditate on the eleven (forms of Rudra).

देवं चन्द्रकलाधरं फणिधरं ब्रह्मा कपालाधरं
गौरीवह्यधरं त्रिलोचनधरं रुद्राक्षमालागलम् ।
गङ्गारङ्गतरङ्गपिङ्गलजटाजूटं च गङ्गाधरं
नीलोग्र भज विश्वनाथसिद्धसहितं सोम शरक्षाकरम् ॥

**devaṃ candrakalādharaṃ phaṇidharaṃ**
**brahmā kapālādharaṃ**
**gaurīvahyadharaṃ trilocanadharaṃ**
**rudrākṣamālāgalam**
**gaṅgāraṅgataraṅgapiṅgalajaṭājūṭaṃ**
**ca gaṅgādharaṃ**
**nīlogra bhaja viśvanāthasiddhasahitaṃ**
**soma śarakṣākaram**

The God who wears the part of the Moon, who wears snakes, the Supreme Divinity who wears skulls. With Gaurī on His left side, displaying three eyes and a garland of rudrākṣa. He supports Gaṅgā who is running down from His matted locks of hair. With a blue throat, the attained ones sing praises to the Lord of the Universe, with full devotion, and seek His protection.

शान्तं पद्मासनस्थं शशधरमुकुटं पञ्चवक्त्रं
शूलं वज्रं च खड्गं परशुमभयदं दक्षिणाङ्गे ।
नागं पाशं च घण्टां डमरुकसहितां साङ्कुशं वामभागे
नानालङ्कारदीप्तं स्फटिकमणिनिभं पार्वतीशं नमामि ॥

**śāntaṃ padmāsanasthaṃ**
**śaśadharamukuṭaṃ pañcavaktraṃ**
**śūlaṃ vajraṃ ca khaḍgaṃ**
**paraśumabhayadaṃ dakṣiṇāṅge**
**nāgaṃ pāśaṃ ca ghaṇṭāṃ**
**ḍamarukasahitāṃ sāṅkuśaṃ vāmabhāge**
**nānālaṅkāradīptaṃ sphaṭikamaṇinibhaṃ**
**pārvatīśaṃ namāmi**

Who is filled with peace, sitting in the full lotus posture with the moon on His forehead, with five faces and three eyes, He holds the trident, thunderbolt, sword and axe, and shows the mudrā that grants freedom from all fear in the (five) hands of His right side. A sword, noose, bell, small drum and curved sword are in those on His left side. His various ornaments are shining like gems and crystal. I bow to the husband of Pārvatī.

कर्पूरगौरं करुणावतारं संसारसारं भुजगेन्द्रहारम् ।
सदा वसन्तं हृदयारविन्दे भवं भवानीसहितं नमामि ॥

**karpūragauraṃ karuṇāvatāraṃ**
**saṃsārasāraṃ bhujagendrahāram**
**sadā vasantaṃ hṛdayāravinde**
**bhavaṃ bhavānīsahitaṃ namāmi**

Of white color like pure camphor, He is the embodiment of Compassion, the Lord of the Ocean of objects and relationships, who wears the King of Snakes as a necklace. I bow to He who always resides in the lotus of the heart of all existence along with the Divine Mother of the Universe.

असितगिरिसमं स्यात्कज्जलं सिन्धुपात्रे
सुरतरुवरशाखा लेखनी पत्रमुर्वी ।
लिखति यदि गृहीत्वा शारदा सर्वकालं
तदपि तव गुणानामीश पारं न याति ॥

**asitagirisamam syātkajjalam sindhupātre**
**surataruvaraśākhā lekhanī patramurvī**
**likhati yadi gṛhītvā śāradā sarvakālam**
**tadapi tava guṇānāmīśa pāram na yāti**

When Śāradā (Sarasvati), who has performed inconceivable austerities of purification and spiritual disciplines, is unable to know or write all your qualities, then what shall we be able to sing?

त्वमेव माता च पिता त्वमेव त्वमेव बन्धुश्चसखा त्वमेव ।
त्वमेव विद्या द्रविनं त्वमेव त्वमेव सर्वम् मम देवदेव ॥

**tvameva mātā ca pitā tvameva**
**tvameva bandhuścā sakhā tvameva**
**tvameva vidyā dravinam tvameva**
**tvameva sarvam mama devadeva**

You alone are Mother and Father, you alone are friend and relative. You alone are knowledge and wealth. Oh my God of Gods, you alone are everything.

करचरणकृतं वाक्कायजं कर्मजं वा
श्रवणनयनजं वा मानसं वाऽपराधम् ।
विहितमविहितं वा सर्वमेतत्क्षमस्व
जय जय करुणाब्धे श्रीमहादेव शम्भो ॥

**karacaraṇakṛtaṃ vākkāyajaṃ karmajaṃ vā
śravaṇanayanajaṃ vā mānasaṃ vā-parādham
vihitamavihitaṃ vā sarvametatkṣamasva
jaya jaya karuṇābdhe srīmahādeva śambho**

Any fault committed by the actions of my hands or feet, speech or body, my eyes, ears or mind, whether authorized or unauthorized, all of that please forgive. Victory! Victory to the Ocean of Compassion, the respected Great God, Illuminator of Peace.

चन्द्रोद्भासितशेखरे स्मरहरे गङ्गाधरे शङ्करे
सर्पैर्भूषितकण्ठकर्णविवरे नेत्रोत्थवैश्वानरे ।
दन्तित्वक्कृतसुन्दराम्बरधरे त्रैलोक्यसारे हरे
मोक्षार्थं कुरु चित्तमचलामन्यैस्तु किं कर्मभिः ॥

**candrodbhāsitaśekhare
smarahare gaṅgādhare śaṅkare
sarpairbhūṣitakaṇṭha
karṇavivare netrotthavaiśvānare
dantitvakkṛtasundarām
baradhare trailokyasāre hare
mokṣārthaṃ kuru cittam
acalāmanyaistu kiṃ karmabhiḥ**

Upon whose head the moon resides, Destroyer of the God of Love, who supports the Gaṅgā, Cause of Peace, at whose throat the snake shines, and also as the ornaments of his ears; in whose third eye resides the fire of Universal Existence, with teeth of ivory, wearing a beautiful garment, He takes away the difficulties of the ocean of the three worlds; for the purpose of liberation, do what is necessary to stop the changes and modifications of consciousness.

ॐ तत् पुरुषाय विद्महे महादेवाय धीमहे ।

तन्नो रुद्रः प्रचोदयात् ॥

**oṃ tat puruṣāya vidmahe mahādevāya dhīmahe**
**tanno rudraḥ pracodayāt**

We meditate on That Universal Consciousness, we contemplate the Great God. May that Reliever of Sufferings grant us increase.

ब्रह्मानन्दं परमसुखदं केवलं ज्ञानमूर्तिं

द्वनद्वातीतं गगनसदृशं तत्त्वमस्यादिलक्ष्यम् ।

एकं नित्यं विमलमचलं सर्वधीसाक्षिभूतं

भावातीतं त्रिगुणरहितं सद्गुरुं तं नमामि ॥

**brahmānandaṃ paramasukhadaṃ**
**kevalaṃ jñānamūrtiṃ**
**dvanadvātītaṃ gaganasadṛśaṃ**
**tattvamasyādilakṣyam**
**ekaṃ nityaṃ vimalamacalaṃ sarvadhīsākṣibhūtaṃ**
**bhāvātītaṃ triguṇarahitaṃ sadguruṃ taṃ namāmi**

This bliss of Supreme Divinity, the highest pleasure, the only image of Wisdom, beyond all changes, the pure perception through the ether, the Highest Goal of all Principles. One, eternal, pure, immovable, the Witness of the minds of all beings, beyond all attitudes, beyond the three guṇas, I bow to He who is the True Guru.

नारायणं पद्मभवं वसिष्ठं शक्तिं च तत्पुत्रपराशरं च ।
व्यासं शुकं गौडपदं महान्तं गोविन्दयोगीन्द्रमथास्य शिष्यम् ॥

**nārāyaṇaṃ padmabhavaṃ vasiṣṭhaṃ**
**śaktiṃ ca tatputraparāśaraṃ ca**
**vyāsaṃ śukaṃ gauḍapadaṃ mahāntaṃ**
**govindayogīndramathāsya śiṣyam**

From Nārāyaṇa (Viṣṇu) to the Lotus One (Brahmā), to Vasiṣṭha, to his disciple Śakti, to his son Parāśara, to Vyāsa, to Śukadeva, to Gauḍapadācārya, to his disciple Mahānta, to the King of Yogis, Govinda, in disciplic succession;

श्रीशङ्कराचार्यमथास्य पद्मपादं च हस्तामलकं च शिष्यम् ।
तं तोटकं वार्तिककारमन्यानस्मद्गुरून्संततमानतोऽस्मि ॥

**śrīśaṅkarācārya mathāsya padmapādaṃ ca**
**hastāmalakaṃ ca śiṣyam**
**taṃ toṭakaṃ vārtikakāramanyānasmad**
**gurūnsaṃtatamānato-smi**

The Respected Śaṅkarācārya and his disciples Padmapādācārya, Hastāmalakācārya, Toṭakācārya and Sureśvarācārya, and thereafter to other gurus, always we bow the head.

अखण्डमण्डलाकारं व्याप्तं येन चराचरम् ।
तत्पदं दर्शितं येन तस्मै श्रीगुरवे नमः ॥

**akhaṇḍamaṇḍalākāraṃ vyāptaṃ yena carācaram**
**tatpadaṃ darśitaṃ yena tasmai śrīgurave namaḥ**

To He who made manifest this infinite existence, and made the individual forms that move and move not; in order to perceive His lotus feet, I bow down to the respected Guru.

गुरुर्ब्रह्मा गुरुर्विष्णुः गुरुर्देवो महेश्वरः ।
गुरुसाक्षात् परं ब्रह्मा तस्मै श्रीगुरवे नमः ॥

**gururbrahmā gururviṣṇuḥ gururdevo maheśvaraḥ**
**gurusākṣāt param brahmā tasmai śrīgurave namaḥ**

Guru is Brahmā, Guru is Viṣṇuḥ, Guru is the Lord Maheśvaraḥ. The Guru is actually the Supreme Divinity, and therefore we bow down to the Guru.

श्रुतिस्मृतिपुरणानामालयं करुणालयम् ।
नमामि भगवत्पादं शङ्करं लोकशङ्करम् ॥

**śrutismṛtipuraṇānāmālayam karuṇālayam**
**namāmi bhagavatpādam śaṅkaram lokaśaṅkaram**

The Repository of Compassion described in the Vedas (śruti), in the histories and commentaries (smṛti) and in the purāṇas, I bow down to the feet of that divinity, the Cause of Peace, Cause of Peace in the worlds.

शङ्करं शङ्कराचार्यं केशवं बादरायणम् ।
सूत्रभाष्यकृतौ वन्दे भगवन्तौ पुनः पुनः ॥

**śaṅkaram śaṅkarācāryam keśavam bādarāyaṇam**
**sūtrabhāṣyakṛtau vande bhagavantau punaḥ punaḥ**

We worship with adoration Śaṅkara and Keśava (Viṣṇu), along with their spokesmen and commentators Śaṅkarācārya and Vedavyāsa (Bādarāyaṇa) again and again.

ईश्वरो गुरुरात्मेति मूर्त्तिभेदविभागिने ।
व्योमवद्व्याप्तदेहाय दक्षिणामूर्त्तये नमः ॥

**īśvaro gururātmeti mūrttibhedavibhāgine**
**vyomavadvyāptadehāya dakṣiṇāmūrttaye namaḥ**

The Supreme Divinity is the soul of the guru, the image of divinity distinguished by attributes. Who is indivisible like the sky, we bow to Dakṣiṇāmūrtti, the Preferred Image.

नानासुगन्धपुष्पाणि यथाकालोद्भवानि च ।
भक्त्या दत्तानि पूजार्थं गृहाण परमेश्वर ॥

**nānāsugandhapuṣpāṇi yathākālodbhavāni ca**
**bhaktyā dattāni pūjārthaṃ gṛhāṇa parameśvara**

Various excellently scented flowers that rise in their time, your devotees are offering for your worship. Please accept them, oh Supreme Lord.

सौराष्ट्रे सोमनाथं च श्रीशैले मल्लिकार्जुनम् ।
ऊज्ज्यैन्यां महाकालमोंकारे परमेश्वरम् ॥

**saurāṣṭre somanāthaṃ ca śrīśaile mallikārjunam**
**ūjjyainyāṃ mahākālamoṃkāre parameśvaram**

In Saurāṣṭra (He is called) Somanātha, and in Śrīśaila, Mallikārjunam; in Ūjjainyāṃ, Mahākālam, in Oṃkāra, Parameśvaram;

केदारं हिमवत्पृष्ठे डाकिन्यां भीमशङ्करम् ।
वाराणस्यं च विश्वेशं त्र्यम्बकं गौतमीतटे ॥

**kedāraṃ himavatpṛṣṭhe ḍākinyāṃ bhīmaśaṅkaram**
**vārāṇasyaṃ ca viśveśaṃ tryambakaṃ gautamītaṭe**

(He is called) Kedāra on the back side of the Himalayas, and in the South, Bhīmaśaṅkaram; in Vārāṇasi, Viśveśaṃ, in Gautamī, Tryambakaṃ.

वैध्यनाथं चिताभूमौ नागेशं दारुकावने ।
सेतुबंधे च रामेशं घुश्मेशं च शिवाल्ये ॥

**vaidhyanātham citābhūmau nāgeśam dārukāvane**
**setubamdhe ca rāmeśam ghuśmeśam ca śivālaye**

In Citābhūmi, the Land of Consciousness, (He is called) Vaidhyanātha, and in the forests of Dārukā, Nāgeśaṃ. Where they made the bridge, (He is called) Rāmeśaṃ, and in the place of Śiva, Ghuśmeśaṃ.

द्वादशैतानि नामानि प्रातरुत्थाय यः पठेत् ।
सर्व पापविनिर्मुक्त सर्वसिद्धि फलं लभेत् ॥

**dvādaśaitāni nāmāni prātarutthāya yaḥ paṭhet**
**sarva pāpavinirmukta sarvasiddhi phalam labhet**

Whoever will read these twelve names upon rising in the early morning, will be freed from the bondage of sin, and will attain the fruits of perfection.

ॐ महादेव महात्रान महायोगि महेश्वर ।
सर्वपाप हरां देव मकाराय नमो नमः ॥

**om mahādeva mahātrāna mahāyogi maheśvara**
**sarvapāpa harām deva makārāya namo namaḥ**

Oṃ The Great God, the Great Reliever, the Great Yogi, Oh Supreme Lord, Oh God who removes all Sin, in the form of the letter "**M**" which dissolves creation, we bow to you again and again.

ॐ नमः शिवाय शान्ताय कारणत्राय हेतवे ।

निवेदायामि चत्मनं त्वं गति परमेश्वर ॥

**oṃ namaḥ śivāya śāntāya kāraṇatrāya hetave**
**nivedāyāmi catmanaṃ tvaṃ gati parameśvara**

Oṃ I bow to the Consciousness of Infinite Goodness, to Peace, to the Cause of the three worlds, I offer to you the fullness of my soul, Oh Supreme Lord.

ॐ नमः शिवाय

**oṃ namaḥ śivāya**

Oṃ I bow to the Consciousness of Infinite Goodness.

## gaṇeśa pūjā

worship of gaṇeśa

### gaṇeśa gāyatrī

ॐ तत् पुरुषाय विद्महे वक्रतुण्डाय धीमहि ।

तन्नो दन्ती प्रचोदयात् ॥

**oṃ tat puruṣāya vidmahe vakratuṇḍāya dhīmahi**
**tanno dantī pracodayāt**

Oṃ We meditate on that Perfect Consciousness, we contemplate the One with a broken tooth. May that One with the Great Tusk grant us increase.

एते गन्धपुष्पे ॐ गं गणपतये नमः

**ete gandhapuṣpe oṃ gaṃ gaṇapataye namaḥ**

With these scented flowers oṃ we bow to the Lord of Wisdom, the Lord of the Multitudes.

**gaṇeśa dhyānam**

meditation

ॐ खर्व्वं स्थूलतनुं गजेन्द्रवदनं लम्बोदरं सुन्दरं

प्रस्यन्दन्मदगन्धलुब्धमधुपव्यालोलगण्डस्थलम् ।

दन्ताघातविदारितारिरुधिरैः सिन्दूरशोभाकरं

वन्दे शैलसुतासुतं गणपतिं सिद्धिप्रदं कामदं ॥

**oṃ kharvvaṃ sthūlatanuṃ gajendra**
**vadanaṃ lambodaraṃ sundaraṃ**
**prasyandanmadagandhalubdha**
**madhupavyālolagaṇḍasthalam**
**dantāghātavidāritārirudhiraiḥ sindūraśobhākaraṃ**
**vande śailasutāsutaṃ**
**gaṇapatiṃ siddhipradaṃ kāmadaṃ**

Oṃ Gaṇeśa, the Lord of Wisdom, is short, of stout body, with the face of the king of elephants and a big belly and is extemely beautiful. From whom pours forth an ethereal fluid, the sweet fragrance of which has captivated with love the bees that are swarming his cheeks. With the blows of his tusks he pierces all enemies, and he is beautified by red vermillion. We bow with praise to the son of the Daughter of the Mountains, Pārvatī, the daughter of Himalayas, the Lord of the Multitudes, the Giver of Perfection of All Desires.

ॐ गां गणेशाय नमः

**oṃ gāṃ gaṇeśāya namaḥ**

Oṃ We bow to Gaṇeśa, the Lord of Wisdom, Lord of the Multitudes.

**kara nyāsa**

establishment in the hands

ॐ गां अंगुष्ठाभ्यां नमः

**oṃ gāṃ aṃguṣṭhābhyāṃ namaḥ** *thumb forefinger*

Oṃ Gaṃ in the thumb I bow.

ॐ गीं तर्जनीभ्यां स्वाहा

**oṃ gīṃ tarjanībhyāṃ svāhā** *thumb forefinger*

Oṃ Gīṃ in the forefinger, I am One with God!

ॐ गूं मद्यमाभ्यां वषट्

**oṃ gūṃ madyamābhyāṃ vaṣaṭ** *thumb middlefinger*

Oṃ Gūṃ in the middle finger, Purify!

ॐ गैं अनामिकाभ्यां हुं

**oṃ gaiṃ anāmikābhyāṃ huṃ** *thumb ringfinger*

Oṃ Gaiṃ in the ring finger, Cut the Ego!

ॐ गौं कनिष्ठिकाभ्यां वौषट्

**oṃ gauṃ kaniṣṭhikābyāṃ vauṣaṭ** *thumb littlefinger*

Oṃ Gauṃ in the little finger, Ultimate Purity!

Roll hand over hand forwards while reciting *karatal kar* and backwards while chanting *pṛṣṭhābhyāṃ*, then clap hands when chanting *astrāya phaṭ*.

ॐ गः करतल कर पृष्ठाभ्यां अस्त्राय फट्

**oṃ gaḥ karatal kar pṛṣṭhābhyāṃ astrāya phaṭ**

Oṃ Gaḥ roll hand over hand front and back and clap with the weapon of Virtue.

ॐ गां गणेशाय नमः

**oṃ gāṃ gaṇeśāya namaḥ**

Oṃ We bow to Gaṇeśa, the Lord of Wisdom, Lord of the Multitudes.

## aṅga nyāsa

establishment in the body

Holding tattva mudrā, touch heart.

ॐ गां हृदयाय नमः

**oṃ gāṃ hṛdayāya namaḥ** *touch heart*

Oṃ Gaṃ in the heart, I bow.

Holding tattva mudrā, touch top of head.

ॐ गीं शिरसे स्वाहा

**oṃ gīṃ śirase svāhā** *top of head*

Oṃ Gīṃ on the top of the head, I am One with God!

With thumb extended, touch back of head.

ॐ गूं शिखायै वषट्

**oṃ gūṃ śikhāyai vaṣaṭ** *back of head*

Oṃ Gūṃ on the back of the head, Purify!

Holding tattva mudrā, cross both arms.

ॐ गैं कवचाय हुं

**oṃ gaiṃ kavacāya huṃ** *cross both arms*

Oṃ Gaiṃ crossing both arms, Cut the Ego!

Holding tattva mudrā, touch two eyes and in between at once with three middle fingers.

ॐ गौं नेत्रत्रयाय वौषट्

**oṃ gauṃ netratrayāya vauṣaṭ** *touch three eyes*

Oṃ Gauṃ in the three eyes, Ultimate Purity!

Roll hand over hand forwards while reciting *karatal kar* and backwards while chanting *pṛṣṭhābhyāṃ*, then clap hands when chanting *astrāya phaṭ*.

ॐ गः करतल कर पृष्ठाभ्यां अस्त्राय फट्

**oṃ gaḥ karatal kar pṛṣṭhābhyāṃ astrāya phaṭ**

Oṃ Gaḥ roll hand over hand front and back and clap with the weapon of Virtue.

ॐ गां गणेशाय नमः

**oṃ gāṃ gaṇeśāya namaḥ**

Oṃ We bow to Gaṇeśa, the Lord of Wisdom, Lord of the Multitudes.

वक्रतुण्ड महाकाय सूर्यकोटिसमप्रभ ।

अविघ्नं कुरु मे देव सर्वकार्येषु सर्वदा ॥

**vakratuṇḍa mahākāya sūrya koṭi samaprabha**
**avighnaṃ kuru me deva sarva kāryeṣu sarvadā**

With a broken (or bent) tusk, a great body shining like a million suns, make us free from all obstacles, Oh God. Always remain (with us) in all actions.

एकदन्तं महाकायं लम्बोदरं गजाननम् ।

विघ्ननाशकरं देवं हेरम्बं प्रणामाम्यहम् ॥

**ekadantaṃ mahākāyaṃ lambodaraṃ gajānanam vighnanāśakaraṃ devaṃ herambaṃ praṇāmāmyaham**

With one tooth, a great body, a big belly and an elephant's face, he is the God who destroys all obstacles to whom we are bowing down with devotion.

मल्लिकादि सुगन्धीनि मालित्यादीनि वै प्रभो ।

मयाऽहृतानि पूजार्थं पुष्पाणि प्रतिगृह्यताम् ॥

**mallikādi sugandhīni mālityādīni vai prabho**
**mayā-hṛtāni pūjārthaṃ puṣpāṇi pratigṛhyatām**

Various flowers, such as mallikā and others of excellent scent, are being offered to you, Our Lord. All these flowers have come from the devotion of our hearts for your worship. Please accept them.

एते गन्धपुष्पे ॐ गं गणपतये नमः

**ete gandhapuṣpe oṃ gaṃ gaṇapataye namaḥ**

With these scented flowers oṃ we bow to the Lord of Wisdom, the Lord of the Multitudes.

## kāmākhyā pūjā

worship of kāmākhyā

ॐ कामाख्ये विश्वजननीं करोतु तव मङ्गलम् ।

काममोक्षप्रदे देवि सततं सिद्धिदं भव ॥

**oṃ kāmākhye viśvajananīṃ karotu tava maṅgalam**
**kāmamokṣaprade devi satataṃ siddhidaṃ bhava**

Oṃ Kāmākhyā, Mother of the Universe, bring welfare to all. Give liberation from desires, oh Goddess. Always give the attainment of perfection.

ॐ कामाख्ये वरदे देवी नीलपर्वत निवासिणी ।
त्वं देवीं जगतं मातार्योणिमूद्रे नमोऽस्तु ते ॥

**oṃ kāmākhye varade devī nīlaparvata nivāsiṇī**
**tvaṃ devīṃ jagataṃ mātāryoṇimūdre namo-stu te**

Oṃ Kāmākhyā, oh Goddess, give boons, you who reside on the blue mountain. You are the Goddess who is the Mother of the Universe. You who are of the form of a female genital, I bow to you.

ॐ ह्रीं कामाख्या देव्यै नमः

**oṃ hrīṃ kāmākhyā devyai namaḥ**

Oṃ hrīṃ I bow to the Goddess Kāmākhyā

**sūryārghya**

offering to the sun

ॐ आदित्याय विद्महे मार्तण्डाय धीमहि ।
तन्नो सूर्यः प्रचोदयात् ॥

**oṃ ādityāya vidmahe mārtaṇḍāya dhīmahi**
**tanno sūryaḥ pracodayāt**

Oṃ We meditate on the son of Āditi who is one without a second, we contemplate he who embodies light. May that Light of divine wisdom give us increase.

ॐ जबाकुसुमसङ्काशं काश्यपेयं महाद्युतिम् ।
तमोऽरिं सर्वपापघ्नं प्रणतोऽस्मि दिवाकर ॥

**oṃ jabākusumasaṅkāśaṃ kāśyapeyaṃ mahādyutim**
**tamo-riṃ sarvapāpaghnaṃ praṇato-smi divākara**

Oṃ With the redness of the Hibiscus flower, O son of Kāśyapa, of Great Splendor. Remover of the Darkness of all sin, I bow in devotion to you, Oh Radiator of Light.

ॐ नमो विवस्वते ब्रह्मन् भास्वते विष्णुतेजसे ।

जगत् सवित्रे सूचये सवित्रे कर्मदायिने ॥

इदमर्घ्यं ॐ श्री सूर्य देवाय नमः ॥

**oṃ namo vivasvate brahman bhāsvate viṣṇutejase**
**jagatsavitre sūcaye savitre karmadāyine**
**idamarghyaṃ oṃ śrī sūrya devāya namaḥ**

Oṃ I bow in devotion to He whose own self is the Universe, Infinite Consciousness, whose own self shines, the Light of Universal Consciousness. To the Light of the worlds, to the One who indicates (or shows), to the Bearer of Light who gives all karma.

## tarpaṇa

guru and ancestral offerings

ॐ कुरुक्षेत्र गया गङ्गा प्रभासे पुष्कराणि च ।

ये तीर्थतानि पुण्याणि तार्पणकाले भवान्ति च ॥

**oṃ kurukṣetra gayā gaṅgā prabhāse puṣkarāṇi ca**
**ye tīrthatāni puṇyāṇi tārpaṇakāle bhavānti ca**

Oṃ Kurukṣetra, Gayā, Gaṅgā, Prabhāsa and Puṣkara: these are the meritorious places of pilgrimage that are to be remembered at the time of offering to ancestors.

यमाय धर्मराजाय मृत्यवे चान्तकाय च ।

वैवस्वताय कालाय सर्वभूतक्षयाय च ॥

**yamāya dharmarājāya mṛtyave cāntakāya ca**
**vaivasvatāya kālāya sarvabhūtakṣayāya ca**

I bow to Yamā, to the King of Dharma, to Death, to the Inner Being; to He who is the universe, to Time, to He who causes the destruction of all existence.

औदुम्बराय दध्नाय नीलाय परमेष्ठिने ।
वृकोदराय चित्राय चित्रगुप्ताय वै नमः ॥

**auḍhumbarāya dadhnāya nīlāya parameṣṭhine**
**vṛkodarāya citrāya citraguptāya vai namaḥ**

To He who lives with the Udumbara tree, to the Giver, to the Dark One, to the Supreme amongst Desired Ones; to the Hidden One, to the Varied One and to the hidden among the Varied Ones, I bow.

ॐ देवांस्तर्पयामि

**oṃ devāṃstarpayāmi**

Oṃ I make offerings to the Gods.

ॐ ऋषींस्तर्पयामि

**oṃ ṛṣīṃstarpayāmi**

Oṃ I make offerings to the Seers.

ॐ पितॄंस्तर्पयामि

**oṃ pitṝṃstarpayāmi**

Oṃ I make offerings to the Ancestors.

ॐ पिता स्वर्गः पिता धर्मः पिता हि परमं तपः ।
पितरि प्रीतिमापन्ने प्रीयन्ते सर्वदेवताः ॥

**oṃ pitā svargaḥ pitā dharmaḥ pitā hi paramaṃ tapaḥ pitari prītimāpanne prīyante sarvadevatāḥ**

Oṃ My ancestors are my heaven. My ancestors are my Dharma. My ancestors are my highest Tapas. If my ancestors are satisfied, all the Gods will be satisfied.

ॐ आशिषो मे प्रदीयन्तां पितरः करुणामयाः ।

वदाः सन्ततयो नित्यं वर्द्धन्तां बान्धवा मम ॥

**oṃ āśiṣo me pradīyantāṃ pitaraḥ karuṇāmayāḥ**
**vadāḥ santatayo nityaṃ**
**varddhantāṃ bāndhavā mama**

Oṃ Oh compassionate ancestors, bless me. Always speak words of peace to me and release me from all bondage.

ॐ गुरुं तर्पयामि

**oṃ guruṃ tarpayāmi**

Oṃ I bow to my guru with the offering of respect.

ॐ परमगुरुं तर्पयामि

**oṃ paramaguruṃ tarpayāmi**

Oṃ I bow to my guru's guru with the offering of respect.

ॐ परापरगुरुं तर्पयामि

**oṃ parāparaguruṃ tarpayāmi**

Oṃ I bow to my guru's guru's guru with the offering of respect.

ॐ परमेष्टिगुरुं तर्पयामि

**oṃ parameṣṭigurum tarpayāmi**

Oṃ I bow to the first guru with the offering of respect.

### guru pūjā

worship of the guru

ॐ अखण्डमण्डलाकारं व्याप्तं येन चराचरम् ।

तत्पदं दर्शितं येन तस्मै श्रीगुरवे नमः ॥

**akhaṇḍamaṇḍalākāraṃ vyāptaṃ yena carācaram**
**tatpadaṃ darśitaṃ yena tasmai śrīgurave namaḥ**

The Guru shows the universality of the entire creation, which is distinguished by movable and immovable objects. Therefore we bow down to the Respected Guru.

ध्यानमूलं गुरोर्मूर्तिः पूजामूलं गुरोः पदम् ।

मन्त्रमूलं गुरोर्वाक्यं मोक्षमूलं गुरोः कृपा ॥

**dhyānamūlaṃ gurormūrtiḥ pūjāmūlaṃ guroḥ padam**
**mantramūlaṃ gurorvākyaṃ mokṣamūlaṃ guroḥ kṛpā**

The root of meditation is the image of the Guru; the root of worship is at the feet of the Guru; the root of mantra is the word of the Guru; the root of self-realization is the Grace of the Guru.

गुरुर्ब्रह्मा गुरुर्विष्णुः गुरुर्देवो महेश्वरः ।

गुरुसाक्षात् परं ब्रह्मा तस्मै श्रीगुरवे नमः ॥

**gurur brahmā gururviṣṇuḥ gururdevo maheśvaraḥ**
**gurusākṣāt paraṃ brahmā tasmai śrīgurave namaḥ**

The Guru (Dispeller of Darkness) is Brahmā, Creative Consciousness; The Guru (Dispeller of Darkness) is Viṣṇu, All-

Pervading Consciousness; The Guru (Dispeller of Darkness) is the Lord Maheśvara, the Great Seer of All, or Great Ruler of All. The Guru is indeed the Supreme Deity, and therefore we bow down to the Respected Guru.

एते गन्धपुष्पे ॐ श्री गुरवे नमः

**ete gandhapuṣpe oṃ śrī gurave namaḥ**

With these scented flowers oṃ we bow to the Respected Guru.

**rāmakṛṣṇa pūjā**

worship of rāmakṛṣṇa

ॐ स्थापकाय च धर्मस्य सर्वधर्मस्वरूपिणे ।

अवतार वरिष्ठाय रामकृष्णाय ते नमः ॥

**oṃ sthāpakāya ca dharmasya sarvadharmasvarūpiṇe**
**avatāra variṣṭhāya rāmakṛṣṇāya te namaḥ**

Oṃ to He who establishes the Ideal of Perfection, the intrinsic nature of all ideals; the manifestation of divinity that grants the chosen boon, to you, Rāmakṛṣṇa, we bow.

ॐ नमो भगवते श्रीरामकृष्णाय नमो नमः

**oṃ namo bhagavate śrīrāmakṛṣṇāya namo namaḥ**

Oṃ We bow to the Supreme Divinity, the Respected Rāmakṛṣṇa, we bow, we bow.

**śrī sāradā devi pūjā**

worship of sāradā devi

ॐ जननीं सारदां देवीं रामकृष्णं जगद्गुरुं ।

पादपद्मे तयोः श्रित्वा प्रणमामि मुहुर्मुहुः ॥

**oṃ jananīṃ śāradāṃ devīṃ**
**rāmakṛṣṇaṃ jagadgurum**
**pādapadme tayoḥ śritvā praṇamāmi muhurmuhuḥ**

Oṃ Mother of the Universe, the Goddess who Flows like the Sea, (considered as) the Supreme Teacher to Rāmakṛṣṇa; we bow again and again to your respected lotus feet.

ॐ श्रीसारदा देव्यै नमो नमः

**oṃ śrīsāradā devyai namo namaḥ**

Oṃ to the Respected Goddess who Flows like the Sea, Sāradā Devī, we bow, we bow.

## shree maa pūjā

worship of shree maa

ॐ सनातनी माया विद्महे ज्ञान प्रकाशायै धीमहे ।
तन्नो श्री माँ प्रचोदायत् ॥

**oṃ sanātanī māyā vidmahe**
**jñāna prakāśāyai dhīmahe**
**tanno śrī māṁ pracodāyat**

Oṃ we meditate on the Eternal Measurement of Consciousness, we contemplate She who illuminates wisdom. May that Shree Maa grant us increase.

## mahiṣāsura pūjā

worship of the great ego

ॐ महिषासुर महावीर सर्वारिष्ठविनाशन ।
देवगृहेऽर्च्चितो भक्त्या पूजां गृह्ण प्रसीद मे ॥

**oṃ mahiṣāsura mahāvīra sarvāriṣṭhavināśana**
**devagṛhe-rccito bhaktyā pūjāṃ gṛhva prasīda me**

Oṃ Mahiṣāsura, oh Great Ego (literally, the Great Ruler of Duality), oh great warrior, who causes all destruction and calamity; devotees make offering to you in the house of the Gods. Please accept the worship and be pleased with me.

महिषात्वं महासुर इन्द्रादिदेवमरिता ।
दिव्यस्त्र तारिता भूपा गच्छा स्वर्गं नमोऽस्तु ते ॥
ॐ महिषासुराय नमः

**mahiṣātvaṃ mahāsura indrādidevamaritā**
**divyastra tāritā bhūpā gacchā svargaṃ namo-stu te**
**oṃ mahiṣāsurāya namaḥ**

Oh Great Ego, great warrior of duality, who even defeats Indra and the other Gods; oh King, you are being conveyed across by means of divine weapons. Go to heaven. I bow to you! Oṃ I bow to the Great Ego.

**siṃha pūjā**

worship of the lion

ॐ सिंह त्वं सर्वजन्तुनामधिपोऽसि महाबल ।
पार्वतीवाहन श्रीमन् वरं देहि नमोऽस्तु ते ॥

**oṃ siṃha tvaṃ sarvajantunāmadhipo-si mahābala**
**pārvatīvāhana śrīman varaṃ dehi namo-stu te**

Oṃ Lion, of all the animals you are the foremost and the greatest in strength. Oh Respected One, you are the vehicle of Parvatī. Give us boons, we bow to you.

असनां चासि भूतानं नानालङ्कारभूषितं ।
मेरु श्रिङ्ग प्रतिकाशं सिङ्गासनं नमोऽस्तु ते ॥

**asanāṃ cāsi bhūtānaṃ nānālaṅkārabhūṣitaṃ**
**meru śriṅga pratikāśaṃ siṅgāsanaṃ namo-stu te**

You are the seat of all existence, shining forth with various ornaments. Even Mount Meru leans upon you and you need not obey Him. We bow down to the Seat of the Lion.

वज्रनखदंष्ट्रायुधाय महासिंहाय हुं फट् नमः ॥

**vajranakhaṃdaṃṣṭhrāyudhāya mahāsiṃhāya huṃ phaṭ namaḥ**

Whose weapons of nails and teeth glisten like lightning, to the great Lion, Cut the Ego! Purify! We bow.

**puṣpāñjalī**

offer flowers

सर्वमङ्गल मङ्गल्ये शिवे सर्वार्थ साधिके ।

शरण्ये त्र्यम्बके गौरि नारायणि नमोऽस्तु ते ॥

**sarvamaṅgala maṅgalye śive sarvārtha sādhike**
**śaraṇye tryambake gauri nārāyaṇi namo-stu te**

To the Auspicious of all Auspiciousness, to the Good, to the Accomplisher of all Objectives, to the Source of Refuge, to the Mother of the Three Worlds, to the Goddess Who Is Rays of Light, Exposer of Consciousness, we bow to you.

सृष्टिस्थितिविनाशानां शक्तिभूते सनातनि ।

गुणाश्रये गुणमये नारायणि नमोऽस्तु ते ॥

**sṛṣṭisthitivināśānāṃ śaktibhūte sanātani**
**guṇāśraye guṇamaye nārāyaṇi namo-stu te**

You are the Eternal Energy of Creation, Preservation and Destruction in all existence; that on which all qualities depend, that which limits all qualities, Exposer of Consciousness, we bow to you.

शरणागतदीनार्त परित्राण परायणे ।
सर्वस्यार्ति हरे देवि नारायणि नमोऽस्तु ते ॥

**śaraṇāgatadīnārta paritrāṇa parāyaṇe**
**sarvasyārti hare devi nārāyaṇi namo-stu te**

For those who are devoted to you and take refuge in you, you save from all discomfort and unhappiness. All worry you take away, Oh Goddess, Exposer of Consciousness, we bow to you.

**praṇām**

दुर्गां शिवां शान्तिकरीं ब्रह्माणीं ब्रह्मणः प्रियाम् ।
सर्वलोक प्रणेत्रीञ्च प्रणमामि सदा शिवाम् ॥

**durgāṃ śivāṃ śāntikarīṃ**
**brahmāṇīṃ brahmaṇaḥ priyām**
**sarvaloka praṇetrīñca praṇamāmi sadā śivām**

The Reliever of Difficulties, Exposer of Goodness, Cause of Peace, Infinite Consciousness, Beloved by Knowers of Consciousness, all the inhabitants of all the worlds always bow to Her, and I am bowing to Goodness Herself.

मङ्गलां शोभनां शुद्धां निष्कलां परमां कलाम् ।
विश्वेश्वरीं विश्वमातां चण्डिकां प्रणमाम्यहम् ॥

**maṅgalāṃ śobhanāṃ śuddhāṃ**
**niṣkalāṃ paramāṃ kalām**
**viśveśvarīṃ viśvamātāṃ**
**caṇḍikāṃ praṇamāmyaham**

Welfare, Radiant Beauty, Completely Pure, Without Limitations, the Ultimate Limitation, the Lord of the Universe, the Mother of the Universe, to you Caṇḍi, to the Energy that Tears Apart Thought, I bow in submission.

सर्वदेवमयीं देवीं सर्वरोगभयापहाम् ।
ब्रह्मेशविष्णुनमितां प्रणमामि सदा शिवाम् ॥

**sarvadevamayīṃ devīṃ sarvarogabhayāpahām**
**brahmeśaviṣṇunamitāṃ praṇamāmi sadā śivām**

Composed of all the Gods, removing all sickness and fear, Brahma, Maheśwara and Viṣṇu bow down to Her, and I always bow down to the Energy of Infinite Goodness.

विन्ध्यस्थां विन्ध्यनिलयां दिव्यस्थाननिवासिनीम् ।
योगिनीं योगजननीं चण्डिकां प्रणमाम्यहम् ॥

**vindhyasthāṃ vindhyanilayāṃ divyasthānanivāsinīm**
**yoginīṃ yogajananīṃ caṇḍikāṃ praṇamāmyaham**

The dwelling place of Knowledge, residing in Knowledge, Resident in the Place of Divine Illumination, the Cause of Union, the Knower of Union, to the Energy that Tears Apart Thought we constantly bow.

ईशानमातरं देवीमीश्वरीमीश्वरप्रियाम् ।
प्रणतोऽस्मि सदा दुर्गां संसारार्णवतारिणीम् ॥

**īśānamātaraṃ devīmīśvarīmīśvarapriyām**
**praṇato-smi sadā durgāṃ saṃsārārṇavatāriṇīm**

The Mother of the Supreme Consciousness, the Goddess Who Is the Supreme Consciousness, beloved by the Supreme Consciousness, we always bow to Durgā, the Reliever of

Difficulties, who takes aspirants across the difficult sea of objects and their relationships.

ॐ महादेव महात्रान महायोगि महेश्वर ।
सर्वपाप हरां देव मकाराय नमो नमः ॥

**oṃ mahādeva mahātrāna mahāyogi maheśvara**
**sarvapāpa harāṃ deva makārāya namo namaḥ**

Oṃ The Great God, the Great Reliever, the Great Yogi, Oh Supreme Lord, Oh God who removes all Sin, in the form of the letter "M," which dissolves creation, we bow to you again and again.

ॐ नमः शिवाय शान्ताय कारणत्राय हेतवे ।
निवेदायामि चत्मनं त्वं गति परमेश्वर ॥

**oṃ namaḥ śivāya śāntāya kāraṇatrāya hetave**
**nivedāyāmi catmanaṃ tvaṃ gati parameśvara**

Oṃ I bow to the Consciousness of Infinite Goodness, to Peace, to the Cause of the three worlds, I offer to you the fullness of my soul, Oh Supreme Lord.

ॐ नमः शिवाय

**oṃ namaḥ śivāya**

Oṃ I bow to the Consciousness of Infinite Goodness

**aśīrbād**

blessings

ॐ श्रीर्वर्चस्वमायुष्यमारोग्यमाविधात् पवमानं महीयते ।
धान्यं धनं पशुं बहुपुत्रलाभंशतसंवत्सरं दीर्घमायुः ॥

**oṃ śrīrvarcasvamāyuṣyamārogyamāvidhāt**
**pavamānaṃ mahīyate**
**dhānyaṃ dhanaṃ paśuṃ**
**bahuputralābhaṃśatasaṃvatsaraṃ dīrghamāyuḥ**

Oṃ You are blessed with the Highest Respect, with Wealth, with Life, with Freedom from disease and freedom to be One with the Greatness; with food, with wealth, with animals and with many children, and with a long life of one hundred years.

मन्त्रार्थाः सफलाः सन्तु पूणाः सन्तु मनोरथाः ।
शत्रूणां बुद्धिनाशोऽस्तु मित्राणामुदयस्तव ॥

**mantrārthāḥ saphalāḥ santu pūṇāḥ santu manorathāḥ**
**śatrūṇāṃ buddhināśo-stu mitrāṇāmudayastava**

May the meanings of the mantras bring excellent fruit, and may the journey of your mind be full and complete. May all enmity be removed from your intellect, and may friendship continuously rise.

आयुष्कामो यशस्कामो पुत्र-पौत्रस्तथैव च ।
आरोग्यं धनकामश्च सर्वे कामा भवन्तु मे ॥

**āyuṣkāmo yaśaskāmo putra-pautrastathaiva ca**
**ārogyaṃ dhanakāmaśca sarve kāmā bhavantu me**

May you enjoy life; may you enjoy fame, children and grand-children throughout the generations; may you all live without disease, with abundance of wealth; and may all your disires be fulfilled.

**visārjaṇa**

removing the divine energy to the unmanifest

ॐ ईतः पूर्व प्राणबुद्धिदेह धर्माधिकारतो ।

जाग्रत् स्वप्नशुषुप्तयवस्थाशु मनसा ॥

**oṃ ītaḥ pūrva prāṇabuddhideha dharmādhikārato jāgrat svapnaśuṣuptayavasthāśu manasā**

Oṃ Thus the full and complete intelligence of the Life Force, the Cause of Dharma, the Way of Truth to Perfection, has been given. Waking Consciousness, Dreaming (or thinking) Consciousness, and Consciousness in Dreamless Dleep (intuitive Consciousness) in which all thoughts are situated.

वाचा कर्मणा हस्ताभ्यां पध्भ्यामूद्रेण शिश्ना ।

यत् कृतं तद्युक्तं यत् स्मृतं तत् सर्वं ब्रह्मार्पणं भवतु स्वाहा ॥

**vācā karmaṇā hastābhyāṃ padhbhyāmūdareṇa śiśnā yat kṛtaṃ tadyuktaṃ yat smṛtaṃ tat sarvaṃ brahmārpaṇaṃ bhavatu svāhā**

All speech has been offered with folded hands raised in respect while bowing to the lotus feet. That activity, that union, that memory, all of that has been offered to the Supreme Divinity. I am One with God!

मां मदीयञ्च सकलं श्री चण्डिका चरणे समर्पये ।

ॐ तत् सत् ॥

**māṃ madīyañca sakalaṃ śrī caṇḍikā caraṇe samarpaye**
**oṃ tat sat**

All of me and all that belongs to me entirely, I surrender to the feet of the respected caṇḍikā, She Who Tears Apart Thought. The Infinite, That is Truth.

ॐ ब्रह्मार्पणं ब्रह्म हविर्ब्रह्माग्नौ ब्रह्मणा हुतम् ।

ब्रह्मैव तेन गन्तव्यं ब्रह्मकर्मसमाधिना ॥

**oṃ brahmārpaṇaṃ brahma havirbrahmāgnau brahmaṇā hutam**
**brahmaiva tena gantavyaṃ brahmakarmasamādhinā**

Oṃ The Supreme Divinity makes the offering; the Supreme Divinity is the offering; offered by the Supreme Divinity, in the fire of the Supreme Divinity. By seeing the Supreme Divinity in all actions, one realizes that Supreme Divinity.

ॐ पूर्णमदः पूर्णमिदं पूर्णात् पूर्णमुदच्यते ।

पूर्णस्य पूर्णमादाय पूर्णमेवावशिश्यते ॥

**oṃ pūrṇamadaḥ pūrṇamidaṃ**
**pūrṇāt pūrṇamudacyate**
**pūrṇasya pūrṇamādāya pūrṇamevāva śiśyate**

Oṃ That is whole and perfect. This is whole and perfect. From the whole and perfect, the whole and perfect becomes manifest. If the whole and perfect issue forth from the whole and perfect, even still only the whole and perfect remain.

ॐ शान्तिः शान्तिः शान्तिः

**oṃ śāntiḥ śāntiḥ śāntiḥ**

Oṃ Peace, Peace, Peace

क्षमास्य *(visārjaṇ mudrā)*

**kṣamāsya**

Please forgive me.

***More Books by Shree Maa and Swami Satyananda Saraswati***

Annapurna Sahasranam
Before Becoming This
Bhagavad Gita
Chandi Path
Cosmic Puja
Cosmic Puja Bengali
Devi Gita
Devi Mandir Songbook
Durga Puja Beginner
Ganesh Puja
Hanuman Puja
Kali Dhyanam
Kali Puja
Lakṣmī Sahasranam
Sahib Sadhu, The White Sadhu
Shiva Puja Beginner
Shiva Puja and Advanced Yajna
Shree Maa Cookbook
Shree Maa: The Guru and the Goddess
Shree Maa: The Life of a Saint
Sundar Kanda
Swami Purana

**CDs and Cassettes**

Chandi Path
Dark Night Mother
Durga Puja Beginner (Instructional)
Goddess is Everywhere
Lalita Trishati
Mahamrtyunjaya Mantra
Mantras of the Nine Planets
Navarna Mantra
Om Mantra
Sadhu Stories from the Himalayas
Shiva is in My Heart
Shiva Puja Beginner (Instructional)
Shiva Puja & Advanced Yajna
Shree Maa in the Temple of the Heart
Shree Maa on Tour 1998
Songs of Ramprasad
Thousand Names of Kali

***Videos***

Across the States with Shree Maa & Swamiji
Meaning and Method of Worship
Shree Maa: Meeting a Modern Saint
Visiting India with Shree Maa and Swamiji

Please visit us at www.shreemaa.org
Our email is info@shreemaa.org